PERSPECTIVE DEVELOPMENTS OF SERIAL MANAGEMENT
A Practical Approach

PERSPECTIVE DEVELOPMENTS OF SERIAL MANAGEMENT

A PRACTICAL APPROACH

S.R. Patnaik

2007

CYBER TECH PUBLICATIONS

4264/3 Ansari Road, Daryaganj, New Delhi - 110 002

Perspective Developments of Serial Management

First Edition 2007

Published by G.S. Rawat
For Cyber Tech Publications
4264/3, Ansari Road, Daryaganj, New Delhi - 110 002
E-mail : cybertechpublishers@yahoo.com
Phone : 011-23244078,
Fax : 011-23280028

Printed at
Tanwar Offset Press, Moujpur, # 9810878184

Preface

There is the challenge of providing the most cost-effective mix of serials that will come as close as fiscal limits permit to meeting customer needs and desires. An attempt has made to explore the new dimension of serial management: electronic journals and full-text journals available electronically. At this point we merely wish to note that the issue exists and is rapidly becoming another major cost concern for libraries. Electronic journals are "publications" that exist only in an electronic format, whereas "full-text" identifies the availability of the text of paper-based journals in an electronic format.

In the modern digital world fast changes are taking place, as a result of which the quantum of knowledge is increasing rapidly. While preparing this work for our readers. Contents of library science of various institutions.

Different sources scholars and institutions for their valuable contribution on this subject. Librarians and their staff members have been kind and helpful. We thank them.

Last but not the least my publishers who appreciated this book and brought this work out in a record time.

– Editor

Contents

CHAPTER 1

Introduction

There is the challenge of providing the most cost-effective mix of serials that will come as close as fiscal limits permit to meeting customer needs and desires. An attempt has made to explore the new dimension of serial management: electronic journals and full-text journals available electronically. At this point we merely wish to note that the issue exists and is rapidly becoming another major cost concern for libraries. Electronic journals are "publications" that exist only in an electronic format, whereas "full-text" identifies the availability of the text of paper-based journals in an electronic format. At present (1999), full-text often does not guarantee that one will find the graphic material and photographs from the print version accompanying the online text.

This will change over time, but it should be kept that graphics often require high-end computers and laser quality printers to handle the material. Serials, regardless of their format, are important sources of current in-formation for the public. Libraries attempt to maintain as large a collection of serials as their budgets will allow, but costs and space considerations have significantly modified the "all and forever" retention philosophy that man serials departments employed in the past. Serial work is interesting, challenging, and frustrating. The following quote sums up the work nicely:

The Publisher is my Tormentor. I shall not smile:

He maketh me to work all day at my desk.

He leadeth me astray with misnumbered issues:

His Roman numerals confound me:

He changeth titles over and over for His own sake.

Yea, when I walk through the shadow of missing or irregular issues, I can find no respite, for He has moved.

He answereth not myletters, nor useth the correct mailing label:

He starteth not when I ask and quiteth before it is time;

My work never endeth.

Rising prices and duplicate issues shall follow me all the days of my life; and

I shall moan and groan in the libraryforever,

Individuals (customers and librarians alike) frequently use the words journals, magazines, periodicals, and serials interchangeably, with no great misunderstanding resulting from the imprecise usage. Thomas Nisonger, in his fine book on serial management, devoted more than six pages to how different groups have attempted to define the material covered in this.

The following definitions are adequate for the purposes of this chapter. The ALA Glossary of Library and Information Science provides the following definitions of two key terms:

> **Serial**—" a publication issued in successive parts, usually at regular intervals, and, as a rule, intended to be continued indefinitely Serials include periodicals, annuals (reports, yearbooks, etc.) and memoirs, proceedings, and transitions of societies."

> **Periodical**—"a publication with a distinctive title intended to appear in successive (usually unbound) numbers of parts at stated or regular intervals and, as a rule, for an indefinite time. Each part generally contains articles by several contributors. Newspapers, whose chief function it is to disseminate news, and the memoirs, proceedings,

journals, etc. of societies are not considered periodicals."

Definitions in general dictionaries have more overlap:

Journal—"a periodical publication especially dealing with matters of current interest—often used for official or semi-official publications of special groups"

Magazine—"a periodical that usually contains a miscellaneous collection of articles, poems, and pictures and is directed.

Periodical—" A magazine or other publication of which the issues appear at stated or regular intervals—usually for a publication appearing more frequently than annually but infrequently used for a newspaper"

Serial—a" publication (as a newspaper, journal, yearbook or bulletin) issued as one of a consecutively numbered and indefinitely continued seris"

We use the term serials because it represents the broadest spectrum of materials.

Some years ago, Fritz Machlup and others developed an 18-part classification system for serials. The following discussion uses their classification system because it covers all types of serials, including serials "not elsewhere classified," we have yet to encounter a serial that does not fit into one of his other 17 categories. Because the system appears to be comprehensive, we will describe the categories.

Reports of Institutions

The first category is "annual, semiannual, quarterly or occasional reports of corporations, financial institutions, and organizations serving business and finance." Academic libraries serving business and management programmes frequently need to acquire this type of serial. Some corporate libraries also actively collect this serial category. Most of the reports available to libraries and information centers are free for the asking. Some organizations will add a library to their distribution lists, but others will respond only to requests for the current edition. Collecting in this area is labour-intensive because it requires maintaining in files and correspondence, especially if one collects much beyond the large national corporations. Without question, having a computer system that has both word-processing and mailing list capabilities will make collecting less tedious, but it will not reduce the need to constantly monitor the programme. Corporate annual reports are issued every month. Many companies issue an annual report for the annual meeting of the management board, owner, or stockholders, which normally occurs in the month the organisation was established. It had been difficult to find a satisfactory vendor for this serials category, except for 10-K reports to the Securities and Exchange Commission, which had previously been available on microfiche from Disclosure, Inc. thanks to the advent of electronic full-text resources, EDGAR-(SEC) filings are now available from a number of sources, including DOW Jones Interactive and Monday's Company Data Direct. (A good discussion of the vendors that offer annual report assistance appears in Judith Bernstein's "Corporate Annual Reports: The commercial. Vendors.")

Yearbooks and Proceedings

A related category is "annuals, biennials, occasional publications, bound or stapled, including yearbooks, almanacs, proceedings, transactions, memoirs, directories and reports of societies and associations." Many libraries collect serials in this class, especially academic, special, and large public libraries. The more libraries that collect a particular society's or association's publications, the more likely it is that a commercial vendor would handle a standing order for the material. Although it is possible to secure some of these serials through a vendor, there are a significant number that one must secure directly from the society or association.

Superseding Serials

Two other labor-intensive collecting categories are (1) "superseding serial services (each new issue superseding previous ones, which are usually discarded) including telephone directories, airplane schedules, catalogs, loose leaf data sheets, etc.," and 2) "non-superseding serial services bound, sewn, stapled, or loose leaf, including bibliographic and statistical data." One must acquire most of the materials in these classes directly from the publisher. Superseding serials are important but problematic; important because people need the correct or current information, problematic as they can be difficult to track and sometimes to secure. Airline schedules, current hotel guides, and other travel-related serial sources have been something of a problem for libraries to acquire. In the past, the publishers would sell the material only to qualified travel agencies. As more and more corporations handle staff travel on their own, it has become easier for libraries to subscribe to such services. In many corporations, the library or information center maintains current travel information. In the United States, since the break-up of AT&T, libraries have found it more difficult and expensive to secure telephone directories outside their immediate area.

Loose-leaf services are particularly important in U.S. law libraries and accounting firms (two examples, Labor Relations Reporter from the Bureau of National Affairs, and Standard Federal Tax Reporter, from Commerce Clearing House). Proper filing and discarding of material is of critical importance in such an environment, because incorrect information can be very costly to a firm (perhaps the clearest way to demonstrate the cost of not having the right information at the right time) With a loose-leaf service, one must make certain that all sections released are received. Many publishers of loose leaf services make their services available through the Internet/Web and some also offer CD-ROM versions. Naturally, there is a substantial cost for the electronic versions; however, e needs to weigh the value of reducing staff labour in filing the material as well as the greater assurance that what is available is in fact correct. (The problem of misfiling or even not filing material can be costly for a organization such as a law firm.)

Non-superseding serials are less of a problem, and some are available from serial jobbers. However, the materials in this class tend to be expensive, and one must order them directly from the publisher. Indexing and abstracting services fall into one of these two classes. All types of libraries need a few of these reference serials. As the serial collection grows, there is an increasing demand from patrons for more indexing and abstracting services.

Newspapers

All types of libraries, with the exception of elementary school media centers, collect newspapers, another serial category. Almost every small public library receives the local newspaper and one or two newspapers from nearby communities. Large public and academic libraries try to have some national and foreign newspaper coverage. Serial jobbers handle subscriptions to major newspapers for libraries. Thus, it would be possible to place one order with a jobber, such as Faxon or EBSCO, for almost all the major newspapers from around the would. At the time the order is placed, selectors and collection development officers must establish the value of the newspapers' content, in the sense of the demand or need to have the latest issue in the shortest time. For example, one can receive the London Times in a variety of packages, each with a different cost: daily airmail edition by air freight, daily airmail edition by airmail (the most expensive option), daily regular edition by air freight, daily regular edition in weekly packets (the least expensive option) or microfilm edition. The New York Times offers a wider variety of editions: city edition, late city edition, national edition, New York edition, large type weekly, same day, next day, two-day, weekly packets, and microfilm.

As is clear, subscribing to a newspaper is no simple matter. Depending on the library's clientele, a certain edition and delivery method will provide the right service at the least cost, but determining the right combination takes more time than selecting a book.

Like other serials, newspapers present special storage and access problems. When a library subscribes to several newspapers, a display of recent issues can occupy a large potion of a current issues area. For research libraries, long-term storage is a problem. Bound newspapers tend to be large, heavy, an awkward to handle. The poor quality of newsprint presents preservation problems.

Today, most libraries use a micro-format for back issue storage, but this adds to the overall subscription cost, because most newspaper companies control the micro-filming of their publication. Access is another problem, except for the largest newspapers, because most indexing services cover only the best-known papers.

A number of the major newspapers are now available online—some from a vendor (for example, LEXIS-NEXIS), some only through the publisher. According to Wallys Conhaim, 600 daily newspapers (about one-third of the U.S. total0 were operating some level of online service in early 1998.7 Electronic versions may solve some of the storage issues associated with newspaper backfiles, at least to a point. They also work well for many readers, as the articles are not very long and people are more willing to read an article without wanting to print a hard copy. Often, however, people demand good-quality printing capability for electronic journal articles because of their length. If one subscribes to a sizable number of regional or local newspapers that are available electronically through a service such as News bank, it may be more economical to choose this option. In any event, choosing the electronic version would lessen the "housekeeping" (storage, reshelving, claims) costs for the print various held. These costs can be difficult to track.

Newsletters

Newsletters, leaflets, news releases, and similar materials represent yet another serial category of major importance for some libraries. Special libraries are the most likely to become involved in the ongoing collection of this class of serial. Many of the items in this class are very inexpensive or free. Others, especially newsletters, can cost thousands of dollars. In either case, someone must put in the time and effort to identify the sources and get on the appropriate mailing lists. Libraries in marketing and public relations firms are likely to be active collectors of this type of material. Any library operating in a disturbed-reactive or turbulent information environment is likely to collect heavily this class.

Magazines

What are the most common serials? Eleven of Machlup's categories cover the variations in the common serials—magazines and journals (scholarly publications). According to Mahlup's definition, magazines are massmarket serials, the ones that almost any serial jobber will handle for a library. His magazine categories include:

- Mass-market serials, weekly or monthly news magazines (such as Newsweek)
- Popular magazines dealing with fiction, pictures, sports, travel, fashion, sex, humor, and comics (an examples is Sports Illustrated)
- Magazines that popularize science, social, political, and cultural affairs (Smithsonian)
- Magazines focusing particularly on opinion and criticism—social, political, literary, artistic, aesthetic, or religious (an example is Foreign Affairs)
- "Other magazines not elsewhere classified" category, An example of an item in this last category is an organisation publication (governmental or private) that is really a public relations vehicle, sometimes called a house orga. These publications often contain general-interest material, but there is usually some clearly stated or implied relationship between the subject covered and the issuing organization (e.g., Plain Truth). Another type of publication in the "other" category is the magazine found in the pocket of airline seats. These publications contains interesting short articles about people, places, and things. Many contain advertising, so the magazine not only helps distract the nervous traveler, but also provides an additional source of revenue for the airline.

Libraries may receive a substantial number of house organs, as their publishers give them away. We do not know of any library collecting airline magazines, but perhaps, somewhere, in a research or corporate library, some collection development officer is trying to work out a play for doing, just that. Who knows when some sociologist may wish to study the reading habits of airline passengers? Vendors seldom handle this type of magazine.

Journals

Machlup similarly divided journals into four subcategories, with one category divided into two smaller units:

- nonspecialised journals for the intelligentsia well-informed on literature, art, social affairs, politics, etc. (Science is an example)
- learned journals for specialist –primary research journals and secondary research journals (American Indian Culture and research journal, for example)
- practical professional journals in applied fields, including technology, medicine , law, agriculture management , library, science, business, and trades (RQ)
- parochial journals of any type but addressed chiefly to a parochial audience , whether local or regional (Kiva)

Again, most titles in these categories are available through vendors, although one must place direct orders for some of the more specialized learned journals. Most parochial journals must be purchased directly from the publisher; local history abd regional archeological publications are examples of this class of serial.

The final serial category identified by Machlup was government publications , reports, bulletins, statistical series , released releases etc. by public agencies, executive, legislative and judiciary, local, state, national, foreign and international." Because we cover this group in chapter 9, no further discussion is offered here.

With the preceding variations in serials in mind, you can understand why there is confusion about terms and challenges in collecting and preserving the. Each type fills a niche in the information dissemination system. Although they do create special handling problems, they are a necessary part of any library's collection, and the public service staff must deal with them.

Several characteristics unique to serials make this format useful. For many patrons, serials are the most important source of printed information. Serials contain the most current information about a topic, other than what may be available on an electronic bulletin board or discussion list. Some professional-society serial publications are very slow to appear, and scholars in the field will known about the material before it is published in the journal; nevertheless, the journal article will be the first published source of information. (Given the importance of currency, providing a system that allows patrons to determine the latest issue received is important.) Related to currency is the frequency with which serials update information. For serials, the update interval can be short; for example, newspapers are updated daily. (In contrast, few monographs get updated, and for those titles that go into second or subsequent editions, the update interval may be several years.) Serial articles can be short and tend to focus on narrow subjects; thus, readers with a specific information need frequently find that serial provide the desired information more quickly than monographic publications. Finally, serials are often the first printed source of information about a new subject or development. People use serials to learn about new ideas, concepts, and information, and they use monographs to gain a broader or deeper knowledge of a subject.

Selection of Serials

Selection and deselection of serials focus on three basic issues: titles currently in the collection, titles not in the collection, and new titles. One uses slightly different criteria in assessing each group. When reexamining titles in the collection, subscription price and use patterns are the two primary issues (see page 165 for an explanation of why periodic reexamination ins necessary).

Looking a t interlibrary loan (ILL) data and citation analysis information helps one decide whether an existing title that is not in the collection ought to be. For new titles, the subject area, cost, and -when available—reviews are they key elements in deciding whether to place a subscription. As with books, one can incorporate some macro selection decisions into the collection development policy for serials. Some possible macro decisions are:

Subscribe to any titles requested by users that match collected subject areas (this rule is often used in special libraries).

Subscribe to any title borrowed through ILL more than X number of times.

Subscribed to all core titles, as identified through citation analysis, in subject areas collected.

Do not subscribe to unindexed titles.

Do not subscribe to journals that contain unrefereed articles.

The list could go on; the point is, the more macro decisions there are, the easier serials management becomes.

One can also make other broad generalizations about serials selection. The fields of science, technology, and medicine (commonly abbreviated as STM in the literature) are very dependent on serial publications. At the opposite end of the spectrum are the humanities, which depend more on books than on serials. Between these two are the social sciences, some of which are more similar to the science disciplines (e.g., psychology, linguistics, physical anthropology), ad others of which are more similar to the humanities (e.g., political science, education, a d social anthropology).

A decision to subscribe to or place a standing order for a serial is a much bigger decision than similar decisions for monographs. Several factors account for the difference. Because serials are ongoing, they can become a standing commitment for the library or information centre and thus become a more-or-less fixed element in the materials budget. Because serials arrive in the library or information centre in parts, there must be an ongoing progress for receiving the parts and maintaining records about what did or did not arrive. Unfortunately, few serials arrive in a form that allows for easy long-term storage or heavy use; therefore, libraries must bind or otherwise develop a means to preserve them. In addition, serials occupy large amounts of storage space, which over time becomes scarce. Gaining access to the contents of most serials unusually requires use of indexing and abstracting services, which are in themselves serials. Adding a new indexing or abstracting service typically results in additional work for the Ill unit, unless the library subscribes to all of the titles covered by the service. A serials collection that does not provide for quick easy, and inexpensive photocopy services will quickly become a collection of covers and advertisements; the articles will disappear. When adding a title that has been published for some time, one must consider the question of back files. Finally, serials change over time. These are the most important differences between selecting a book and a serial.

Unlike a monograph, a serial normally implies a long-term commitment. Subscriptions require renewals, but with most vendor plans the renewal process is automatic, requiring no actión on the part of the collection development staff. When the subscription renewal requires a positive decision by the library staff, the serial holdings are more likely to reflect the current interests of the library's customers. With automatic renewal, there is a substantial chance that the library will continue inappropriate serials long after the serial ceases to meet community needs.

A long-term commitment to a serial results in subscription costs becoming a fixed feature of the budget. With rapidly rising pries and small budget increases, each year serials take up an increasing proportion of the total materials budget. Chapter 13 on fiscal management provides more information about this problem, but in general, serial price have been increasing at a much faster rate than general inflation. Thus, each year the amount of money required to maintain the present serials subscriptions increases at a rate greater than many libraries are able to sustain.

Another fixed cost is processing. When ordering and receiving a monograph, the library incurs a one-time cost. Serials have ongoing receiving and renewal costs, in addition to the cost of placing the initial order. Claiming missing issues is a normal part of maintaining a serials collection. A staff member records each issue when it arrives in the library. When the person notes that an issue is missing or that a number has been skipped, the library contacts the publisher or agent to attempt to secure the missing material. (This is called placing a claim.) Acting promptly on claims is important, because serials publishers print only slightly more copies than the number of subscribers. Serial publishers know that a certain percentage of issues sent will go astray in the mail, and they print extra copies to cover the expected claims. However, at times the number of claims is greater than the number of available copies. When happens, a number of unlucky libraries receive out-of-print notices. The closer the claim is made to the publication date, the greater the chances are of receiving the missing issue. (The consequences of small print runs appear again when it is time to bind the volume and the library discovers that one of the issues is missing. Locating a copy can be time-consuming, if not impossible.) Daily serial check-n is a must to avoid missing issues. Automated serial systems. Help speed routine serials work, including providing automatic claiming but in a library with a large serials list, one or more full-time staff may work exclusively on processing serials. Clearly, each new serial adds to the workload on an ongoing basis.

By their nature, serials arrive in successive issues, normally as paper-backs. If the library maintains serials for long periods of time or the titles receive relatively heavy use, the library must repackage the serial for more convenient handling. One method is to store the loose issues in a cardboard or metal container (sometimes referred to as a Princeton File) that keeps a limited number of issues together in a vertical position. This makes I easier to shelve the loose issues alongside bound materials. The container must have room on its outfacing side to record the title and issue or volume number of the items in the box. The most common long-term storage treatment is binding. A third alternative, micro-format storage, represents an additional cost. Whatever choice is made, there is an ongoing cost to package each serial year after year.

Eventually, finding storage space for collections becomes a problem for all libraries and information centers. Storing long runs of serials can consume large quantities of limited shelf space. Using microforms as the long-term storage for at for long runs of low-use serials will help with the space problem for a time. However, microforms also present some problems. Customers usually resist and complain about using microforms, so there is a public relations issue to address when shifting to microforms. Microforms also mean acquiring equipment: microform readers at a minimum, with reader-printers being the best solution. Libraries usually have at least two types of microform readers, film and fiche. Most machines have several lenses to accommodate various reduction ratios. The library must maintain the equipment and provide users with assistance as needed, especially when it is necessary to change lenses. As the size of the micro-for collection increases, more equipment will be needed to meet ser demands. Finally, microform storage cabinets are heavy when empty and very heavy when full. Libraries may face problems in locating a growing collection of such cabinets if the floor cannot sustain their combined weight. Clearly, microform brings with it new costs and concerns.

Another solution for storage is to move low-use items to a less accessible and less costly facility. Yet another solution is to deselect some titles. As space becomes scarce, decisions about what to keep and for how long become more and more difficult. Given the current nature of most serials, older holdings are prime candidates for remote storage. After making the first, relatively easy decisions about which titles to store, weeding decisions become increasingly complex, take more time, and can lead to conflicts between staff and patrons.

An important consideration in serials selection is how the patron gains access to the information each issue contains. Going through each issue is not efficient, and few patron are willing to do this. Many serials produce an annual index, but this is of no help with current issues. An entire industry has developed around providing access to serials. A variety of indexing and abstracting companies now provide services that assist in locating information in serials. Naturally, most of these services are expensive and are a hidden cost of building a serials collection. Though Harvard's Tozzer Library (an anthropology library) is atypical, it illustrates the nature of the problem. That library receives more than 1,200 anthropology serial each year. If it did not do its own indexing, the library would have to spend more that $30,000 per year for indexing and abstracting services to achieve only 83 percent coverage of its serial holdings. Tozzer's solution to the indexing problem is to index all the serials it receives. It publishers the index an Anthropological literature, which helps offset the indexing costs.

One selection question is, "Should one subscribe only to commercially indexed serials?" If a library subscribes to an unindexed title, does that library do anything to help patrons locate information in the new serial? Specialised (subject) indexing services lead to patron requests for titles indexed in the service but not held by the library. The library must then decide whether to add yet another title to the serials list, increase the interlibrary loan (ILL) department's workload, or made patrons unhappy. Copyright law limits the library's ability to use ILL in place of subscribing to a particular title; copyright law limits the library's ability to use Ill in place of subscribing to a particular title; copyright law imposes legal constraints on the frequency with which one may borrow articles from a single serial title.

Document delivery services for journal articles are changing the nature of the selection decision. These systems, such as CARL Uncover (originated by the Colorado Alliance of research Libraries), allow libraries and information centers to offer customers access to thousands of serial titles and their tables of contents. Not only can one identify articles through an index service (presently search capabilities are not very sophisticated), but one can also order the items. The services have taken care of copyright, and the patron receives the full text. There are substantial costs ($10 to $20 per article on average) which the library or customer must pay. Mode of delivery varies from postal service to facsimile, with corresponding price differences. For low use titles, document delivery (DD) services may be the most cost-effective way to provide series. As of 1993 in the United States, the DD business was small ($60-70) million) compared to the subscription business (about $1 billion).[7] today the gap is much narrower and will, in all likelihood, continue to lessen in the future.

Selecting a document delivery or full-text vendor requires as much consideration as selecting a serial title. One must assume that funds to pay for the documents, unless the users are to pay the full costs, are likely to come from collection development allocations. Like all aspects of collection development, one must have a clear understanding of the purpose of and need for the service. Some of the possible reasons for employ in a service are:

To provide faster service than through traditional ILL service

To reduce the overall cost of ILL by having less mediation

To reduce subscriptions to high-cost, low-use journals

To provide a supplement to course reserve usage.

Other issues include the type of equipment required to implement the service and what, if any, remote access is available. The factors one uses to evaluate possible vendors are the same as for other library vendors, such as service and size. As popular as document delivery services are electronic indexing and full-text deliver services. These are discussed in greater detail in chapter 7.

Serial tend to increase the volume of photocopying activities. Serial articles are short (seldom more than 25 pages); as a result, many people prefer to photocopy the article and consult the material at their leisure. Also, many libraries do not allow serials, or at lest journals, to circulate, which further encourages photocopying. The amount of library or information center photocopy in is another copyright issue. Although the copyright law covers photocopying of monographs, it is the serials photocopying that is the major issue among serial publishers, librarians, and users.

When a library does not start a subscription with volume I, number I, the librarian must decide whether and to what extent to acquire back issues or volumes. Are backfiles needed? Some serial publishers have full runs available, but most do not. Titles widely held by libraries may be available from reprint houses. Backfiles are expensive, they may be difficult to find, they may require binding, they certainly take up valuable shelf space, and many receive little use. Libraries also cannot assume that vendors handling online full-text serials will maintain backfiles or make them available for all titles.

Serials can and do change over time. New editors, governing boards, or owners make major and minor shifts in the content and orientation. A major shift in emphasis usually is well publicized. As selectors become aware of such shifts, they can reassess the serial. A title change is something librarians. Frequently complain about, primarily because of internal concerns (see articles by Foggin[9] and Nelson[10]). From a collection development point of view, a title change should be welcome because it probably signals a significant change in the serial's content. For that reason, the selectors should review the changes in content to determine whether the item is still appropriate for the collection. Moe difficult to identify is a slow shift over a number of years. The final result may be a greater difference in content than a well-publicised major change, but few people will notice the shift. Periodic examination of incoming serials by the selection officers is an excellent method for checking on changes in emphasis.

Given all of these factors, one can see why serials selection is a major decision. Yet, all too often, libraries treat it as being no different from the decision to acquire a monograph.

Selection Models

There are fie basic approaches to selection: cost, citation analysis, worth or use, polling, and core lists. There are many variations, but the five listed form the basis for models for selecting serials. Much of the work done in this area is relatively recent and more the result of having to cancel rather than to start subscriptions.

Cost models of selection are the oldest and have the greatest number of variations. One of the most complex models deals with the real annual cost of a serial. The annual cost consists of six elements: acquisition cost, processing cost, maintenance cost, storage cost, utility or use cost, and subscription price. Acquisition costs include such things as selection, order placement, and time spent in working with the subscription agent or publisher. Processing costs cover check-in, claiming routing, cataloging or other labeling, adding security strips, and shelving in public service for the first time. Maintenance costs involve binding, microfilming or acquiring microform, selecting for remote storage, and possibly discarding. *Storage costs* entail calculating the linear feet of storage space (either or both shelf and cabinet space) used by the title and the cost of the space. *Utility or use* costs are the most complex to calculate. They incorporate costs of time of or such things as retrieval from a storage location (library staff only), pick-up and reshelving, answering questions about the title ("Do you have ...?", "I can n't find...", and "What is the latest issue you have?"), and all other required assistance (assistance with microform readers, for example). The last, and often the lowest, cost is the subscription price. The sum of these costs represents the real annul cost of the title for the library. Looking over the list of costs makes it clear that it will take some time to calculate the individual cost centers. However, once one determines the unit costs (for example, the average time to shelve an issue), it is fairly easy to calculate the cost for a given number of issues of a title. With an annual cost for each title, selectors can determine which titles title. With an annual cost for each title, selectors can determine which titles to continue or discontinue. Several articles describing variations on this approach are included in the "Further Reading" section at the end o this chapter.

Like cost models, citation analysis paradigms take several forms. The main objective, from a selection point of view, is to identify frequently cited titles. Citation analysis can help identify a core collection for a field and provide a listing of titles ranked by the frequency with which they are cited. Another collection development use of citation analysis is in evaluating a collection. (Could a set of papers/reports have been done using this collection?)

Citation analysis information is most useful in large or specialized research collections, although core collection information is valuable to smaller and non-specialised collections a well.

It is important to understand certain certainassumpitonsabotu cittion analysis before deciding to use this approach. The underlying assumption is that the subject content of the cited documnt relates to that of the citing document. A second assumption is that the number of times a document receives a citation is proportional to the value or intrinsic worth of the document. Another assumption is that all the publications an author cites were, in fact, used. (A related assumption is that authors list all the sources they used.) One other major assumption is that the sources used to secure the citation data are representative of the field under investigation. These are the major assumptions; others do exist. However, many people do not accept all the assumptions. If one cannot accept the assumptions, one should not use citation data for collection building.

There are two major sources of citation data; research reports and articles in the professional press, and data from the publishing firm institute for Scientific Information (ISI). ISI publishes Science Citation Index (SCI), Social Sciences Citation Index (SSCI), and Humanities Citation Index (HCL). These publications provide citation information for many journals. For example, SSCI covers almost 1,500 social science titles and provides selective coverage of about 4,500 nonsocial science journals that contain some social science material. On an annual basis, ISI also produces Journal Citation Re-science material. On an annual basis, ISI also produces Journal Citation reports (JAR), which provides a useful analysis of the journals ISI covers. Some of the major features of JAR are:

- a listing of the number of articles a title contained for the year
- how many citations were made to articles that appeared in the title through time.
- a ratio of articles published to articles cited (impact factor)
- a ratio of articles published during they year to citations to those articles (immediacy index)

- a cited half-life, that is, how far back in time one needs to go to retrieve 50 percent of all citations appearing during a year to all articles that ever appeared in the title.

Such information can be helpful in making continuation and storage or deselection decisions.

Using the Bradford Distribution, one can rank titles to develop information for collection policy use as well to make decisions regarding current subscriptions.11 The goal of this ranking is to identify all journals containing articles relevant to a given subject and to rank them in order based on the number of relevant articles they publish in a year. The pattern, according to Bradford's Law of Scattering, will show that a few journals publish the majority of articles and a large number of journals publish only one or two cited articles. If one equates a basic collection (level 2 in the conspectus concept, see pages 78-79 with holding journals that contain 20 per cent of the relevant material, one might subscribe to only three or four titles. For libraries with a comprehensive collection (level 5), the subscription list may contain several hundred titles. For example, Tozzer Library has a current subscription list of more than 1,200 titles for its coverage of anthropology. Journal worth models usually involve some information about title usage along with there data. An article by Dawn Bick and Reeta Sinha described one of the many worth models,[12] one that is reasonably easy to implement. The model involves cost, use, impact factor, and information about the nature of the publication (core subject, for example) to calculate a cost-benefit ratio.

As one might assume, most of the models require a substantial amount of data collection. If their only utility lay in making selection decisions, few libraries would use them. Their major value comes into play when the library must cut subscriptions. Having collected data that is similar for all the titles makes the unpleasant task a little easier. What librarians hoped would be a rare occurrence has, for some libraries, become an almost annual task. Each time the task becomes more difficult, and the models demonstrate their value.

Polling experts and using lists of recommended journals are other methods for identifying what to buy or keep. Both suffer from being less directly linked to the local situation, unless the experts are local users. One can find lists of journals in relatively narrow subjects, often listed with recommendations, or at lest comments, in journals like *Serials Librarian* and *Serials Review*.

Maria Janowska described a rather complex model to use when making the choice between paper and electronic materials.[13] She drew on a publishing method known as Multiple Criteria Evaluation (MCE). Her approach used content, publication cycle, number of subscribers, overall cost, and price as the criteria. She then used a matrix that allows one to compare the criteria against one another, which allows consistency in the decision-making process. The process is somewhat complex but is worth considering when making a series of decisions regarding paper or electronic journals.

Identifying Serials

Serials employ a different bibliographic network than that used for monographs. Few of the selection aids for books cover serials. However, there are several general and specialized guides to serial publications. Reviews o serials are few and far between. Bill Katz's column in *Library Journal* is one regular source of serial reviews. In the past, when publishers would supply several free sample copies of a title for the library to examine, the lack of reviews was not a problem. Today, many publishers charge for sample issues, and though it depletes the funds for subscribing to serials and adds to the time it takes to acquire them, it is useful to get sample issues before committing the library to a new serial.

Four useful general guides are Ulrich's International Periodicals Directory (R.R. Bowker), Irregular Serials & Annuals (R.R. Bowker), Serials Directory (EBSCO) and Standard Periodical Directory (Oxbridge Communications). All employ a subject arrangement, and entries provide all necessary ordering information. Bowker updates the annual Ulrich's with Ulrich's Update. Another resource, Standard Periodical Directory, covers American and Canadian titles and has a reputation for providing the best coverage of publications with small circulations, lesser-known organizations, and processed materials.

Newspapers, newsletters, and serials published at least five times a year are identifiable in guides like Gale Directory of Publications and Broad-cast Media (Gale Research) and *Willings' Press Guide* (Thomas Skinner Directories). For literary publications; on should use *International Directory* of little magazines and Small Presses (Dustbooks), MLA *International Bibliography* (Modern Languae Association), and L'Annee Philosogique (Societe International de bibliographie Classique).

All of the above, with the exception of *Ulrich's Update*, have limited value in identifying new titles, because they are annuals and the information is therefore at least several months old. (As noted earlier, serials change in a variety of ways—titles, frequency, editorial policy, and so on—and keeping up with existing titles is enough of a problem without addition the need to identify newly created serials.) the best source of information about serials acquired by American libraries is the Library of Congress's *New Serial Titles (NST)*, which reflects data in OCLC. Te data in NST is the result of a cooperative effort called Cooperative Online Serial Programme (CONSER). One gains a useful sense of the number of existing serial titles when one considers that in 1981, there were 339,000 CONSER records in OCLC; in 1997—1998, there were 856,618 records, with the addition of almost 34,000 new records. If one can justify costs, online systems provide the most current information. Certainly OCLC is one source as are BRS and DIALOG. The latter services have information from Ulrich's. Such services are current but costly; $75 per hour is not an uncommon charge, so one must be certain that the speed and currency are essential. Some serial vendors also supply new serial title information online.

Using a review of serials presents certain difficulties. Most serials that receive reviews are popular magazines rather than scholarly journals. Given the propensity of serials for change, a completely accurate assessment of a title is possible only when the serial ceases publication and the reviewers can examine all the issues. All that on should expect from a review of a serial is an accurate description of the content of the issue(s) available to the reviewer, usually not more than six issues. What a selector wants from the review is as much information about the purpose, audience, and editorial policy as the reviewer can identify; information about publisher, price, frequency, and other technical matters; and, if appropriate, comparisons to other related serials. Unfortunately, some of those limited data may be lacking, because it is sometimes difficult to determine purpose and editorial policy, even with the volume 1, number 1, issue in hand. Information about the publisher is less important in serials selection than in monograph selection because many times the serial is the publisher's only publication, and only time will reveal the publisher's reliability.

Serials Review (Pierian Press) publishes some reviews prepared by serials librarians and, occasionally, subject experts. The journal started as both a reviewing journal and a professional journal for serials librarians. Today it is primarily a professional journal, with only a few pages *Serials Reviews* in each volume. Occasionally, Serials Review reviews an established serial. Such reviews help librarians monitor changes in the editorial policy of titles to which the library subscribes.

Library Journal (R.R. Bowker) offers a regular section focusing on new periodicals. Each issue contains brief annotations describing 6 to 10 new titles. Because of the breadth of coverage, most types of libraries will find some titles of interest covered in the course of a year. Every few years, Bill Katz and Linda Sternberg Katz compile Magazines for Libraries,[14] in which they list 6,000 to 7,000 recommended titles.

New magazine review (new magazine review) covers titles of particular interest to librarians. Choice (association of college and research libraries feature a column, "periodically for college libraries". an additionally way to see new titles is to check at book and serial exhibitor booths at professional association meeting.

One van also uses core or recommended lists for a variety

of subject fields. Two examples are; A. Brandon and D.Hill's "selected lists of books and journals for the small medical library" bulletin of the medical library association 83 (April 1995); 151-75; and Selma Richardson's magazine for children, 2d ed (Chicago; American library association 1991). Some caution is in order when using core lists; one must understand the methodology employed to generate the list and know that it fits the needs of the library.

Serial Vendors

For most libraries, it is not economical to place serial subscriptions directly with the publisher. As we have seen, the amount of work required to monitor expiration dates, place renewals, and approve payments repeatedly for title is too great. In any sizable serial collection, a few titles will be direct orders to the publisher; however, if a library uses a serial vendor for most orders, there will be ore time for problem-solving activities related to serials.

Serial jobbers trend not to handle monographs, just to look jobbers tend not to handle serials. Tend is the key word here, given the variety of serials; in the area of annuals and numbered monographs series, lines, become blurred and jobbers overlap. Given the nature of serial publications, one is better served by an experienced serials jobber than by a friendly and willing book jobber who offers to handle the serials list along with book orders. Many serials librarians find it best to use domestic dealers for domestic serials and foreign dealers for foreign titles. Choosing a foreign dealer can be a challenge; for American libraries, the American Library Association's International Subscription Agents: An Annotated Directory is helpful. The 1994 edition lists agents and provides information about countries and regions covered, types of material serviced, catalogs or listings provided to customers, notes about special services (standing orders for monographs, for example), and name and address. It is advisable to ask other librarians about their experience with the dealers one is considering. If the librarian cannot identify anyone using a dealer, he or she might start by placing one or two subscriptions with the dealer and increase the volume of business if service is satisfactory.

Service is what one is looking for in a serials vendor. To provide service, the company must make a profit. How does it do that? In the past, vendors offered discounts. Today, libraries pay a service charge based on a percentage of the total subscription price. Serial vendors have one minor and two major sources of income. One major source is the discount publishers offer vendors. (Publishers offer these discounts because it is more convenient for them to deal with one billing/ordering source rather than subscriptions to many individual subscribers.) Recently, librarians have blamed publishers for rising subscription costs, but a few publishers claim that vendors share the blame because vendors are not passing on a share of the discount they receive from the publishers. Whatever the case may be, vendors depend on publisher's discounts to make a profit.

The second major revenue source for vendors is the service charge they add to their invoices to libraries. The service charge varies from library to library, depending on several factors. It often requires a good deal of work to determine just what the service charge is. When a subscription list contains thousands of titles, it is unlikely that there will be only one invoice, if for no other reason than that prices change during the year; supplementary invoices will arrive. Sales representatives may not know all the factors involved in calculating the charge and can give only an overview explanation. There may be various rates for various types of publications: in part, the service charge depends on the size of the discount the vendor receives.

Another variable in the calculation of a library's service charge is what services the library uses. Often, there is an extra charge for handling unusual serials, such as government publications. The types and number of management reports the library receives from the vendor also affect the service charge. Title mix is another factor, just as it is with book jobbers. For serial vendors, it is more a matter of knowing which titles generate additional work for the vendor, rather than a bookseller's pricing concerns with popular titles (low price/high discount) versus scholarly titles (high price/ low discount). If a library has a high percentage of problem titles, its service charge may be somewhat higher than for another library with a similar number of subscriptions, costing about the same, but with fewer problem titles.

The setting of the service charge is an art, and the service charge is open to negotiation. A good book on the acquisition aspects of serial work is N. Bernard Basch and Judy McQueen's Buying Srials.[15] A growing source of income comes from a variety of extra services most agencies offer, such as automation packages, publishing and electronic services (CD-ROMs, for example), custom lists.

What does the customer receive beyond the basic advantage of one order, one invoice, and one check for multiple subscriptions? Automatic renewal by a vendor saves library staff time, and when the invoice arrives, there is the opportunity to cancel titles no longer needed. Jobbers may offer multiple-year subscription rates that will save the library money. Notifying libraries about discontinuations, mergers, changes in frequency, and other publication alternations is a standard service provided by a serials jobber. The jobber is more likely to learn of changes before a library does, especially if the jobber has placed hundreds of subscriptions with the publisher.

Vendors also provide some assistance in the claiming process (missing issues, breaks in service, and damaged copies). Several of the large American subscription agents (for example, EBSCO and Read more) have fully automated serial systems that libraries use to handle their serials management programmes, including online claiming. (Fazon supports a backfile service serials Quest, that includes data from libraries and dealers.) For libraries with manual claiming systems, cost vendors offer two forms of claims: one by which the library notifies the vendor, which in turn contacts the supplier; and one by which the vendor supplies forms for he library to use to contact the published. Assistance in claiming has become more important in the past 10 to 15 years as more and more popular-market publishers use fulfillment centers. These centers serve as a publishers' jobber; that is, a center handles a number of different publishers' titles by receiving, entering subscriptions, and sending copies to subscribers. (For such centers, the mailing label is the key to solving problems; until recently, few libraries worried about serials' mailing labels.) Often the subscription vendor is more effective in resolving a problem with a fulfillment centre than is a single library.

Management information is another service serial vendors offer. Their information regarding price changes can be most useful in preparing budget requests. (A sample of this type of data appears.

Other types of management information that may be available (at an extra cost) are reports that sort the subscription list by subject or classification category, accompanied by the total amount spent for each group or (if there are several groups) a record of how many titles and how much money were charged to each group.

A good place to learn about the variety of services available, and who offers which services, is at the national meetings of various library associations. For example, representatives of most national serial vendors, as well as a number of foreign vendors, attend the ALA annual conventions. They will supply more than enough promotional material to fill a suitcase. Collect the information (including a formal request to quote), make comparisons, and talk with other librarians about their experiences with various vendors; this is the best way to go about selecting a vendor for one's library.

Cooperation in Serials Work

No library can acquire and keep all the serials that its patrons need or will at some time request. Knowing who has what serial holdings is important to serials librarians and anyone involved in interlibrary loan activities. The CONSER project and NST help to identify holdings in American and Canadian libraries. It is interesting to note that, despite the long-time concern about serial holdings, it was not until early 1986 that a national standard for serials holding statements was adopted in the United States (ANSI Z39.44). The standard provides for the same data areas, data elements, and punctuation in summary holding statements in both manual and automated systems.

Although the Centre for Research Libraries (CRL) is much more than a cooperative serials programme, CRL serial holdings have been effective in holding down the amount of duplication of low-use serial titles in American and Canadian research libraries. Bibliographic utilities such as OCLC and RLIN, whose databases include serial holdings, provide a type of union list service that H.W. Wilson's Union List of Serials provided so well in the past. To some extent, even vendor-based systems offer a form of union listing. Though it is possible to use such union lists and shared holdings to cover some low use serial requirements, the librarian must be certain to comply with copyright regulations before deciding not to buy.

Many libraries using the same serials vendor are able to acquire union lists form the vendor. For example, the four largest Catholic universities in California (University of San Francisco, Santa Clara University, Loyola Mary mount University and the University of San Diego) use EBSCO and have a union list produced each year to coordinate serial holdings. The libraries have agreed that when only one institution holds a title, there will be consultation with other libraries before the library drops the title.

Issues and Concerns

Several major issues face libraries today in regard to their serial collections. Cost is perhaps the major concern (cost of subscriptions, processing, storing, changing value of currencies, and tight budgets). Another issue is the delivery of serial information to customers without subscribing to the title busing document delivery or, as some librarians phrase it, "just in time rather than just in case." Related to document delivery are questions about copyright and traditional ILL services; on a percentage basis, ILL does more work with serials than monographs.

Continued growth in the number of serials and their spiraling costs are two issues of grave concern, especially for scholarly journals. Areas of knowledge are constantly being divided into smaller and smaller segments; at the same time, these smaller audiences want more information about the narrower topic. An example of the problem may be seen from the journal department of Academic Press, which announced one new journal, Applied Computational Harmonic Analysis: one journal dividing into two parts: Journal of Magnetic resonance—Series a And Series B: and seven titles increasing the number of issues per volume. All these changes carried price increases with them.

Costs of producing a special-interest journal will rise, no matter how many or how few people are interested in reading about the subject. When a journal reaches a certain price level, the number of individual subscribers drops quickly. More often than not, any price increase to individual subscribers only makes the problem wore. Increasingly, journal publishers have adopted a dual pricing system, one price for individual and another, higher price (often double or triple the individual rate) for institutions (read: libraries). The publishers' premise is that an institutional subscription serves the needs of many readers, which justifies the higher price. An interesting ethical question for librarians in general, and collection development personnel in particular is: Is it ethical for a library to regularly accept an individual's gift of journal that has a high dual-rate subscription? (Our view is no, the library should not do that. If not for ethical reasons, there are practical concerns about the regularity with which the person delivers the issues, as well as with securing missing issues).

If publishers take the dual-pricing concept to its logical conclusion, publishers will demand that libraries track the use of each serial and pay an annual service fee based on that number. Or, as one occasionally sees in the literature, publishers will make the title available only on a site-licensed basis. Before dismissing the idea as unrealistic, one should consider two things. First, for years libraries subscribing to H.W. Wilson's periodical indexes have been paying an annual service fee or subscription fee based on the number of journals indexed to which the library subscribes. Second, some countries, including Canada, now have a lending fee, that is, a fee paid to the author for each circulated use of his or her booking a pubic library.

There are two types of journal price studies with which collection development staff should become familiar: macro pricing and micro pricing. Macro information deals with subscription prices, rates of increase, and projections of coming price increases. One can obtain this type of data about the library's subscription list from the library's serials vendor. Information about overall price changes appears in several sources for U.S. serials, including *Library Journal* and *American Libraries*. One problem for many libraries is that data about projected price changes appears at a time when it is of little help in preparing the budget request for the next fiscal year. The data may be useful, but it is about a year behind the budget. That is, one uses 2001 projections for preparing the 2002-2003 budget request. What was clear at the time we prepared this edition was that no relief is in sight in terms of price increase. (One serials vendor issued a information sheet in late 1998 indicating that the price escalation had not really slowed. The vendor projected the 1999 increases in prices to range from 9.5 to 11.5 percent.) This pattern has been facing libraries for many years. Publishers don't understand why libraries cut their subscription lists and libraries and users don't understand why the prices must rise by so much more than the consumer price index.

Micro studies examine cost of the information in the journal, number of articles per volume, number of pages, page size, and cost per thousand words or characters. Such studies are helpful in the retention and cancellation activities in which more and more libraries must engage on an annul basis. (Finding micro studies takes a little effort; one good article dealing with the subject and presenting some examples is by Barbara Meyers and Janice Fleming.16) Not all publishers are pleased to see micro studies published, but such studies do provide useful data for building a cost-effective serials collection. Naturally, one must use these data in conjunction with their information, such as local use patterns.

Robert Pikowsky published a good article outlining both the history of journal price problems and the potential for electronic journal's solving the problem at least for academic and speciallibrries.[17] Not surprisingly, he did not see how e-journals would change the picture, and presently it appears that he was correct.

As journal prices rise and serial budgets fill to keep pace with the increases, collection development staff face the unpleasant task of deciding what to keep and what to drop. No one lies the process, especially the customers. Every one has er or his favorite candidates for keeping and dropping. A library's first cancellation project may be relatively easy, but after the initial round of cuts, the process becomes project may be relatively easy, but after the initial round of cuts, the process becomes progressively more difficult. The usual response is to assist decision makers by developing a model that takes price and use information into account. Price data are easy to acquire, at least at the macro level, but use data are more difficult to come by. Many libraries do not circulate journals, so circulation data analysis is not an option. In such cases, the library must establish so e process for collecting the data. Though one can find a number of articles about journal use data and cancellation work, the true task is to find a method that will work in the local situation.

For the most part, serials will continue to escalate in price and budgets may or may no keep pace. Clearly, serials will continue to play a major role in meeting customer information needs, and likewise may command a growing share of a limited collection development budget. How far can a library or information centre go in cutting back on the acquisition of other formats to maintain the subscription list? Will switching to electronic sources for on demand material really help with the budget problem, or just made matters wore? Answer to such questions vary from institution to institution.

Many librarians and information centers face the problem of buying the journal twice in paper and electronic formats. Even in the network environment, it is likely that potential users will not have network access. Does the library ignore these users and provide only the electronic versions? One think twice about dropping the paper version , because some publishers (Biological abstracts, for example) charge higher fee for the CD-ROM version if the library does not have a paper subscription as well. Often the higher fee is equal to the price of both subscriptions. With the ADONIS product (biomedical titles) the price of each article printed is based on whether the library has a paper subscription to the journal. Networking the material also entails extra expenses, such as license fees, that can equal or surpass the basic subscription price. Additionally, some products have a per-page or per-view charge that increases the overall cost. For example, Bell & Howell Information and Learning company has a 10 cents per printed page copyright charge for its full-text material on CD-ROM. Libraries should not expect to save money by shifting from paper to electronic formats, unless they also shift some of the costs to the users.

Short of providing full text in electronic form, the library can provide document delivery services bracket by index in and abstracting and table of contents access in electronic form. (A summary article about these services and their costs is by Ronald Leach and Judith Trible. Although the specific information in this article is outdated, the issues and consideration sthey raise remain valid.) Commercial services, such as Bell & Howell Informaton and Learngin Company's Article Clearninghouse and ISI's Genuine Article, provie documents based on thos ecompanies' indexing and abstrctign services. Newer services ar ebased upon the tables of contents of a large number of titles (11,000 to 12,000 titles). Subject searching is generally limited with the table of contents approach; basically, searching is keyword in title. In essence, with table of contents services, one gives up depth of subject access for broader scope in title coverage. Most table of contents services have also entered the document delivery field. CARL UnCover 2 is the oldest such service, with OCLC's Content First and Article First and RLG's CitaDel also available to users. As with full text, there are a variety of charges to consider before one can decide to drop a paper subscription. They are complex and costly, regardless of their format. Cost is probably going to remain the primary concern for some time.

For the past 15 years, serial prices have had double-digit rate increase, higher than anything else a library adds to its collection. Thus, serials continually take a larger and larger share of the materials budget, or the library must begin to cancel titles and provide access to the information in some other manner. Technology is changing the way libraries handle serials and is making it possible to provide access to more titles. However, technology will not solve the economic concerns of either the publishers and producers or the consumers.

REFERENCES

1. Thomas Nisonger, *Management of Serials in Libraries* (Engleood, Colo: Libraries Unlimited, 1998).
2. Heartsill Young, e.d., ALA Glossary of Library and Information science (Chicago: American Library Association, 1983).
3. Webster's *Third New International Dictionary* (Springfield, Mass.: G& C Merriam, 1978).
4. Fritz Machlup et al., *Information Through the Printed Word* (New York: New York University, 1978).
5. Judith Bernstein, "Corporate Annual Reports; The Commercial Vendors," *College & Research Libraries News* 47 (March 1986): 178-80.
6. Wallys Conhaim, "Linking up to the Global Network," LinkUp 15 January/February 1998): 5-11.
7. Janice Kuta, "AAP Seminar Explores Document Delivery," *Publishers Weekly* 239 (November 30, 1992): 20
8. Carol Foggin, "Title Changes: Another View," *Serials Librarian* 23, nos. ½ (1992); 71-83.
9. Nancy Nelson, "Serials Title Changes: What's in a Name?" *Computers in Libraries* 1 (February 1993): 4.
10. Robber Silvers, "Partitioned Bradford Ranking and the Serials Problem

in Academic Libraries," *Collection Building* 8, no. 2 (1986): 12-19.

11. Dawn Bick and Reeta Sinha, "Maintaining a High-Quality, Cost-Effective Journal Collection," *College & Research Libraries News* 51 (September 1991): 485-90.

12. Maria A. Janowska, "Printed versus Electronic: Policy Issues in the Case of Environmental Journals," *Serials Review* 20 (Fall 1994): 17-22.

13. William Katz and Linda Sternberg Katz, *Magazines for Libraries*, 9th ed. (New York: R.R. Bowker, 1997).

14. N. Bernard Basch and Judy McQueen, *Buying Serials* (New York: NealSchuman, 1990).

15. Barbara Meyers and Janice Fleming, "Price Analysis and the Serial Situation: Trying to Solve an Age-Old Problem", *Journal of Academic Librarianship* 17 (May 1991: 86-92).

16. Robert Pickowsky, "Electronic Journals as a Potential Solution to Escalating Serials Costs," *Serials Librarian* 32, nos. ¾ (1997): 31-55.

17. Marifran Bustion, John Eltinge, and John Harer, "On the Merits of Direct Observation of Periodical Usage," College & Research Libraries 53 (November 1992): 537-50; Anna Price and Kjestine Carey "Serials Use Study Raises questions About Cooperative ventures," Serials Review 19 (Fall 1993): 79-84; Christie Degener and Majory Waite, "Using an Automated serials System to assist with collection Review and Cancellations," *Serials Review* 17 (Spring 1991): 13-20; Maiken Naylor, "A Comparison of Two Methodologies for Counting Current Periodical Use," *Serials Review* 19 (Spring 1993): 27-34, 62.

18. Ronald G. Leach and Judith E. Tribe, "electronic Document Delivery: New Options for Libraries," *Journal of Academic Librarianship* 18 (January 1993): 359-64.

CHAPTER 2

Issues in Serials Cataloguing

Traditionally, the majority of serials are acquired through subscription, although serials are acquired through such other means as gifts, exchange or deposit. This section discusses the basic methods where by libraies acquire serials, except the change of serials is covered in more detail later in this chapter.

Subscription is the most frequently used serial order method. The *Serials Acquisition Glossary* defines *subscription* as "the arrangement by which, in turn for the sum paid in advance, a periodical, newspaper, or other serial is provided for a specific number of issues or a specific period of time." Typically, a serial subscription begins in January or covers a bibliographical volume (which often but not corresponds to a calendar year) or both. A *rolling*-year *subscription* is for a consecutive 12-month period, beginning with the month the subscription is placed. A bulk subscription is for a large number of copies (usually10 or more, according to the Serials Acquistion Glossary) of a particular title to be sent to a single address often for further distribution. A serial subscription is ocassionally obtained through membership in a society, association , or an organisation.To city a well-known example, national geographic is acquired through membership in the national geographic society.

In some cases membership is required to procure the subscription; in other instances optional membership provides a lower cost subscription or some other benefits, such as a right to purchase the organization's monographic publications at a discount. Some memberships receive all an organization's publications, both monographic and serial, and thus may be considered the equivalent of a *blanket order*.

A *standing order*, sometimes called a *continuation order*, is officially defined "a general order to vendor or publisher to supply the volumes or parts of a particular title or type of publication as they appear, until notified otherwise". The terms *until forbidden* or *Til forbidden* are particularly synonymous with standing order. In other words the library is telling the vendor to continue sending the item until told to stop, i.e., until the standing order is cancelled. A standing order is not normally used for periodicals but is used for annuals, monographic series, and and such law series as pocket parts. Two crucial elements distinguish a standing order from a subscription. A subscription must be renewed (usually on an annual basis), whereas a standing order, once placed, remains in force until cancelled or the ordered item ceases publication. Moreover, subscriptions are paid in advance, but standing orders are paid after each item is received.

A one- item, definite order for one or more items, the firm order is closed after the ordered material has been supplied. This order type is often contrasted to an approval plan (discussed below), subscription, or standing order. Film orders are commonly used to acquire monographs. They are generally unsuitable for serials (because of the format's characteristic of continuing indefinitely), but in certain circumstances, firm orders are used in serial acquisition. For example, single serial issues (needed for idiosyncratic collection development reasons or, more commonly to replace missing copies) or so-called non-subscription serial (defined as one for which the publisher refuses to accept subscriptions or standing orders) might be acquire through film orders. Both solicited and unsolicited gifts may include serials. Examples of the later would be

* newly founded serials that publisher send without charge to entice a library interest;

* publications by political groups that are more concerned with disseminating their view points than with financial remuneration; and
• individuals "cleaning out their closets."

Unsolicited serials whose sources are not readily can create numerous processing problems, i.e., it is unclear why they are arrived, there is no check-in record for them etc.

Solicited gifts include

• complimentary copies of journals published by the library itself or its parent organization and
• items subscribed by benefactors and turned over to a library.

Chiou-sen Dora Chen classifies serial gifts into three categories: backfiles, continuous donations, and miscellaneous. In the past many libraries have assigned a staff members to handle gifts or had a combined "gifts and exchange unit." Libraries should avoid giving the donor a statement of gift's value for income tax purposes because under Internal Revenue Service regulations the donor rather the recipient is supposed to evaluate the gift. Also ascertaining a gift's fair market value requires much time and effort.

Approval plans

Approval plans were developed in 1960s as a method for quickly and efficiently bringing books into the library and giving overall direction to the collection's development. The library writes a vendor indicating the subject areas and non-subject parameters (language, level, publisher type, etc.)in which it is interested in receiving materials. Book matching profile are shipped to the library on a regular basis (typically week) for review the library is to return unwanted items – thus the name *approval* periodicals are not received on approval plans, but such serials as annuals, yearbooks, and numbered monographic series can be included.

Deposit

The U.S. Federal Depositary Program, whose purpose is to

make federal government document available to the citizenry, was formally established in 1895 and included 1,400 libraries by the early 1990s both monographic and serial items are available. Participating libraries may be full depository or select depository. A full depositary library receives all documents distributed by the Government Printing Office. For select depositary libraries, the Government Printing Office provides a list of available items and the library creates profiles of what it wishes to receive, often listening specific serial titles. Select depositary academic libraries must consider the information needs of the local community members when selecting material. That the federal government is shifting towards the electronic distribution of information that will have a profound effect on the depositary system. Most states have depositary programs for state documents. Government document serials are typically administered by the government document rather than a serial unit.

Check-in

Check-in entails maintaining a record that a particular periodical issue has been received. Prior to automation, a Kardex file was traditionally used for serial check-in. Normally a Kardex is arranged alphabetically. Each entry might hold such basic information as title, place of publication, frequency, the vendor, the order type, the date of order was placed, the original requestor's name, routing instructions, binding instructions, payment record and each number's receipt date. (The precise information will vary from library to library.) Check-in achieves the following objectives: inventory control for current received periodicals, identification of missing or late issues for claiming and tracking of payment records. Discussion on SERIALST concerns whether the old Kardex file should be retained after automation. Marcia Turtle notes in an integrated, automated system, a check-in record need contain only details on receipt because it can be linked to the order and many bibliographic records that contain the order information traditionally found in the Kardex.

Claiming

In essence, a claim is gentle little remainder to vendor asking,

"Where the heck is my serial issue?" or pointing out some other problem. Yet serial claiming is more complex than is initially apparent. Six types of serial claims or reasons foe claiming have been defined have been defined by J. Travis Leach and Karen Dalziel Tallman and in the association for Library Collections and technical services (ALCTS) *Guidelines for Handling Library Orders for Serial and Periodicals.*

1. A skipped issue. If issue number 4 arrives before number 3 was received, it is evident that an issue was skipped.
2. A lapsed subscription. In this instance, issues stop arriving because the subscription has expired.
3. A doorman standing order. The major question, of course, concerns how much time must have elapsed before a standing order must have dormant.
4. An inactive new order. Although a subscription has been placed the issues do not arrive.
5. A replacement. An issue actually received requires replacement because it is defective or was damaged in the mail.
6. An incorrect number of copies supplied. No further explanation is required.

How long should one wait before placing the claim? Tuttle states, "There is no agreement among vendors or among librarians as to timing claim." The ALCTS Guidelines for handling Library Orders for Serials and Periodicals recommends a library wait 45 to 60 days after the anticipated publication date before submitting a claim for a new subscription. The B.H. Blackwell's Periodicals Services recommended the following guidelines for ongoing subscriptions: for daily publications, wait ten days since the receipt of the last issue wait two weeks for weekly publications, two months for monthlies, and five months for quarterlies. Tuttle provides a table of recommended claiming periods, ranging from 30 days for a domestic daily to 300 days for a foreign semiannual. If the first is not successful, she recommends a second claim after six to eight weeks for domestic publications and three months for foreign ones. Claiming policy and practice vary significantly among libraries and are influenced by such factors as available staff time and the automated system.

According to the ALCTS *Guidelines* for handling library orders for serial and periodicals, five factors should be considered prior to placing a claim: the title's publication frequency; the issues anticipated receipt date; vendor reports; a subscription's beginning date; and the other considerations "such as country of origin, method of delivery (air or surface mail), external matters (strikes, political developments, etc.)."

In the past claims were usually sent through the regular mail system. New electronic mail (e-mail) is increasingly used to transmit claims or more publishers develop electronic capacity. In mid –1996 an Indiana university claim specialist reported that she half her claims through e-mail.

Payment

Payment may be viewed as a final steps in the serial acquisition. It involves processing publisher or subscription agent invoices, a function often termed *payment authorization.* Tuttle stresses this should be done promptly, with careful checking and in accordance with accounting principles. checks are normally issued by an accounting office outside the library to insure a librarian does not go to Argentina or Brazil on a serial budget!

Periodical orders are normally renewed each year and paid in advance. A library typically receives an annual voice during the late summer or early fall. Added charges through supplemental invoices have traditionally cause much concentration to librarians. Reasons for added charges include a price increase by the publisher after the subscription agent sent the invoice, a influctuation in foreign currency exchange rates, and additional volumes issued by the publisher. Tuttle emphasises linking order, receipt, and paymet records to, among other things, support claiming and create an audit trail to demonstrate that the serials librarian really did not go to Argentina on the serials budget.

Periodicals are sometimes paid for through a depositoryaccount, in which a sum of money is paid in advance. The cost of subsequent orders is the deducted from the account's balance. Normally, a depository account would not be exclusively for serials.

One occasionally hears that libraries—to take advantage of subscription prices that are less expensive for individuals than institutions—should reimburse supporters who subscribe to journals in their own names and then turn over the received issues. This tactic entails both practical and ethical problems, however, and should be avoided. Such a tactic should not be confused with an "adopt-a-Serial" programme, in which a benefactor pays the subscription cot for a particular serials title, because, in the latter situation, the order would be placed through the library.

Fund Accounting

Sometimes termed budget control, fund accounting entailskeeping track of serial expenditures as the library prograesses through the fiscal year. Traditional financial accountign categories for librarymaterials include allocation, encumbrance, expenditure, and balance. Allocation represents the initial amount of budgeted money. Encumbrance refers to funds that have been committed but not yet actuallyspent. The term expenditure is self-explanaory, as it reflects funds that have been paid out. Balance refers to the amont still availabel when encumbrances and expenditures are subtracte from the allocaiton. A related concept, sometiems termed free balance, reflects all unexpended funds.

Monthly financial reports accordign to these categories, whih have been traditioanlly used for monographs, do nto lend themselves eepeciallywellto serials for a variety of reasons, includign add-on charges, the fact that serials expenditures are driven by a renewal cycle rather than uniform expenditures throughout the fiscal year, and the problem that the major serials budgetary issue cocerns advance predicton of the current subscription list's inflation rate.

Many libraries find it helpful to keep track of serials expenditures according to such variables as subject or department; venor; publisher;

time period (e.g., on a monthly basis); counter of origin; and expenditure category (i.e., current subscriptonal, standing orders, replacements, etc.).

Automated serials control systems, generally include a budgeting and financial accounting system. Serial subscription agent reports can provide assistance. Various software programmes can support serials budgeting and financial control. Lynne Myers Hayma describes the use of dBase III+ at Beaver College library, and Helen M. Shuster depicts the use of dBase III+ and Lotus 1-2-3 at Worcester Polytechnic Institute.

Other Acquisition Functions

Because of space limitations and the fact that this book emphasizes serials collection management rather than processing, other serials acquisition issues will not be noted but not discussed, including preorder searching and verification, order preparation maintaining invoice files, renewals, cancellation, and mail sorting. Two textbooks, *Chen's Serial Management:* a practical guide offer through discussions of these issues as well as the entire serial acquisitions process.

Cataloguing of Serials

This section introduces the important tools and major issues for serials cataloguing and briefly describes the Cooperative Online Serial Program (CONSER) project plus union list of serials. The machine readable cataloguing (MARC) record and format integration. Frieda B. Rosenberg's chapter on serial cataloguing in Tuttle's *managing serial* offers an excellent analysis of contemporary serial issues.

Cataloguing Tools

As stated in recent cataloguing textbook, "in current United States cataloguing practice there is no comprehensive code of rules" that covers all aspects of cataloguing. Yet some tools are available for serial cataloguing.

Codes of descriptive cataloguing are often traced to Anthony Panizzi's so called 91 rules published in 1841. The code currently in forced is the revised version of the *Anglo-American cataloguing rules,* second edition, issued in 1988, amended 1993, and often abbreviated AACR2R. Descriptive cataloguing of serials is covered in AACR2R's chapter 12, organized according to the eight areas of International Standard Bibliographic Description: title and statement of responsibility; edition; numeric/ alphabetic/chronological or other designation; publication or and distribution or both; physical description; series; note; standard number and terms of availability choice of access points.(i.e., ascertaining main and added entries). A vital supplement to the AACR2R is the *Library of Congress Rule Intepretations (LCRI), Published in its Cataloguing Service Bulletin.* As promised by its title, the LCRI outlines Library of Congress (LC) interpretations of the cataloguing code as well as LC policies, which are generally followed by north American libraries.

Specific tools for serial cataloguing have been produced by the CONSER project, described in the subsequent section. The CONSER Editing Guide provides practical instruction on MARC "tagging" (i.e., use of MARC fields and application of codes.) Its companion piece, the CONSER *Cataloguing Manual,* may be viewed as a training guide and reference source for serial catalogers. Also of use are some cataloging textbooks, such as Carol L.H. Leong' serial Cataloging Handbook, Bohdan S. Wyner and Arlene G. Taylor's Introduction to Cataloging and Classification, and maxwell's handbook for AACR2R: *Explaining and Illustrating the Anglo-American Cataloging Rules and the 1993 Amendments.* The latter two contain a chapter on serials. The CONSER World Wide Web (WWW)site provides E-mail addresses for submitting the serials cataloguing question to the LC.

Bibliographic utilities, which offers databases of cataloging records, might also be viewed as cataloguing records. William Saffady has thoroughly documented the history of these organizations, which originated during the 1960s. The OCLC Online Computer Library Center (OCLC), originally founded the in 1967 to support the cataloging function among academic libraries in Ohio, was providing 24,000 libraries in 63 countries by 1997 the world cat item database items through OCLC contained 34378135 unique records of which 1,786,063 were for serials. the two other major U.S. bibliographic utilities are theWestrn Library Network (WLN) and th eResearch Libraries Information Network (RLIN) Th efourth North American bibliographical utility, Utlas International Canada (formerlythe University of Toronto LIbrary Automaton System) was purchased by ISM Informaiton Systems Management Corporation in December 1992 and renamed the ISM Library Inofrmaiton Services. Bibliographic utilities support serials catalogng in a variety of ways, including providing cataloging records, retrospective conversion, authority control, and creatign union lists. CONSEr records, discussed below, are availabel through OCLC. Problems wit bibliographic utility databases include duplicate records for the same title, substandard records input by members, and the fact a serial may have changed (title, frequency, publisher, etc.) since a record was input.

Issues in Serials Cataloging

Instruction on cataloging serials is clearly not this chapter's purpose. Readers interested in practical guidance are referred to the various tools mentioned above. This section discusses some major serials cataloging issues.

- *To Catalog or Not*: Whether serials need to be cataloged has been a long-debated issue, with Andrew D. Osborn taking an ambivalent position. Arguably, the major cataloging purpose—helping patrons access the collection—can be accomplished by creating a serials holding list rather than cataloging. In fact, holdings were often not included with the bibliographic record in the old card catalog and early OPACs. However, because OPACs can now easily link bibliographic records with holdings statements, cataloging of serials would be the desirable option.
- *Extent of Cataloging*: Even cataloged serials may not receive complete cataloging treatment (i.e., subject headings and classification numbers in addition to descriptive cataloging). Libraries that shelve serials alphabetically

may both perceive a need to assign classification numbers. Ironically, Wynar and Taylow state that determining classification numbers and subject headings for serials may be less complex than for monographs because they are assigned at a more general level.

- *Unit That Is Cataloged*: Cataloging of periodicals could theoretically focus on any of three units: title, issue, or article. For fairly obvious reasons, serials cataloging as usually focused on the title. It would be highly expensive t catalog issues or articles. Moreover, access to specific issues can be provided through holdings statements, and indexing and abstracting services provide access to individual articles. However, some academic libraries (e.g., the College of Charleston and Carnegie-Mellon University) plan to catalog individual articles.
- *Level of Cataloging*: The AACR2R offers three levels of cataloging. The higher the level, the more detail included in the cataloging record. The LC uses an "augmented" level on e for serials. The following is added to the bare-bones first-level one for serials. The following is added to the bare-bones first-level description: A "general material designation" when appropriate (a serial computer file would be designated as such), parallel title or titles, the first statement of responsibility, the first place of publication, the first publisher, additional physical details, and series. In practice, the amount of detail in the bibliographic description of serials varies widely among libraries.
- *Source of Information for Cataloging*: AACR2R specifies that the chief source of cataloging information for a print serial is the title page of the first issue. If the cataloger does not have access to the first issue, the first a available issue can be used. Prior to AACR2, cataloging was based on the latest issue. If there is not title page, as is often the case in a serial's first issue, an alternate title page, cover, capitation masthead, editorial pages, colophon, or other pages can be used.

- *Choice of Entry*: Only infrequently is a serial's main entry an individual author. Thus, the usual choice is between title and corporate author (e.g., is the Bulletin of the American Cat Fanciers Society entered under title or the American Cat Fanciers Society?). In the 1970s considerable debate in the profession concerned a proposal to catalog all serials under title main entry, but the proposal was rejected by the Joint Steerign Committee for revision of AACR in 1976. However, AACR2 (published in 1978 and implemented by the LC in 1981) did restrict corporate author main entry in favour of more entries under title. In accordance with rule 21.1B2 of AACR2R, a serial is entered under corporate author only if it "emanates" fro the corporate body and more than 50 percent of its content deals with the body's policies, procedures, and operations. In contrast, pre-AACR2 policy allowed corporate main entry based on wording in the title.
- *Latest Entry Versus Successive Entry*: Because serials frequently change title and, thus, form of entry, a long-standing issue that is still debated concerns which form should be used in the catalog. Three major options exist: earliest entry, latest entry, and successive entry cataloging. In earliest entry cataloging a serial is cataloged under the earliest or original form of entry—an approach broached by Charles A. cutter in 1876 and adopted in the United Kingdom in 1908. This approach offers the advantage of a single, consistent form of entry. The clear disadvantages is that a periodical could be entered under a vastly outs dated title. Latest entry cataloging lists a periodical under its most current title. This option was included in the 1908 and 1949 cataloging codes. A "Title Varies" note is used to link the current title with previous titles by presenting the history of title changes. Successive entry cataloging uses a separate catalog record for each significant title change. Successive entry cataloging, which conforms to international standards, was contained in the 1967

Anglo-American Cataloguing Code and adopted by the LC in 1971. Notes, such as "Continues" and "Continued by," connect a title with its immediate preceding title and its immediate following title. This arguably constitutes a more economical, efficient approach than latest entry cataloging because no attempt is made to trace a journal's entire history in a single "Title Varies" notes. Successive entry cataloging can lead to a proliferation of records in the catalog, although this is not a significant issue in an automated environment. The Northwestern University Library began using a modified form of latest entry cataloging in 1985 because "meaningless title changes" required new successive entry records. A fourth theoretical possibility is to catalog under the "best known title." This approach has not received much attention in the literature or actual practice because of the strong subjective and relativistic element in determining which title is the "best known."

- *Electronic Journals and access versus Ownership*: chapter 9 addresses electronic journal cataloging issues and the associated question on whether items not physically housed in the library should be entered into the OPAC.
- *Format Integration*: The question of format integration—consolidating seven separate MARC records for different formats (e.g., book, serials, computer files, etc.) into a single record—has received considerable attention from serials catalogers in recent years. Because this issue relates to the structure of the MARC record.

The Conser Project

The CONSER project deserves attention because of th eimportnt roel it has played in serials cataloging during the last two decades. The project began during the early 1970s under th eauspices of th eCouncil on Library Resources as a major ooperative effort to support serials retrospective conversion by creating MARC records, but it later shifted emphasis to support the cataloging of current serials. The acrony CONSER originally stood for Conversion of

Serials Project, but in 1986 the name was changed to Cooperative Online Serials programme to reflect its new focus. According to the current CONSER mission statement, the programme "facilitates identification a of and access to serials by cooperatively building and maintaining a database of authoritative bibliographic records." Useful histories or descriptions of the CONSER project have been written by a number of authors, including Suzanne Striedieck and Bill Anderson.

Since its inception, the number of CONSER members has increased. As of December 17, 1996, there were 31, organized into five membership categories. "National Members," The 16 "Full Members" include the Center for Research Libraries; the U.S. government Printing Officer; Harvard, Cornell, and Indiana Universities; and the University of Pittsburgh. The remaining categories are "Associate" (four members), "Affiliate" (three members), and "Enhanced' (four members). The U.S. Newspaper Programme, jointly administered by the LC and the National Endowment for the Humanities, contributes records for U.S. newspapers to the CONSER database.

Prior to 1984 cataloging records from CONSER embers were authenticated by the National Library of Canada (for Canadian records) and the LC for all other records. Once authenticated, a record could only be changed by these two national libraries. Due to the backlog caused by these policies, self-authentication by CONSER members was introduced in 1984, except for certain fields.

A few CONSER projects should be noted. The A & I overage Project adds abstracting and indexing notes to bibliographic records. A large number of records have been contributed by the U.S. Newspaper Programme. A Subject and Classification Task Force was appointed in 1988 to development CONSER guidelines For subject analysis (the majority but not all CONSER records contain subject headings). CONSER is presently addressing cataloging issues posed by electronic serials.

The CONSER database contained about 260,000 records in January 1980, 437,623 "fully authenticated" records at the end of 1988, and 697,000 authenticated records by the beginning of 1995. The database is contained within the OCLC Online Union Catalog. Each week OCLC sends tapes containing authenticated CONSER records to the LC and the national Library of Canada, who distribute them through their marc services. The entire CONSER database is available in CD-ROM through CD-MARC Serials, which can be purchased from the LC. The National Library of Canada distributes CONSER records in microfiche through CONSER Microfiche. Paper-format CONSER records appear in NEW Serial Titles, except those contributed by the U.S. Newspaper Programme.

Beginning in 1976 a newsletter Conser, provided news about the project. In January 1994 this newsletter was renamed Conserline and converted to electronic-lonely format to be distributed free of charge on a semiannual basis in January and June. Two major publications are the previously mentioned CONSER Editing Guide and the CONSER Cataloging Manual.

Although a major thrust of the CONSER project has been editing or updating records to reflect title changes, it has also addressed the issue of duplicate serial records in the OCLC database. The project's obvious benefit is the provision of reliable serials cataloging records that can be used for copy cataloging and retrospective conversion. CONSR records also support numerous other serials functions, such as collection management, library automation, inter library loan, the creation of union lists, and check-in. Furthermore. CONSER has played an important role in developing and maintaining serials cataloging standards. The CONSER project is generally viewed as a successful cooperative effort that created a high-quality national database of bibliographic records for serials. Striedieck asserts, "Most references to the CONSER database generally express satisfaction with the size and scope (with some notable gaps), though some have decried inconsistencies among records."

Union Lists of Serials

A union list contains the holdings of two or more libraries. According to the Serials Acquisitions Glossary, it lists "items of a given type, in a certain field, or on a particular subject.' The list can assume a paper or electronic format. In recent decades considerable effort has been devoted to creating union lists of serials. These lists typically contain he periodical holdings of a consortium of libraries or the libraries in a geographical region such as a metropolitan area or a state.

The world's first serials unionlist was supposedly a 20-page pamphlet issued in Milan, Italy, in 1859; the initial American list, Check List of Periodicals, was published by Johns Hopikins University in 1976. In1927 the American Library Association (ALA) published the Union List of Serials in Libraries of the United States and Canada, for which a second edition was published in 1943 and a third in 1965.

In 1981 the Directory of Union lists of Serials identified 60 separate serials union lists. The number had increased to 137 by 1988 when the Directory's second edition was published. The second edition, based on a survey conducted in spring 1986, summarized serials union list project sin 37 different states and the Distribute of Colombia as well as Canada, Belgium, and India.

Union lists can contain bibliographic data and holdings or location data (Or both) while serving as a "finding" tool. A serials union list can support serials collection development and management and resource sharing by indicating a title's availability elsewhere. Such lists can also support a variety of other library functions, including technical a services interlibrary loan, and reference.

Other Processing Functions

The serials processing functions previously discussed are arguably the most important. This section directs attention to some additional functions (e.g., routing, replacing missing issues, and binding).

Routing

Distributing a serial issue to a select group of individuals is termed routing. Typically, library science journals are routed to staff members, who use them for selection or general professional development. Occasionally, an academic library will route journals to faculty as a form of current awareness or selective Dissemination of Information (SDI). Special libraries often route journals to their clients because they tend to emphasize customized service. An issue is usually routed before being placed on the shelves for use by patrons, although in some cases libraries ma purchase duplicate subscriptions for routing. The major processing issues concern maintaining a list of individuals to whom the issue is to be circulated, integrating routing into the serials workflow, and retrieving issues.

A system for routing new journal issues to faculty at the University of New Hampshire's Biological Sciences branch Library has been described in the literature. Deborah Naulty has explained the use of Lotus 1-2-3 software to support routing.

Replacing Missing Issues

A replacement issue has been defined by Beth Holley and others as "a substitute for an item once purchased and received, which now requires reordering/repurchasing to complete a binding unit." The term replacement is also applied to purchasing issues that were never received (i.e., the claim period lasped or a subscription began after the first issue). A periodical issue may be missing because it was lost, stolen, or damaged after receipt. Mutilation by patrons who cut out pages or articles (inexcusable behaviour in the age of photocopying machines) represents a major cause of damage. To share an anecdote from the university of Manitoba during the 1970s a patron once entered the Current Periodical Reading Room and asked for a pair of scissors. When asked why he needed them, he replied, "to cut an article out of a magazine!"

Issues are commonly identified as missing through the check-in and claiming process (if they were never received), during preparation for binding (for numbers that were lost, stolen, or damaged), or the public service function (If patrons cannot locate a desired issue). In some instances, a library may decide not to replace the issue (e.g., it is superseded by a later cumulation or from allow-priority title). To help, one can compile a list of missing items to replace, arranged by title and number, termed a *Desiderata* or *Want* list.

Options for obtaining missing issues include purchase (from the publisher, a serials subscription agent, or a periodical backrun dealer), duplicate exchange, gifts, micro for, or getting reprint. Under certain circumstances, copyright law allows photocopying an item from another library for replacement purposes—see the later section on copyright. The most appropriate option will vary depending upon the missing item and the resources (i.e., funds plus staff time) available to the library.

As Geraldine f. Pionessa comments, "Special procedures must be followed to handle the idiosycraises of replacement orders since they are more like monographicir orders than subscriptions or standing orders." Her article contains a more-detailed discussion. A replacement programme at the University of Alabama library has been briefly depicted in the literature.

Binding

Binding is a major and labour-intensive operation in many libraries. During 1995-96 Association of Research Libraries (ARL) libraries spent more than $25 million on contract binding—of which approximately two-thirds was spent for serials. This section addresses the processing aspects of binding after the collection management decision to bind a particular title (discussed in chapter 4) has been reached. The discussion assumes that serials are bound at a commercial bindery rather than in-house. Major steps in the binding process are briefly outlined below:

- *Identifying titles ready for binding.* A binding schedule should be established for each title. Most periodicals are bound once a year, when a complete bibliographical volume is bound as a physical volume. Frequently issued titles that will be bound in more than a single physical volume may be sent to the bindery two or more times per year. Some libraries avoid sending the most recent issue to reduce patron inconvenience. Instructions on the binding schedule and binding requirements for periodical titles can be kept in a check-in file, a bindery field, or an automated system. Some automated systems contain a "binding Information File" that serves as a master file of pertinent binding data.

- *Preparing binding shipments*. This is the process's most labor-intensive aspect. The issues are pulled from the shelves and taken to the binding preparation area. Generally a bibliographical volume should be bound as a physical volume, although Milan Milkovic states a thickness greater than 4 ½ inches is undesirable. The contents are checked for completeness and collated. Tables of contents and indexes would normally be included. Whether to bind covers and advertising is debatable, although the front cover should definitely be bound if it has artistic value or contains bibliographic information. The contents to be bound as physical volume will be tied or bundled together. (A bottle of aspirin may be needed in cases where a title has switched size or when issues or pages are missing.) The shipment is normally packed in boxes, which are often supplied by the bindery. A binding ticket is printed or written in duplicate (one copy for the library, the other for the bindery) containing instructions for each volume to be bound. Typically, this includes the title, an identification number, account number, the date sent, type of binding, binding style, buckram color, lettering color, spine information (i.e., title, volume, date), slot (location on spine where information appears), and special instructions-often odes are used to save time and space.
- *Bindery pickup*. Generally, commercial binderies pick up and deliver binding shipments on a predetermined schedule. In some cases commercial trucking companies or the post office might be used. A binding or packing list of the included titles and volumes (arranged in alphabetical or some other systematic order) is usually created to accompany the shipment. The number of items is a shipment should be tabulated for record keeping.

- *Keeping record of volumes at bindery.* A temporary record of volumes sent of binding, the date sent and the expected return date can be quite important for public service purposes. Some automated systems contain a "Binding Shipment File" and can print an "at bindery" list. Many integrated automation systems indicate items at the bindery and the return date in the OPAC.
- *Receiving shipments form binding*: reshelving items; adjusting records to indicate return from bindery; preparing bindery invoice for payment. These self-evident steps require little elaboration. The invoice and the bindery's packing slip should be checked for accuracy. Final processing steps, such as marking with the library's ownership stamp or inserting security strips may be performed prior to reshelving, although, depending upon contractual terms, the bindery might perform these steps.

During the last two decades, automated binding preparation systems have been developed by binderies and marketed by automation vendors (including subscription agents and bibliographic utilities) as part of serials control systems. Moreover, serials control systems that lack a separate binding module can sometimes be manipulated to support the binding process. These systems can make binding procedures easy by automating record keeping and billing and printing binding slips. Yet much of the labour involved in the binding process such as carrying items to and from the shelves and transporting items back and forth form the bindery, can not bee limited by automation. Toby Heidtmenn described the University of cincinnati's use of Help-Net, a microcomputer-based binding preparation system from the Heckman Bindery, and Harry H. Campbell and Wesley. L. Boomgaarden wrote about the Ohio State University library's use of the General Bookbinding Company's automated binding system.

Other issues include selecting and negotiating term with a bindery, deciding whether to sign a contractor use a profile, determining standards of acceptable workmanship and service, budgeting for binding and keeping track of expenditures, ascertaining what type of binding is most appropriate for a particular periodical, migrating from a manual to an automated binding system, evaluating the interface between the binding component of one's automated system and the requirement's of one's commercial bindery, and handling incomplete volumes. A detailed discussion of binding may be found in Tuttle's Managing Serials.

Duplicate Exchange of Serials

Exchange of materials (often duplicate or unneeded items) among libraries has been a long-standing practice. Although most types of material can be exchanged, serials are a major focus of duplicate exchange activity. For illustration, at the University of California at Berkeley Library in the mid-1980s, 90 percent of exchange activity involved serials. During the 1990 fiscal year, 75.8 percent (387,651 of 511,139) of the pieces acquired by the LC exchange and Gift Division were serials. Generally, either subscriptions or replacement issues are exchanged.

Library exchanges have usually been orgnised according to two models: one-on-one exchanges between libraries and organized exchange unions. The LC's Surplus Book Programmes does not precisely correspond to either model. Both organizational models and the LC programme will be discussed separately.

Direct Exchanges Between Libraries

As implied, this organisational model refers to an explicit exchange agreement between two libraries (or other education entitles, such as museums or scholarly societies). The exchange can be with domestic or foreign institutions, although the later is more common. These exchanges are usually for ongoing subscriptions rather than replacement issues, and non serial items can also be included. Material published by the library or its parent university are frequently offered in the arrangement.

The three types of direct exchange used by the LC exchanges and Gift Division illustrate different theoretical approaches; priced, piece-for-piece, and open. In a priced exchange, the partners agree to provide each other materials of a set monetary value within a particular time period. Considerable bookkeeping is obviously required. A piece-for-piece exchange tabulates the number f specific items that have been exchanged, usually similar type items that have been exchanged, usually similar type items (i.e., "book for book, pamphlet for pamphlet, microform for microform"). The LC uses this approach to acquire serials, usually published by the exchange partner, that are not available through regular market channels. In an open exchange, libraries donate and receive without recording the number of exchanged pieces or their monetary value.

The traditional motivations for entering direct exchanges follow:

- to obtain journal as inexpensively;
- to obtain journals that are difficult or impossible to procure through regular subscription (for example, in the late 1970s only 8 of the 555 serial titles received on exchange by the Johns Hopkin University Library were available through regular subscription channels); and
- in a more idealistic sense, to contribute to a wider dissemination of publications from one's institution or country.

The origin of direct exchange between libraries has been traced to an 1840 Joint Resolution of the U.S. Congress authorising the LC to exchange materials with foreign libraries. During the late nineteenth century, many U.S. academic libraries established exchanges with foreign institutes. For example, in 1882 the Johns Hopkins University library instituted an exchange with the Royal Swedish Academy of Sciences' Mathematics Institute. The University of California at Berkeley Library began its exchange programme in the 1880s. The number of exchange programmes between U.S. and foreign libraries expanded in the post-World War II period.

Considerable evidence suggests libraries have been scaling down or eliminating their exchange activities. In the early 1970s the Johns Hopikins Library had 390 exchange agreements, from which they received more than 800 serial titles and provided 660; but by the late 1970s, the figures had been reduced to 555 titles received and 325 supplied, based on 250 exchange agreements. In 1995 it was reported that the Ohio State University libraries had recently eliminated 5000 exchanges, keeping only a small number for such crucial areas as the former Soviet Union.

Organized Exchange Unions

In contrast to direct agreements between two libraries, exchange can be organized among a large number of libraries, often under the auspices of a professional orgnisation. Although precise details very among exchange unions, material may be offered for free, for a set free, or for reimbursement of postal costs. Typically, lists of materials available for exchange are circulated to members.

Perhaps the best-known duplicate exchange union is the United States Book Exchange (USBE). The USBE, originally termed the Universal Serials & Book Exchange and located in Washington, D.C., was founded in 1948 to help acquire material for European libraries that were damaged or destroyed in World War II. The USBE relocated to Cleveland, Ohio, in spring 1990. A duplicate exchange programme among libraries in the greater Dallas-Fort worth area was run for a brief period during the mid-1980s by the University of Texas at Dallas Library.

The ALA's Library Collections and Technical Services Division manages an exchange programme termed the Duplicates Exchange Union. This exchange operates the DEU-L listserv. The materials is provided free except for postage reimbursement.

Some more-specialised duplicate exchange unions are briefly summarized below:

> ASEE/ELD Duplicates exchange. (For engineering materials)
>
> This exchange union is managed for the American Society for Engineering Education Engineering Libraries Division (ASEE/ELD) and coordinated at the North Carolina State University libraries. Lists of available materials along with claiming instructions can be sent to the coordinator, who will post them to members and on BACKSERV (see below).

In the last few years, several Internet-based listservs have been created for exchanging serials and other materials among libraries.

Backserv. In autumn 1994 the serial subscription agent Readmore announced a new listserv, entitled BACKSERV, for the exclusive purpose of exchanging serials back issues among libraries. BACKSERV's scope was soon expanded to include books.

BACKMED. IN July 1995 BACKSERV was split in half when Readmore founded a second list, BACKMED, for the exchange of medical serials and books. Both BACKSERV and BACKMED are now administered by Blackwells, which recently merged with Readmore.

DUPSTM-L. This list offers STM journals and backruns for exchange among Australian libraries.

COLLIBS. Although not explicitly created for exchange purposes, COLLIBS< a list for academic and research libraries in Australia, frequently offers serial backruns for exchange among Australian libraries.

EUROBACK. This French-language list is for the exchange of serial backruns and books among European libraries.

LIS-MEDJOURNAL-DUPLICATES. This list is primarily for the exchange of medical and health science journals among medical libraries in the United Kingdom, although non-U.K. libraries can also participate.

NEEDSANDOOFFERS-L. This listerv is for the exchange of legal materials, including law serials.

Subscription addresses for most of the above lists can be found in the WWW site "back Issues & Exchange Services."

Lydia A. Morrow's 10-week study of the ALA's Duplicates Exchange Union, conducted at the Governors State University library in Illinois, indicates that procuring missing serial issues through exchange is inexpensive but highly labor-intensive. She found that 33 hours and 22 minutes were required to review 66 lists (30.33 minutes per list), resulting in the procurement of 45 items (out of 183 requested). Although not stated by Morrow, the required staff time for reviewing lists averaged 44.5 minutes for each item obtained. However, the total out-of-pocket expense of $16.23 for postage reimbursement to the supplying library amounted to only 36 cents per item.

The Library of Congress Surplus Book Programme

A surprisingly large proportion of librarians are unaware that the LC acts as the official disposal agent for books and serials that have been discarded from U.S. federal libraries. Often termed the Surplus Book programme, the procedure apparently dates from the post-World war II period. This rather obscure programme, administered by the LC Exchange and Gift Division's Receiving and routing section, has rarely been described in the literature (e.g., by A.. Aime Deschamps, R. Neil Scott, and Thomas E. Nisonger).

More than two million items per year are normally transferred from other federal libraries to the LC for disbursement through this program. The LC uses a seven-level hierarchy for disposing of the material:

1. Selection for its own collection
2. Transfer, whereby federal libraries and agencies select item for transfer to their collections.
3. International Exchange, in which staff select material for use in the LC's exchange agreements with overseas libraries, universities, museums, and scholarly societies.
4. Domestic Exchange, in which LC staff select items for exchange with such U.S. partners as universities, museums, and historical societies.
5. Project Ex, in which book dealers and libraries select sets of material and submit financial bids; if the bid is accepted, the money is used to purchase microfilming services for the LC, which are given "in exchange' for the selected items.

6. Domestic Donation, whereby any tax-example U.S. library can select free material for its own use.
7. Final disposition, that is, the remaining items are contracted out for paper recycling

Federal libraries select free material at level two. Most other libraries tae apart at level six, in the Domestic Donation program; although they are also eligible to bid on material at level five, through Project ex. The Domestic Donation programme is open to U.S. university, college, school, and public libraries that qualify as tax-exempt institutions. however, special libraries attached to for-profit corporations as well as non-U.S. libraries are ineligible.

Serials represent a significant portion of the available material. Most of what the LC selects for its own use at level on in he the disposal hierarchy are bound serials volumes, which are used to replace missing issues. During the mid-1980s the University of texas at Dallas Library successfully filled numerous gaps in periodical backruns through the Domestic donation programme. The LC stresses that one should not make a trip to Washington, D.C., simply to select material because no guarantees exist about how much useful material will be available at any particular time.

The exchange function is closely tied to the paradigm of traditional librarianship, which focuses on the ownership of materials. Moreover, exchange can be costly because of its labour-intensive nature—although exchange listervs on the Internet should reduce the required labor. As noted above, considerable evidence shows libraries are downsizing their exchange operations; and with the increasing emphasis on electronic resources and access, one can assume this trend will continue. Yet a need for a limited number of serials exchanges, especially on the part of large research libraries seeking material from such locations as the former Soviet Union, will probably continue indefinitely.

Housing, Arrangement, and Circulation

Within the traditional library paradigm, a strategy must be adopted for housing and arranging serials (articles acquired through

ILL or document delivery as well as electronic journals do not require housing or arranging in the library).

Several issues will be discussed here:

1. alphabetical versus classified arrangement,
2. integrated versus separate shelving,
3. open versus closed access,
4. other formats, and
5. circulation.

These issues often interconnect with each other as well as with other questions about cataloging policy (e.g., whether journals are classified).

Alphabetical Versus Classified Arrangement

These two basic approaches to the arrangement of periodicals do not require explanation. According to Glenda An Thornton, who offers a well-done review, this issue has been debated in the library literature since at least the 1940s. It is argued that an alphabetical arrangement offers the following advantages:

- The patron can retrieve periodicals more directly because it is not necessary to first look up a classification number.
- Processing costs are less expensive because classification numbers do not have to be assigned.
- Rearrangement is easier because periodicals will not be interfiled with books.

The disadvantages associated with an alphabetical approach follow:

- Titles dealing with the same subject will not be grouped together.
- Seemingly insignificant words in the middle of the title—such as the, of for, etc.—can influence the arrangement and confuse the patron.
- Generic titles—such as Journal of, Transactions, Proceedings,

or Bulletin—may cause many different but similar-sounding titles to be grouped together, possibly confusing patrons.

- Different titles from the same organisation (e.g., Journal and Bulletin) would be shelved apart (this could be remedied by shelving under corporate author, although AACR2R has moved in the direction of title main entry).
- The patron may not know whether to look under a periodical's title or corporate author (e.g., would the journal of the American Society for Information Science be shelved under J or A?).
- Title changes may cause the splitting of backruns (although using cross-reference shelf "dummies," i.e., wooden blocks representing journal titles, can help rectify this problem).
- Unindexed titles "tend to be more or less overlooked."

A classified approach offers these benefits:

- Periodicals on the same or similar subjects will be grouped together, thus making browsing easy.
- The current and superseded forms of a journal's title will be grouped together (unless the title' subject focus has changed).
- Periodicals issued by the same corporate body would normally be collocated.
- Similar-sounding titles are usually scattered, thus possibly reducing patron confusion.
- In significant words in the middle of the title will not confuse patrons.

On the negative side, a classified approach does have disadvantages:

- Patrons can not go directly to periodicals because they must locate the call number.
- Assigning classification numbers requires staff time and processing costs.

Indexing and abstracting may be more important than subject classification for providing access to periodicals.

Numerous surveys exist on how libraries arrange their periodicals. Although their results are somewhat inconsistent, these surveys generally indicate that a majority of libraries use the alphabetical method, larger libraries are more likely to use a classified approach, and that a slight trend toward the classified arrangement exists.

Integrated versus Separate Shelving

Classified bound periodical volumes can either be housed in a separate areas or integrated with the book collection. Integration with the book collection means books and periodicals on the same subject will be housed close to each other, thus making browsing easy. However, integration with the books means that periodicals will be dispersed throughout the collection and thus may be located a significant distance from the periodical indexes, which are required to access their content. Nancy Jean Melin even suggests that interfiling books and periodicals may require "extensive duplication" of periodical indexes. Also, interfiling can complicate stack maintenance by requiring frequent resifting caused by the rapid growth rate of periodicals. A survey conducted at the 1990 North American Serials interest Group (NASIG) Conference revealed that of 50 libraries classifying periodicals, 28 (56 percent) inter shelved them with monographs, 18 36 percent) did not, and 4 (8 percent) used both methods.

In their 1989 survey of American academic libraries, Jim Segesta and Gary Hyslop identified three basic patterns for arranging periodical backruns:

1. alphabetical—used by 59 percent;
2. classified and integrated with monographs—used by 21 percent; and
3. classified and separately shelved—used by 15 percent.

They also found that about three percent of the responding libraries, half of which were associated with community colleges, maintained periodical backruns only as unbound issues or on microfilm.

Open Versus Closed Access

The terms open access and closed access are fairly self-explanatory. In open access the patrons directly retrieve items from the shelf, whereas in closed access the library employs a paging system to retrieve material for the patron. Open periodical stacks obviously offer greater patron convenience and allow browsing. Closed stacks may cost more because it is necessary to staff a paging system for retrieving patron requests. Melin notes that closed stacks can create political problems because inevitably some patrons will request special access. From the positive perspective, closed stacks are presumed to reduce loss, theft, and mutilation. It is easier to conduct a use studying a close-access setting. Moreover, incomplete volumes can be tied together on the shelves. If access is closed, a classified arrangement is not needed, and an alphabetical sequence makes reshelving by library staff easier.

Other Formats: Unbound Periodicals and Non-periodical Serials

Most of the professional literature's discussion focuses on bound periodical volumes. Yet the basic issues discussed above also apply to unbound periodical issues and non-periodical serials.

If bound periodicals are integrated with books, non-periodical serials would obviously be treated in the same fashion. Tuttle asserts that if periodicals and books are shelved apart, a separate decision should be made for each type of non-periodical serial. She offers the general guideline that noncirculating materials should be shelved with periodicals, and circulating items, such as analysed monographic series, should be housed with books.

Segesta and Hyslop's survey identified four approaches for unbound periodical issues:

1. alphabetically on open shelves in a current periodicals collection—used by 41 percent of responding libraries;
2. interfiled with bound volumes—used by 33 percent;

3. maintained in a closed area—used by 13 percent; and
4. an open shelf classified or subject arrangement in a current periodicals section—used by 11 percent.

This discussion presupposes that serials are maintained as part of the library collection. Some serials are kept in library departments (such as the Cataloging department) for in-house use by staff, and occasionally serials may be located in faculty or administrative offers external to the library. A few additional issues beyond this book's scope include creating and maintaining current periodical reading rooms, handling serials on microform, staffing serials serve counters, maintaining stacks, and providing security.

Circulation

Variables affecting the circulation of serials include type of library, patron category, the loan period, type of serial (periodical or non periodical), and format (bound, unbound current issues, or micro-format). Periodicals are usually circulated may be restricted to certain patron categories (e.g., faculty or graduate students). Some research libraries don't allow periodicals to circulate. Yet non-periodical serials are often circulated according to the same policy that applies is so great that it is impossible to summarize them all. Indeed, the various branches and departments of a large library system may have different serials circulation policies.

University libraries sometimes allows periodicals to be checked out to a desk or study carrel wit the provision they not leave the building. Melin stresses that the abstracts and indexes, which are necessary for accessing periodicals, should never be allowed to circulate. Tuttle argues that libraries should provide a written statement of their circulation policy for all types of serials. Other issues include policies on renewals, recalls, and fines for overdue items.

The basic policy issues discussed in the preceding sections all directly or indirectly affect two vital issues: availability and accessibility. Availability may be defined as success in finding an item on the shelf when the patron wants it; accessibility refers to the length of time required to place the item in a pattern's hands. (For a discussion of availability studies as a collection evaluation method,) Obviously, if an item is available, it is immediately accessible.

Trade-offs do occur between the concepts of availability, accessibility, and patron convenience. Circulating periodicals may be more convenient for the patrons who check them out, but it reduces overall availability and accessibility. Closed access may be less convenient for patrons wishing immediate access, but it probably increases availability.

As with many administrative questions, these fundamental issues do not necessarily have unambiguously right or wrong answers and, as pointed out by Thornton, have not been fully researched. Such factors as library type and size, patron needs and expectations, indexing, available resources, and past practice will determine the best policy in any given case. A library is often "locked in by past decisions. If periodicals have not previously been classified, a major commitment of resources, depending on library size, would be required to change the policy. Thornton describes a proposed periodical reclassification project at the university of North Texas library with an estimated cost of $100,000. According to Segesta and Hyslop's survey, only 5 percent (19 of 377) of U.S. academic libraries changed their basic arrangement of bund periodicals during the 1980s.

According to Tuttle, serial subscription agents are on of six types of vendors that market serials to libraries, along with standing order dealers, back issue dealers, publishers, distributors, and magazine fulfillment centers (see Tuttle for definitions of each of these). Arguably, serial subscription agents are the most important players from the librarians' perspective. As the name implies, this commercial entity acts as a library's agent in acquiring current periodicals subscriptions.

For exceedingly useful practical guides to selecting and using serial subscription agents, refer to Buying Serials: a How-to-Do-It Manual for Librarians, by N. Bernard Basch and Judy McQueen, or, more recently, Tuttle's Managing Serials. The latter includes appendixes listing specific telephone questions for subscription agents and other serial vendors about orders, claims, invoicing, management reports, and costs. Arnold Hirshon and Barbara Winters publish a sample request for Proposal for libraries wishing to select a subscription agent through competitive bidding.

Services performed by serial subscription agents include

- placement of new subscriptions,
- subscription renewal,
- subscription cancellation,
- consolidation of serial orders,
- customized invoicing, Claiming,
- replacement of mission issues,
- management reports analyzing serial collecting and expenditure patterns,
- projection of future serial costs,
- obtaining sample issues,
- table of content services,
- document delivery, and
- access to electronic journals.

The major benefits of using a serials subscription agent are the economies of scale and service. Perhaps the major drawback associated with agents is the cost of the service. Serial subscription agents are analogues to book wholesalers such as Baker & Taylor or Blackwell North America in that they act as a middle person between the publisher and the library.

However, some differences between serial subscription agents and book wholesalers should be noted. Book wholesalers generally offer a discount, but serial subscription agents often do not. A book wholesaler is a dealer who, like an automobile dealer, purchases the item and then resells it to the customer. A serial subscription agent is a broke who, analogues to a stockbroker, acts and an agent in the purchase of an item but never actually owns it.

Librarians sometimes forget that subscription agents provide services to publishers as well as libraries. Among these services are consolidating subscription payments into large lump sums, listing a publisher's titles in the subscription agent's catalog, and providing sales statistics. Some subscription agents such as B.H Blackwell's Periodicals Services, directly market periodical titles for which they receive a discount on the subscription price.

How does a librarian find out about subscription agents and their services? Lenore Rae Wilkas provides a practical guide to serial subscription agents arudn the world entitled International subscription Agents. Arranged alphabetically by cuntryand byagents within a country, the book lists more than 250 agents in 63 differnet countries including the United States. All continents except Antarctica are represented. Upto 28 different ctegories of informtionare provided for each company, including postal address, cable address, phne nuber, fax umber, the tpe of mateias handled, the ability to support automation, service and handling charges, and invoicing policy. One should also mention Book and Serial Vendors for Asia and the Pacific, edited by Thelma Diercks.

Most of the leading serial subscription agents, including Faxon, EBSCO, Readmore, and Swets & Zeitlinger, now have home pages on he WWW that offer useful information on their policies and services. See appendix 3 for a listing of these sites, brief annotations, and their Uniform Resource Locator (URL) addresses.

A survey of 80 ARL university libraries, conducted in 1985 by Jan Derthick and Barbara B. Moran, found that all responding to the question used serial subscription agents, 76 percent of paid periodical subscriptions and 64 percent of paid non-periodical standing orders were received through serial subscription agents; and that the average library used 17 different agents (ranging from 1 to 60).

In an era that increasingly emphasizes smaller collections,

access rather than ownership, and electronic publications, a question might arise about the future need for serial subscription agents. Yet, subscription agents appear to be striving to redefine their role by providing automated services, document delivery of specific articles, table of contents services, access to electronic journals, etc.

A relatively new phenomenon that might rival or eventually transform subscription agents is what Hirsohon and winters term a "pass-through fiscal agent." The agent provides Windows-based software that allows a library to directly order, claim, and transfer payment funds over the Internet using Electronic Data interchange (EDI)—a concept explained in chapter 10. Furthermore, the library is supposed to receive a discount from list subscription price instead of the surcharge normally added by subscription agents. This service was first introduced by RoweCom, founded in 1994 by Richard Rowe, a former Faxon Chief Executive Officer (CEO). RoweCom offers Subscribe software for conducting serials business transactions over the internet. By means of a Bank One serve, located in Columbus, Ohio, funds are transferred from the ordering library's to the publisher's bank account. In late 1996 the RoweCom WWW page asserted that their service eliminated supplemental invoices because the catalog reflects current prices, customers were paying 8 percent less than with their previous subscription agent, and an agreement has been reached with Ameritech for interfacing Subscribe with the not is system. The university of California at Berkeley, the University of Pittsburgh, and the Massachusetts General hospital libraries were listed as major RoweCom customers. In October 1996 Library Journal reported that the University of California at Berkeley library had saved more than $200,000 on its periodicals subscription s through this service.

Before using a pass-through fiscal agent service, Hirshon and Winters recommended that a library test a service's software (which usually can be downloaded for free form the Net) and compare the cost of a 625 title sample, taken from its current renewal invoice, with the price quoted by the pass-through agent.

They also warn that any subscription cost savings might be partially offset by the need for more staff at the local library level to handle problems. Because pass-through fiscal agents are a relatively new development, many unanswered questions remain about their benefit to libararies, the ultimate form of their services, and their effect on traditional serial subscription agents. However, these agents clearly represent yet another example of the Internet and WWWs potential impact on serials operations as well as the broader socioeconomic trend toward commerce on the Internet.

Vendor Evaluation

The term vendor is a derivative of the Latin word vender, which means "to sell." In a technical sense, a serials vendor is the entity from which the item was purchased and might be a serial subscription agency, a book jobber who sells standing orders, a back issue dealer, or the publisher. However, in common usage, the publisher is not considered a vendor.

A significant body of literature exists concerning book vendor evaluation. In1988 the ALA issued guidelines for the evaluation of book vendors, and the Vendor study Group published an annotated bibliography listing more than 15 book vendor evaluation studies. Unfortunately, considerably less has been written about the evaluation of serials vendors. The 1997 ALCTS Guide to Performance evaluation of Serials Vendors states that in late 1994 only four published serials vendor evaluation studies could be identified. In general, vendor evaluations may be conducted for the following purposes: monitoring a vendor's conformance with contract terms, comparatively evaluating different vendors, comparing service quality over a period of time to see whether its is increasing or decreasing, and establishing a benchmark on the level of service that should be expected. Moreover specifically, the Guide includes improving vendor performance, providing data for bid situations, improving library procedures, providing management information, and promoting better communications among the library, vendor, and publisher among its reasons for doing a serials vendor study.

A formal vendor evaluation study requires careful planning

and implementation. Most of the steps outlined for a periodical use study in chapter 6 (problem definition, design, implementation, data tabulation, interpretation of findings, and action or recommendations) would also be applicable to a vendor evaluation study and need not be discussed here. However, the criteria and methodological techniques would obviously different. The Guide outlines the major criteria for evaluation of serials vendors, including order placement, order renewal, claims, order fulfillment, materials' condition on receipt, accurate pricing, service charge or discount rate or both, invoices and credit, and "database quality and automated services." The reader is referred to the Guide for specific methodological techniques—many of which involve gathering various types of statistics—for evaluating each of these criteria. The Guide correctly observes that different approaches may be needed for subscription agents and standing order vendors; one should ensure results are not affected by the library's own operations or factors beyond the vendor's control, such as mil strikes; vendors can be validly compared only if they have received similar order mixes; and study results obtained in one library may not be transferable to another. Moreover, a good study should combine objective and subjective methods: the former for criteria that can easily be measured, the latter for difficult-to-quantify factors such as the expertise and service quality of the vendor's staff. It goes without saying that an automated system can greatly help data gathering.

Vendor evaluation and vendor selection are frequently juxtaposed in the serials literature—presuably because the two are logically connected and use the same criteria. For illustration, Derthick and Moran's 1985 survey of ARL library is used a modified semantic differential rating scale (in which respondents rated terms from "very important" to 'not important") to analyse the importance of 28 factors in the selection of serial subscription agents. They identified six factors as the "most significant:" "prompt renewals,' "accurate invoices," "seedy claims," "rapid placement of orders," "country of serial's origin," and "agent experience."

Serials vendor evaluation origin," and "agent experience."

Serials vendor evaluation originally focused on subscriptions or standing orders. In recently years, however, attention has turned to the evaluation of commercial document suppliers, which provide individual articles. The basic evaluative criteria for a document supplier would be fill rte, cost, speed, and quality of reproduction. Examples of serials vendor evaluations reported in the literature include studies at the University of Leeds (in the United Kingdom) and the University of Kentucky. Evaluations of document delivery supplies have been reported at the University of Tennessee at Knoxville, Iowa State University, and Vassar College, among other institutions.

Organization of Serials Work

Prior to the 1930s most libraries combined the processing of serials and monographs, and only a few major libraries had a separate, centralized serials department. Among the first libraries to create separate serials departments were the Boston Public Library in 1858, the LC in 1897, and the New York Public Library in 1911. A significant movement toward creating separate serials departments can be traced to the mid-1930s, with Minneapolis Public Library and the New York University library cited as notable examples of the earliest libraries that did so. This movement was apparently given impetus by J. Harris Gable's influential article in the 1935 Library Journal advocating the creation of separate serials departments. The development of technical service divisions as an administrative layer between departments and the library director dates to the late 1930s. The prosperous 1960s have been termed the "high point for the establishment of serials departments, and in 1980 Mitsuko Collver noted a continuing trend towards centralized serials departments. Beginning in the mid-1980s, several authorities (for example, DonLanier and Norman Vogt) noted a reverse trend toward the decentralization of serials operations, with budgetary concerns and the impact of automation acting as major factors.

The organisation of serials work has frequently been couched in terms of "form versus function." –an issue that has received considerable discussion, sometimes highly emotional, in library literature. Note that organisation by form implies a separate serials department to which the terms ccentralised, integrated, or unified have been applied. Organisation by function logically implies a decentralised model, with the handling of serials dispersed through several departments and the absence of a serials department—a reality that exists in many libraries. Arguments in favour of a separate serials department follow.

> Serials are important enough to warrant separate treatment.
>
> Specialised knowledge and skill are required to handle serials.
>
> Serials' unique nature requires different treatment tan other formats.
>
> Better coordination, cooperation, and communications are fostered.
>
> Duplicate record keeping is avoided.

Arguments against an integrated serials department follow.

> A serials "mystique" is created.
>
> Automation can make decentralisation of processing activities easy.
>
> Although duplication is avoided in some areas, it may be created in others.
>
> The department assumes a life of its own and protects its turf.

Although recommending a centralized serials department base don the theoretical principle of "reciprocal interdependence" for effectively coordinating interdependent functions, Collver noted three reasons "for remaining unconvinced by arguments that one form is preferable to another": most serials organisation has been based on the idiosyncratic requirements of particular libraries rather than long-range planning theory, research is lacking about the two forms' relative effectiveness, and it is uncertain which model will work best for future technological developments. Although written in 1980, her cogent arguments remain valid today.

The slogans "form versus function" or "centralised versus decentralized" significantly oversimplify the issue's complexities. In the absence of a serials department, a serials unit may exist in one or more other departments (e.g., cataloging, acquisitions, or public services). Most unified serials departments do not perform all serials functions. Indeed, the definition of what constitutes a 'department" can be ambiguous because such terms as department, division, section, and unit are used inconsistently among libraries. Moreover, these slogans do not address the relationship between a central library and branch locations or the type of materials handled by the serials department (e.g., periodicals only, periodical plus standing orders, etc.).

Numerous studies address the organization of serials work, Fred B.Rothman and Sidney Ditzion wrote in 1940 that 7 of 22 large academic libraries had independent serials departments, although 12 of 22 had serials units—presumably in other departments. Gloria Whetstone's October 1959 survey found that 6 of 16 college and university libraries reported a separate serials department, 9 reported "Separately-administered serials units" in larger departments, and one responded that both the cataloging and acquisitions departments were responsible for serials. However, none of the six serials departments were responsible for al serials functions. Donald H.Dyal revealed in 1976 that 74 percent of 46 academic and large public libraries in Texas had serials departments. In 1981 Diane Stine reported that 67.7 percent (21 of 31) of the medium-sized ARL libraries she surveyed had separate serials departments. In terms of functions handled, she identified seven different patterns:

1. order/payment, check-in/claiming, bindery and serials cataloging
2. order/payment, check-in/claiming, ad cataloging
3. order/payment, check-in/claiming, and bindery
4. order/payment, check-in/claiming
5. cataloging, check-in/claiming, and bindery
6. cataloging and check-in/claiming.

7. check-in/claiming

Other studies also note the wide diversity of organisational models for serials. A 1990 survey of Canadian university libraries by K. Krishan revealed that 56.1 percent (32 of 57) had a separate serials department.

One of the major unresolved issues concerns whether serials cataloging should be under the jurisdiction of the cataloging or serials department. Almost invariably serials collection management is not under the serials department's direct control.

Many libraries use a structure, which may be variously termed the "serials Committee," "Periodicals Committee," "Periodicals Review Committee" or some variation thereupon for formal approval of serials collection management decisions such as subscription and cancellation. These committees often seek to represent diverse interests, such as public and technical services as well as the central library and its branches.

Applying such business concepts as outsourcing, reengineering, downsizing, and the team approach to library management has recently become fashionable—some libraries now accept credit cards for fine payments! Outsourcing—which a library contracts with an external agency to perform specific functions—has generated considerable interest and concern within the library community. Although frequently used for cataloging, the concept is clearly applicable to serials processing. For a long time libraries have used commercial binderies to outsource the binding function. In their work on outsourcing, Hirshon and Winters suggest that libraries already outsource serials acquisition through the use of subscription agents. In September 1996 a SERIALST posting noted that an unnamed "large university library' was considering outsourcing serials check –in, and a follow-up posting asserted this option was being considered by "many universities." However, Hirshon and Winters state that outsourcing serials check-in and claiming "should probably be done on a limited scale...where other attempts to increase in-house productivity failed," with the subscription agent the logical external candidate to perform these functions. The obvious benefit of outsourcing is potential savings in staff cost. A drawback would be loss of local autonomy.

In conclusion, the innumerable models and permutations for the orgnaisation of serials work can be partially explained by so many different functional areas being involved with serials. Yet no "ideal" model exists. The most appropriate organisational structure will vary from library to library, depending on the particular needs of each. Moreover, the ultimate impact on serials organisation of such factors as electronic journals, commercial document delivery automation, and the application of business trends to library management cannot be predicted. The organisation and staffing for the handling of electronic journals will be covered.

Copyright

This section briefly introduces copyright law and examines its ramifications for handling serials in U.S. libraries. Serials lend themselves to copyright concerns because of the ease with which articles may be photocopied in full. For useful sources of information on U.S. copyright law, the reader is referred to the Copyright Primer for Librarians and Educators, second edition, by Janis H. Bruwelheide; Libraries and copyright: A guide to Copyright law in the 1990s, by Laura N. Gasaway and Sarah K. Wiant; the section on copyright in the third edition of G. Edeward and Sarah K. Wiant; the section on copyright in the third edition of G. Edward Evans's textbook, Developing Library and Information Center Collections; and the Copyright Clearance Centre and the U.S. Copyright Office WWW home pages. The full complexity of copyright cannot be addressed within this book's confines. Moreover, nothing stated in this section should be interpreted as constituting legal advice, which requires consulting an attorney—a frequently expressed caveat in books that address copyright.

Copyright Law

The copyright concept originated in English statutory and common law. It has been traced to the Court of Star Chaber's Royal Charter to the stationer's Company in 1557 and the statute of Anne, enacted in 1710. In 1783 the Continental Congress proposed that the states enact copyright laws, and all but Delaware did so. The legal underpinning for copyright law in the United States may be found in the U.S. Constitution. Article 1, section 8, clause 8, states that Congress has the power "to promote the progress of Science and useful Arts, by securing for limited times to Authors and Inventors the exclusive Right to their respective Writings and discoveries." The first U.S. copyright law was passed in 1890, and major revisions were passed in 1831, 1870, and 1909. The current U.S. copyright law, the Copyright Act of 1976, went into effect on January 1, 1978. The United States adhered to the Universal Copyright Convention in 1955 and the Berne Convention in 1989. (A short summary of U.S. copyright law may be found in Arlene Bielefied and Lawrence Cheeseman's Libraries and Copyright Law.

The fair use doctrine dates to the nineteenth century and, according to Clara D. Brown and Lynn S. Smith, was incorporated in the so-called Gentleman's Agreement of 1935 between the National Association of Book Publishers and the Joint Committee on Materials for Research. Although fair use ha no statutory basis until the 1976 copyright law, the concept received earlier recognition by the courts. Section 107 copyright law, the concept received earlier recognition by the courts. Section 107 of the Copyright Act of 1976 outlines four criteria for determining fair use:

1. the use's purpose (i.e., commercial or educational),
2. the copyrighted work's nature,
3. the amount used in proportion to he whole work, and
4. the effect upon the copyrighted work's potential marked value.

Nevertheless, in actual practice considerable ambiguity exists about the definition of fair use. One cannot assume that a use for educational purposes automatically qualifies as fair use.

Section 108(a) of the 1976 copyright law allows a library or archives to photocopy one copy of a work under certain conditions: the copyright is not done for "direct or indirect' commercial advantage; the library is "open to the pubic," or available to other researchers not affiliated with its institution; and copyright notice is included on the copied item.

Impact of Copyright on Serials Management in Libraries

This section examines seven areas in which copyright affects serials and their management by or use in libraries:

1. library photocopying for patrons,
2. in-house photocopying by patrons,
3. photocopying for reserve,
4. digitizing for electronic reserve,
5. interlibrary loan borrowing,
6. photocopying to replace damaged or missing periodicals,
7. photocopying for classroom teaching purposes.

Library Photocopying for Patrons

Many libraries operate a photocopying center or otherwise provide photo-copying services to their clients. According to section 108(d) a library can made for a patron a single copy of one article per journal issue if four conditions are met: the copy becomes the patrons' property the library has not knowledge the copy will be used for any purpose other than private study, scholarship, or research; a copyright warning is displayed in the area where photocopy requests are accepted; and the warning is also displayed on the request form. Gasaway and Wiant stress that when photocopying requests are telephoned, faxed, or e-mailed to the library, an alternative method must be devised for delivering the warning at that time—such as reading it over the telephone or creatigna fax submission form that includes the warning. If the photocopy is faxed to the patron, the library must destroy its copy because only one copy is allowed. No record keeping is required.

In-Housing Photocopying by Patrons

Most libraries contain public access photocopying machines

that patrons use on an unrestricted basis. Section 108(f)(1) states that neighter libraries nor their employees will be held legally accountable for unsupervised patron photocopying if an appropriate warning sign is posted nearby photocopying machines. The first edition of the Copyright Primer for librarians and Educators recommended use of a warning worded approximately as follows:

Notice: The copyright law of the United States (Title 17 U.S. Code) governs the making of photocopies or other reproductions of copyrighted material: the person using this equipment is liable for any infringement.

Gasaway and Wiant caution that if a library fails to post a warning notice it might face liability for copyright violations. The Copyright Primer for Librarians and Educators recommends that libraries inventory and place appropriate warnings on all their reproducting hardware as well as consider attaching the warning on equipment that circulates to clients.

Photocopying for Reserve

Academic libraries maintain a separate reserve section for teaching materials supporting the institution's courses. For serial materials, photocopies of journal and magazine articles are typically placed on reserve. Unfortunately, as stated by Kenneth D. Crews, "the copyright implications of reserves receiving little attention in the legislative history of the 1976 Copyright Act," Indeed, section 108 does not mention photocopying for reserve.

To address this dilemma, the LA published in 1982 the Model Policy Concerning College and University Photocopying for Classroom, Research and Library Reserve Use, often termed the Model Policy. The policy states that if a faculty member requests only one copy be placed on reserve, the library may photocopy an entire article for that purpose. It also states that requests for multiple copies must conform to the following four guidelines:

1. "the amount for material should be reasonable in relation to the total amount of material assigned," considering the

course's nature, subject matter, and level.

2. a "reasonable" number of copies may be made, considering the number of students in the course, the assignment's difficulty, and the number of other courses that use the same item.
3. Copyright notice should be attached to the item.
4. Photocopying should not be "detrimental to the market for the work," and at least one copy of the photocopied material should "generally" be owned by the library.

The Model Policy elaborates that "in most instances" a reasonable number of copies is less than six, but in "unusual circumstances" (e.g., considering the number of enrolled students the assignmnet's difficulty, and th etime available for completion), more are permitted. It also sttes that several photocopiesof copyrightd articles, citing recent issues of time or the New York Tiemes as Examples, can be placed on reserve if there is not sufficient time to request copyright permission. As with classroom, use, "repetitive" photocopying of an tem for different courses or successive years of the same course "normally' requires copyright permission.

According to the Copyright Primer for librarians and Educators, a library may place on reserve a photocopy made by a professor—the presumption being that the photocopy was made legally. Gasaway and Wiant state a library can "occasionally" put on reserve a photocopy of an item not held in its collection—one owned by a faculty member or obtained on interlibrary loan (ILL)—so long as this is not a "general practice." They also recommend that the library rather than faculty decide what is a "reasonable" number of copies for reserve.

Crews's study of university copyright policies found-wide variety in reserve policies: 21 percent (17 of 80) were based on the ALA's Model Policy, described above; whereas 30 percent (24 policies) were based (presumably because reserve is viewed as a teaching function) to some degree on the Classroom Guidelines (discussed later) even though the guidelines do not explicitly address copyright. This diversity in library reserve policies undoubtedly reflects the lack of legislative direction and the numerous issues involved.

Digitizing for Electronic Reserve

In recent years numerous academic libraries have created "electronic reserves," which digitize articles and other documents. An ALA survey indicated that by sprint 1996, 27 percent of Ph.D. Granting-institution libraries had an electronic reserve project in process.

The electronic reserves working group of the Conference on Fair Use began meeting in September 1994 to develop fair use guidelines for placing material on electronic reserve. After several of their drafts were rejected by same professional organisations (notably commercial publishers, the working group reached the conclusion that consensus was not feasible and that each library will have to develop its own policy. One of these drafts, dated March 5, 196, appears as an appendix in Bielefield and Cheeseman's Technology and Copyright Law. Links to WWW sites addressing electronic reserve copyright issues may be found on Columbia University's Electronic Reserves Clearinghouse (on the Web).

After examining university electronic reserve polices posted on the Internet, Bielefield and Cheeseman identified the following common stipulations: the system is restricted t students, faculty, and staff affiliated with the institution; one article per serial issue can be entered into the system; and items on electronic reserve must contain copyright notice as well as be deleted from the system when each semester is completed.

Interlibrary Loan Borrowing

ILL sharing of journal articles is the aspect of serials management most affected by copyright. Section 108(g)(@)(d) of the 1976 statute authorizes ILL borrowing consistent with 108(d) described earlier, stating 'nothing in this clause prevents a library or archives from participating in interlibrary arrangements that do not have, as their purpose or effect, that the library or archives receiving such copies or phonorecords for distribution does so in such aggregate quantities as to substitute for a subscription to or purchase of such work," In 1976, the Commission on New Technological Uses of Copyrighted Works (CONTU), appointed by congress to address diverse copyright issues, issued a set of guidelines covering ILL borrowing by libraries. The so-called CONTU Guidelines are not statutory law, but they have been used by libraries for the last two decades with no reported case of a library in compliance with them having been sued for copyright infringement. Although some commercial publishers are challenging CONTU as too lenient for libraries, the guidelines remain the only widely accepted standard for ILL photocopying.

If a library does not currently subscribe to a journal, it is limited to five request per year from the journal's most recent five years. (The presumed rationale for this limitation is that a library is not supposed to use ILL as a substitute for a current subscription.) Termed the "Rule of Five," this policy is based on section 108(g)(2) of the 1976 copyright law, as interpreted by CONTU.

To comply with copyright, the requesting library must keep a written record of each request for an item from the proceeding five years of a journal to which it does not currently subscribe. Moreover, the records must be maintained for three years after the end of the calendar year in which the request originated. (As previously noted, these records provide a serendipitous source of potentially valuable serials management data.) The requesting library must state on its request that it is following the CONTU Guidelines. The "Rule of Five' applies regardless of the technology used to coy and transmit the article: photocopying, facsimile machine, or the Internet using Ariel. However, the Copyright Primer for Librarians and Educators advises that the photocopy form which a facsimile was transmitted should be destroyed to avoid making two copies. A request for a currently unavailable article from the last five years of a periodical held by the library or to which a subscription has been placed does not count in the total.

Although the "rule of Five" ostensibly seems clear-cut, some ambiguities exist in its interpretation. Periodicals older than the five-year limit are not explicitly mentioned in the CONTU Guidelines, but, as noted in the Copyright Primer for Librarians and Educators, "they are not to be considered as fair game for unlimited copying Copyright term is still in effect." Does a multi-campus library system, such as Indiana University, count as one library, eight libraries (if each campus is counted), or fifty-seven libraries (if each branch is counted)? A library may exceed the annual limit by paying a copyright fee on each request beyond five.

Photocopying for Replacement Purposes

Replacing missing or damaged periodicals is a well-known library problem that a photocopy may be made to replace a "damaged, deteriorating lost, or stolen" published item if the library, "after a reasonable effort, determined that an unused replacement cannot be obtained at a fair price.' The Copyright Primer for librarians and Educators identifies "fair price" as "the prevailing retail price for an unused copy," although Gasaway and Wiant asset "it is impossible to define for all circumstances." They also state a "reasonable effort" requires contacting "commonly known U.S. trade sources" and the publisher or copyright owner or using an authorized reproducing service. Gasaway and Wiant further advise that a library probably does to need to replace an entire bound periodical volume if a single article has been cut out and that a photocopy for replacement purposes may be requested from another library if the requesting library originally owned the missing item, attempted to obtain a replacement, and certifies conformance with section 108©.

Photocopying for Classroom Use

Although not strictly a library unction, photocopying for classroom use is an important issue that may affect library serials control. On March 19, 1976, the ad Hoc Committee on Copyright Law Revision, the Author. Publishers Group, and the association of American publishers signed the "Agreement on Guidelines for classroom Copying in Not-for-Profit Educational Institutions with Respect to Books and Periodicals," a document often called the "Classroom Guidelines."

The Classroom Guidelines specify that a single copy of a newspaper or periodical article or a single "chart, graph diagram, drawing, cartoon, pr picture' from a periodical can be made by or at the request of a teacher for research, teaching , or classroom preparation. Multiple copies for classroom teaching or discussion (not to exceed one per pupil) can be made by or for a teacher provided three conditions are satisfied: the brevity and spontaneity tests, the test of cumulative effect, and the placement of copyright notice on each copy the brevity test allows photocopying "a complete article" of less than 2,500 words and one illustration, such as a chart, graph, diagram, drawing, cartoon, or picture per periodical issue. The spontaneity test requires the copying e caused by "inspiration of the individual teacher," and "the inspiration and…its use for maximum teaching effectiveness are so close in time that it would be unreasonable to expect a timely reply to a request for permission." According to the cumulative effect test.

1. an time can be copied for only one course in the school,
2. no more than two articles from the same author or three form the same periodical volume can be copied during a semester, and
3. there shall be no more than nine instances of copying for one course during a semester.

However, newspapers, current news periodicals, or other periodicals' news sections do not count in the limits under two and three. The guidelines conclude that photocopying cannot be substituted for purchase of a periodical, a teacher can not repeatedly copy the same item form semester to semester, and students cannot be charged a fee beyond the copying cot.

The Copyright Primer for Librarians and educators advises that the term course refers to a specific subject, so someone teaching several subjects to the same students can made nine copies a semester for each subject. Moreover, an instructor teaching two sections of the same course can made photocopies for both sections. However, items copied for a fall course can not be used again in the spring course because there would be sufficient time to obtain copyright permission.

Additional Copyright Issues

The above review makes it apparent that to conform with specified conditions and restrictions, periodical articles may be photocopied for a variety of purposes. The question is less clear in regard to newsletters. Gasaway and Wint assert that photocopying an entire newsletter is not permissible, but Crews states that in some circumstances this might be considered fair use.

The Copyright Clearance Center (CCC), a not-for-profit organisation located in Danvers, Massachusetts, was established in 1978 to license photocopying. Its purpose is to made payment of copyright fees easy and to distributed the fees to the appropriate publishers. In1990 more than 600,000 journals were registered wit the cc, and the figure now approaches two million.

The CCC is presently developing the Academic electronic Reserves programme for collecting copyright fees for items placed on electronic reserve by academic libraries. Crews pints out some limitations to using the CCC: fees are set by the publishers and thus vary widely; not all journals can be licensed because some publishers do not participate; and "an administrative and financial burden" can result. Many serial publishers have created a formal provision for directly paying them the copyright fee at the time photocopies are made in the local library. For example, Haworth Press includes a "local photocopying royalty payment form," a part of the Document Delivery Service form reproduced in its publications.

CHAPTER 3

New Technologies in Cataloguing

New technologies in libraries arises from the simple belief that technology, if intelligently applied, can bring three important benefit. It can improve the efficiency of our service to library users; it can enable us to spend our limited resources more sensibly; and it can improve the nature of the work of all employed in the library. The last of those advantages is too often ignored. The ideal of a technically improved library system can be found in the words of William Morris written nearly one hundred years ago: "Work in a duly ordered community should be made attractive by the consciousness of usefulness, by its being carried on with intelligent interest, by variety, and by its being exercised amidst pleasurable surroundings." I believe that ideal is as valid now as then, and that it constitutes a primary factor in the appeal of the new technologies.

Efficiency is not the only criterion, we must also pursue the improvement of the lot of the library worker. An interestign aspect of the new technology is the widespread fear of change and cynicism about change among many people whomight expect to benefit from it. This is, of course, due in great part of an entitely udertnadable reaction to the ills, real and imagined, that can be seen as resulting from many modern technical advances. We strongly believe that we must cultivate a more positive attitudetowards change in the field of librry work, and that this attitude must pervade all levels of great responsibility in this respect. Only when this more positive attitude is wide-spread can be begin to achieve the real benefits of the new technology.

A common attitude to the mechanization of library technical services is that the machine can be used to accomplish many of our current practices more quickly. In my opinion this approach is incorrect, and the use of computers to speed up and perpetuate outdated systems is a perversion of technology. The best use of mechanisation will be founded on a complete reconsideration of all of our systems, an examination of what we are doing and why we are doing it. If this process leads to radical change, so be it. If it means the abandonment of cherished ideas of the past, then let us abandon those idea. We must emphasise that this does to mean a supine acceptance of temporary technical and financial limitations of the present stage of automation. In this country it is scarcely necessary to point out that what human beings can imagine, human beings can do. We should think of the eventual possibilities of machine systems and what they can achieve, and not be diverted by short-or medium-term problems.

First, let us took at the physical nature of the end product of our work: the catalogue. Too often the prevalent attitude towards the physical form of the catalogue is that expressed by a student of mine in an essay which began "As well as normal catalogues there are book and microfilm catalogues." We will divide these forms into what we call the *old* forms (that is, the card and the book catalogues) and the *new* forms (that is, the microform catalogue produced from machine-readable records and the on-line computer catalogue). If we contrast these two categories, certain qualitative and quantitative differences become apparent. The old forms are either unique (that is, located in one place) or, in the case of the book catalogue, expensive to duplicate and heavy to transport. The new forms can be made available in many places, both inside and outside the library. The old forms are perpetually and inescapably out of date. The new forms are capable of speedy updating and near complete currency. The old forms are inflexible in that they allow limited and highly structure access to information. The new forms, either because of their nature (as with the on-line computer catalogue) or because of the cheapness of the material on which they are produced (as with microform catalogues) allow the possibility of many more points of access to information. The old forms arise out of previous technologies, and have the restrictions and limitations of those technologies. The new forms arise out of our current and emerging technologies, and do not suffer from those restrictions and limitations.

These changes in the physical form of the catalogue have implications which go far beyond changes in form or even in improvements in speed and convenience to the catalogue user. They should be seen as changing the nature of what we are doing, or, at least, as forcing a reconsideration of our cataloguing practices. To take an obvious example, in a new catalogue how does our old friend the main entry fare?

As with all emerging technologies, the computerisation of catalogue records has had to develop both technically and conceptually. It has had to go through various stages, each of which is both a prerequisite of, and paradoxically a hindrance to, the next stage. It is only now, after 15 years, that we can see the shape of computer records of the future. Those records will be true products of their technology, as opposed to what we have now-a computer record which amounts to little more than an electronic version of a familiar and much-loved artifact measuring approximately three inches by five inches. The developed catalogue record that is emerging is multi-layered and multi-dimensional. It uses computer technology to achieve far more than the mere mechanisation of catalogue entry production.

To take a fairly simple example, we can imagine a user who is searching for information about a particular edition of Dante's *Divine Comedy*. The user can approach the system by mane, by title, by subject, etc. In this instance, let us imagine that the approach is by one of the forms of name by which Dante is identified—ALIGHIERI. This name would live access to the package of information relating to Dante. This package will include two important pieces of information. First, that the standard form oaf citation for Dante is DIVINA ALIGHIERI. Second, that name is linked with a number of works, among which is one sometimes identified as the DIVINE COMEDY. The work package contains the information that the standard title for the work is DINA COMMEDIA. It also contains links with packages describing particular manifestations of the work. The user would then be presented, on a screen or in a print-out, with the information about the standard citations of the work and descriptions of those editions which were English translations entitled the DIVINE COMEDY. This process of assembling and presenting information is done automatically within the machine system by programme and it is done extremely quickly. The user is only aware of the way in which the assembled information is presented to him or her. The example used is extremely simple. Other packages relating to the work and its manifestations are also present in the system. For example, there will be links to individual parts of the DIVINE COMEDY (INFERNO, PURGATORIO, etc.); to series in which items have been issued; and to the subjects, names and titles of the work; its parts, and of the series.

We do not wish to discuss the mechanisms by which this developed record works, but to concentrate on it conceptually. In looking at this diagrammatic representation of the system, we can see the essential difference between it and catalogue entries or bibliographic records found in previous systems. Because of the way in which the developed record is structured, it is possible to approach information from any level, and by way of any access point within one of those packages. For example, if a series package is associated with subject package, information relating to that series will be retrieved in a subject search. It is he that the multi-dimensionality of the developed machine system lies.

We embarked on this somewhat lengthy description of a system with a question about the main entry. In fact, we believe that the idea of the main entry as a particular physical entity in the catalogue arose out of our previous technologies. What remains of the main-entry idea is the fact that the developed machine system, if it is to be capable of carrying out all its functions, allows for, and indeed demands, an indication of the standard manner of citing the name of each person and each body and the title of each work. In the example I used there is a standard citation for Dante and a standard citation for the *Divine Comedy*. As the link between them will contain an indication of their relationship (in this case, that of primary responsibility or authorship), the standard citation for the work emerges as DANTE ALIGHIERI. DIVINA COMMEDIA. This enables the machine system to fulfill all the remaining useful purposes of the main entry idea. Individual items can, however, be equally accessed by any variant forms of that name or of that title. What has happened is that we have been released from the tyranny of the idea that there is only one place in which full information is to be found, and that there is only one place in which full information is to be found, and that there is only one way in which an item should be approached. We are left with the concept of standard citation.

The likely contents of two of the packages of information are: (1) a name package and (2) a work package. The replacement of the main-entry idea by that of a standard citation can readily be seen. In the name package there is a place for the preferred form of the name. In the work package there is a place for the preferred form of the title. Each package will contain links which not only connect one package to another but also define precisely the nature of the relationship between them.

It is evident that the work of the cataloguer in preparing these packages is very different from the work involved in preparing conventional catalogue entries. A complete aggregation of related information is presented, rather simplistically, as a set of building blocks. Using this analogy, the task of the cataloguer can be seen as that of constructing new building blocks and fitting them into an existing structure. These new modules will be standard descriptions of items newly acquired, new subject packages, new name packages, and new work packages. Once these are created the cataloguer must perceive the links between new and existing packages, and build them into the system. Familiar injunctions such as "Enter under..." seem to have been lost. In fact, in many applications the choice of main entry (or standard citation) is unimportant. A standard description will be accessible by a number of characteristics, each of which has equal validity. As far as the user is concerned, all access points are main access points because they all provide an equal amount of information. In other applications the choice of standard forms is very important, so this task remains when constructing multipurpose records.

The multidimensional nature of the developed machine record. The subject of a series, an item, or a part are equally accessible, as are the names associated with a series, an item, or a part. The user can approach information either horizontally, that is, at one level containing subject name, and descriptive information; or vertically, that is, by category of information irrespective of level. The catalogue no longer has to concentrate on one level of information to the complete or partial exclusion of all others.

We have seen that the work of the cataloguer is different in that such work demands as must, if not more, professionalism and commitment to standardisation as before. There is one more, professionalism and commitment to standardisation as before. There is one further important difference between such work and conventional cataloguing; his lies in the fact that the element of repetition that our present system demands is all but eliminated. Once a package of information is established and its links to other packages are made, it remains as the package for that name, subject, item, etc., and subsequent work connected with the same data consists simply of citing the control number for that package in the appropriate field. Thus the machine system can be used to eliminate busy work and to leave the cataloguer with the task of establishing new information in a standard manner that is, the truly professional task. To return briefly to the quotation from Morris, we believe that this aspect of technological change goes a long way towards the realization of the ideal of "useful" work.

Another change that technology can bring to cataloguing is the possibility of resolving what have hitherto been considered irreconcilable problems. Take, for example, Russian names. No one has yet come up with a satisfactory solution to the problem of whether one should use a romanised form of name or the *popular* English form of name. Another instance is the difference between the English and North American practices in adding dates to personal names. In English practice they are added only when there is a conflicts; in North American practice they are added, when available, in anticipation of conflict. Another instance is that of the choice between pseudonyms and *real* names of persons. Other instances of unresolved or partially resolved conflicts of this type abound in our precomputer cataloguing codes. Using a developed machine-readable record these problems can be resolved. First, the question of whether one uses the systematic popular form of name for a Russian: In the developed machine system, each of these forms will be present, and each will be accompanied by an indication of the type of name. A particular printed catalogue using that record could select, by programme, the form which is preferred for that catalogue. Even within one library one could use the systematic form for a general catalogue and the *popular* form for a reading list. The other example, that of dates added to personal names, is resolved by the fact that, in the name package is created (or subsequently) and remain in the package only to be printed when conflict occurs. In that way, the irreconcilable problem in our premachine systems—the necessity to record dates and use then or not to record them at all-is overcome. They are recorded in all instances, but only used in instances where they are relevant and necessary. Again we see that the impact of technology is to alter the cataloguing task and to alter the nature of the decisions that the cataloguers have to make.

An impact of computer technology which has already occurred is the system-atisation of the description of library materials. This was brought about by the introduction of *International Standard Bibliographic Description (ISBD).* We do not wish to discuss the merits or demerits of this particular way of systematizing description, but to make some deductions from its occurrence. The *ISBD* has been through a lengthy process of development. It will be seen that the second edition of *AACR* contains complete scheme for the description of library materials based on *ISBD*. A fundamental aspect of *ISBD* is that the description is formalized in two ways. First in the standard order in which the elements of the description are presented. Second, in the formalized punctuation that is used to separate one element of the description from another. This formulisation was intended to have two purposes. The first was to enable the automatic translation of human-readable data into machine-readable data. Fairly simple programmes can be used to recognise the various elements of the description. The second, and to my mind, much more important, purpose was to aid the human comprehension of descriptive data. Here we can see the interaction of machine systems and cataloguing standards; The desire to make information more understandable to the user meets the necessity in the machine system for pieces of information (in this case elements of descriptive data) to be clearly delimited. Some people have said that this implies some kind of sacrifice of standards and the imposition of alien conventions on cataloguing. I would reject both of these assertions as it seems to me that the systemisation arises from an increased desire to communicate and from an enhanced understanding of the interaction of cataloguing and machine-and human-readable systems. This interaction is entirely desirable and furnishes a good example of the sort of cooperation and growth that should take place in the future.

English speaking cataloguing community. No such universal system exists for the formulation of headings and uniform titles, though there has been much discussion of the possibilities of such a system. There are a number of reasons why this universal system does not exist. The most important reasons are that the differences between different codes are far greater as far as access points are concerned than they were as far as description was concerned; and the fact that the question of the choice and form of headings is perceived to be far more important in its implications than the question of description.

We would suggest, arrived at a point where many of the differences regarding access points are either resolved or on the point of resolution because of the introduction of machine systems. In a developed machine system a name package can carry a number of preferred forms of name, each of which is accompanied by an indication of the environment in which it is preferred. For example, the name package for the government of the U.S.A. can include the forms *United States*, *Elalts-Unis* and *Estados Unidos* with an indication that these are the preferred forms in an English language, French language, and Spanish language environment, respectively. Thus the machine can be used to resolve a fundamental problem in international standardization. There still remain certain problems that cannot be resolved by the manipulation of name packages. One problem which is representative of these is the question of standard entry element for persons with family names that include a prefix. Some codes enter all such names under the part following the prefix, others (as in the case of *AACR*) base the decision on the language of the person bearing the name, and others base the decision on the nationality of the person. There are two ways to solve this problem. We can either aim at complete international agreement on entry elements or we can use the computer to arrive at a solution acceptable to all. This second solution presupposes that there is no one way to enter such a name. The cataloguer's task is to recognize and code each element of the name, and to add other necessary indications. Programmes can then be used to cite the name in the form appropriate total particular output. If we take the example of the name VINCENT VAN GOGH, we find that it consists of three elements: a forename VINCENT, a prefix VAN, and a main element of surname GOGH. The cataloguer would add codes to each of these and an indication of the language of the person, the nationality, etc. An *AACR* progrmme would use the indication that the person's language was Dutch to assemble the name for printing in the form GOGH, VINCENT VAN. Other systems would use different programmes to achieve different results.

The implication of all this is that we no longer need an international code of cataloguing rules, whether based on the Paris Principles or not, because of the introduction of machine systems. We no longer need a single of options in a standard and controlled manner, and permits these options to be selected by programme depending on the purpose for which a particular record is used. To return to a prevailing theme of this paper-the impact of technology on the work of the cataloguer-the cataloguer is then entrusted with the task of analyzing data and ensuring that alternative treatments are possible. He or she is no longer required to decide on one solution, and is therefore no longer presented with the kind of invidious choice that our present rules demand.

Our last instance of the changes being brought about by technology is that which is commonly, though inaccurately, in known as alphabetical filing. Library Filing Rules Committee, are much simpler than their predecessors. This simplicity depends, to a great extent, on an principle which states that one should file a character as it is and not as if it were something else. For example, the number 3 occurring in a title is filed as a number, in with other numbers, and in a order dictated by its numerical significance. One does not file it as if it were *t-T-r-e-e or d-r-e-i- or l-r-o-i-s*. This change has resulted from a reconsideration of all our filing practices which itself resulted from the use of the computer in filing. This does not mean that it would be impossible to file 3 as if it were a word, in fact such a thing is perfectly simple. What it does mean is that the use of the computer in filing, has made it necessary to look at our filing practices and to ask ourselves why we file one thing as if it were something else. The conclusion that most of us have come to is that such a practice may have had some validity in the past but has no validity now. It now seems a manifest absurdity to say that if this elephant were an orange, it would file in such-and-such a place. This is an illogical premise upon which to base an agreement. An elephant is not an orange, it belongs with the elephants and not with the oranges. Why, again have we chosen to file names beginning with MC as if they began with Mac? The answer is that they (almost) sound the same. Why base can aberration in arrangement on sound? These are awakward questions which the process of mechanising filing poses. We donot wish to argue for one filing arrangement or another though we do believe that the simpler the arrangement and the fewer other rules, the more change users have of finding information speedily. We wish merely to point out that the reconsideration of filling practice which as necessitated by the introduction of computer filing has been a healthy and fruitful process. It has made us examine every aspect of the process, to stop doing things out of habit, to retain those principles which are logical and comprehensible and to discard those which are simply the accretions of the years.

Online Service

Online catalogue in libraries is mainly a phenomenon of the 1980s. Only a few academic and some special libraries had implemented them earlier. In mid-1983, Hildreth reported that OPACs were in use in more than 100 libraries in the United States. These and subsequent systems have evolved from several different directions and variety of sources. For example, of 34 OPACs described by Matthews in 1982, about half had been developed by libraries; the other half were developed commercially. OPACs developed by libraries generally are in use only at the originating institution although an increasing number of libraries gave sold or leased their software to other libraries.

Commercially developed systems are already in use in a substantial number of libraries. Some OPACs in use today emerged from online circulation systems. Probably the best example of a long-standing library-developed OPAC with origins in an online circulation system is LCS at the Ohio State University. In the commercial area, all of the largest-and longest-established online circulation system vendors have developed OPAC modules, including such firms as CLSI, Data Phase, Geac and Universal Library Systems. The evolution from circulation system into a system that incorporates a pubic-access component has been fairly common in the commercial areas, but a number of OPACs developed by libraries were designed first and foremost as online catalogues, independent of circulation functions. The University of California's MELVYL system and the catalogue Access system of the Minnesota State University System Project for Automated Library Systems (MSUS/PALS) are two examples. Whichever component of a large-scale, in-house automated system is developed—circulation or OPAC—development of the other may follow. Some of the systems developed by libraries, such as VI designed by Virginia Polytechnic Institute, also incorporate function in addition to circulation and public access; acquisition capabilities are the most common, and some provide serials control capabilities. Locally designed OPACs are found in many types of libraries, although the most widespread development has occurred in the academic library. Some of the better known include systems developed by Ohio State, the University of California, Northwestern University, the Minnesota State University System, Virginia Polytechnic Institute. Dartmounth College, the Claremont Colleges, Washington State university and Pennsylvania State University OPACs have also been developed in medical libraries, such as systems at the National Library of Medicine (NLM), the Washington University School of Medicine in St. Louis, and the Beth Israel Hospital in Philadelphia. OPACs developed by public libraries have not been as numerous, although the Pikes Peak Library District in Colorado and the Dallas Public Library are examples of public libraries that have developed and currently use the own online catalogue systems. In addition to academic, medical, and public libraries, some smaller special libraries, especially in corporations, use locally developed online catalogues. In the commercial field, the almost universal tendency has been to offer OPAC capabilities as only one of several system component.

Earlier we noted various vendors initially offering online circulation systems; large-scale multipurpose systems with pubLic-access modules are also available from a number of other commercial vendors, such as Advanced Library Concepts. Biblio-Techniques. Data Research Associates, Dynix, Easy Data Electronic Memory, Inc., and OCLC. Carlyle, Inc., founded by some of the individuals involved with the development of the University of California's MELVYL system, was for a long time unique in the commercial sector in offering a large-scale system that is exclusively an OPAC, without capabilities for circulation or other applications. As more libraries can afford online catalogues, activity in the commercial market place it likely to density. New vendors will appear, and some of the existing ones will undoubtedly go out of business. Among the bibliographic utilities in North America, at least three can be said to be involved in OPAC development in one way or another. The University of Toronto Library automated Systems

((UTLAS) markets INFOQUEST, a microcomputer-based OPAC software package. OCLC is vending modified versions of the NLM Integrated Library System. The Washington Library Network's (WLN) involvement has been in the form of licensing its software, which has been used by the Southeastern Library Network (SOLINET) in its LAMBDA system, is in several other library projects, and is also the basis of the commercially available Biblio-Techniques Library and Information System (BLIS); which includes a public-access component.

Online catalogues can be looked at from several perspectives. Many issues pertain to their design and use in libraries, ranging from the number of terminals required to service a given number of users, to the ergonomics of terminal placement, to the types and amount of information to be included in a catalogue, as well as its arrangement on a screen display. But in examining any from of library catalogue, online or other, the distinction between its implications for the internal operations of the library and its implications for library users must be kept in mind.

Even though these two perspectives do act on one another in the creation and use of the final product, the distinction is important. The internal-operations perspective has to do primarily with the production and maintenance of a catalogue; the library-user perspective has to do with presentation and use of it.

Computer Output Microform (COM)

The introduction of offline, computer-produced book and Computer Output Microform (COM) catalogues was a significant step in the evolution of the library catalogue, but almost exclusively in terms of production and maintenance. Computer-produced, offline catalogues addressed many of the problems inherent in card catalogue production and maintenance, and many labor-intensive tasks that were fundamental to card catalogues were eliminated with the use of computers and machine—readable records. With offline computerized catalogues, only one unit entry record had to be created for each item; the computer expanded this record in to as many individual catalogue entries as necessary and performed all alphabetisation and filing tasks to maintain the catalogue. It was also much easier, at least in theory, to change a major catalogue heading; the change could be made once and applied to all effected entries by the computer-quite a difference from manually typing a new heading onto each which a change applied. However, as far as the library user was concerned, the benefits of computer-generated offline catalogues were far less pronounced. The actual format of the catalogue certainly changed in some instances, but the basis content, and the basis avenues through which records in the catalogue could be found, rally did not.

The principles used for access to entries in computer-generated book and COM catalogues mirrored those of the card catalogue, and the information was often identical and sometimes even less in amount. From the users stand point, computer-produced book catalogues were little more than card catalogues in bound volumes, and COM catalogues little more than card catalogues in a box. Given such frustrations as dealing with multiple parts of a catalogue issues in editions and supplements, and equipment breakdowns with COM catalogues, more advantages of computer-produced offline catalogues were not noticeable to the user and, at any rate, could often be overshadowed by the logistical difficulties in using them. In contrast, many OPACs, represent a radical departure both from card catalogues and from offline computerized catalogues in their implications for the user.

Access to records can be enormously broadened in an online catalogue over what had typically been provided in other forms, but these benefits are accompanied by a new set of requirements and demands on the catalogue user. The relationship between user and online catalogue is fundamentally different from that in use of other catalogue forms. The online catalogue is interactive, not passive, and requires the user to engage in a dialogue quite uncharacteristic of card, book and COM catalogues. Just to look into the catalogue requires new procedures on the part of the user. A search must be physically, not just mentally, initiated by typing onto a keyboard issuing a command through some other means. The system will respond according to the very specific action initiated by the user. In many instances, the user will then have to initiate further action based on the system's response, and so on back and forth until the user arrives at the desired end of the search or otherwise terminates the dialogue. This interaction and the nature of system responses represent a significant departure for the user from simply thumbing through catalogue cards or pressing a button, turning a knob, or sliding a handle on a microfilm or microfiche reader.

The fact that a OPAC is intended for users of library materials in perhaps the fundamental distinction between this application of automation and those which serve strictly internal processing functions. Such matters as simplicity of operation or sophistication of retrieval capabilities should be important considerations in the design and selection of any automated system regardless of application, but self-evidence in operation may be less important in a technical processing system in which the library is able to exercise a certain degree of control over the selection training, and monitoring of system users.

The design of an online catalogue must take into account a quite different set of circumstances. Considerable diversity exists among users in their level of knowledge about library catalogues and in the extent to which they are familiar with the use of computerized systems. The library will usually have little or opportunity to balance its diversity though a planned programme of controlled instruction and monitoring. Most people will not use the OPAC as part of everyday routine, and hence their knowledge and skills will not be constantly reinforced. An example of the well-placed emphasis in discussions of OPACs on users and their interaction with the catalogue is the series of studies sponsored by the Council on Library Resources (CLR) during the early 1980s, aimed at gaining a better understanding of what users want and need in online catalogues, their likes and dislikes, and the dynamics of their interaction with catalogues. Despite the vast array of differences among existing OPACs and lack of specific guidelines for development, at the base of these differences is a common goal: to design online catalogues that will allow the user maximum flexibility and yet will be easy to use. Investigations like those sponsored by CLR should help to establish a stronger foundation for realizing such a goal.

Phrases such as "user friendly" have become almost meaningless because of their sometimes indiscriminate use to describe systems or features that commonsense observation show are 'anything but.' Yet the overuse, and ever misuse, of well-worn phrases does to negate the relevance of the concepts they represent. The degree to which OPACs are willingly accepted by library users will indeed depend in large part on just how user friendly these systems are. Technical processing systems can be evaluated largely in terms of functional capabilities, or what a system can do. But the circumstances in which OPACs are still used are too different for such a simple evaluation. Equally and perhaps more important is the question of how easily system functions can be learned, understood and applied to the fullest extent by a diverse group of users. For any given characteristics in their operation, OPACs are still simply too new, and their use still too little understood, to be able to state categorically that one approach is somehow 'better" than the other. Fundamental to all of the features described is the most basic improvement that OPACs have made on other forms of the library catalogue: The expansion of avenues of access to catalogue records. Some of the techniques used to accomplish this are reviewed in the next section. The usefulness of different forms of library catalogues can be compared in a variety of ways. One of the most important criteria is simply the exent to which a catalogue fulfills its basis purposes.

Although the purposes of the library catalogue are not case in stone and depend on one's perspective, one set of standards by which library catalogue functions have been measured throughout the twentieth century is the principles of Charles Ammi Cutter as noted in his Rules for a Dictionary Catalogue.

The three major "objects" of library catalogue, enumerated by Cutter are the following:

1. Catalogue should allow someone to find book if its author, title, or topic is known.

2. Catalogue should fulfill a gathering function, showing what a library owns by given author, on a given subject or in a given type of literature.
3. Catalogue should provide assistance in the change of a book, either as to its edition or its literary or topical character.

Collection, a fourth commonly recognized catalogue function, having to do with the arrangement and relationship of headings within the catalogue. Underlying most of these functions is the fundamental matter of access top bibliographic records in the catalog: the points of entry through which a record for an item may be found.

The finding function is the essential basis for access, nut the gathering and collocation functions also have to do with accessibility to records. The function least directly related to access is assistance in the choice of materials, which has more to do with content of a bibliography record than access to it. Whether Cutter's objects still provide the most viable criteria for defining the purposes of a library catalogue in an online era is debatable , and some have questioned the degree of completeness to which these objects have ever actually been realised in libraries. Cutter's principles stem from a time quite different from the 1980s. New factors including but not limited to those of a technological nature—should not be disregarded in defining the purposes of a library catalogue. Nevertheless, cutter's principle serve as a point of departure in many decision so online catalogues, and concerning access to bibliographic records they still provide a convenient framework for comparing online catalogues with one another and with other forms of the library catalogue. Access to bibliographic records in library catalogues has traditionally been marked by a high degree of rigidity, requiring considerable knowledge and exactitude on the part of the user.

Generally, access is gained through four types of bibliographic elements: author, title, series, and subject. Multiple author and subject headings are assigned to an item as rules or judgement dictates, but the number is usually kept to a minimum. The terminology selected for headings is also tightly controlled, with the library usually trying to establish a one-to-one correspondence between headings and the persons, corporate bodies, or concepts they represent. These practices may be understandable from a practical point of view, but they do impose certain limits on accessibility to records. The user can indeed locate an item in the collection for which the author, title, or subject is known, but only under some rather inflexible conditions. To find a record under the title, the user must know the full and exact wording of the title—to some or most of the words, but all of the words, and in their correct order.

For access by author, because of the pre-AACR practice of establishing full and singularly valid forms of names, it has not always been enough to know the from of an author's name as it appears on publications or by which the person is popularly known. It has been necessary for the user somehow to know the exact from of a person's or corporation's name as it has been established by the library, often on the basis of considerable research. Where there are discrepancies in name form, it has been up to the user to figure out the form selected by the library.

Access by subject is even more problematic. Singularly valid forms of headings are selected from among all possible equivalents, but because of the greater conceptual complexity involved, there is even greater likelihood in subject searching that discrepancies will arise between the terminology selected by the library and the vocabulary chosen by the user. The problem is further compounded by the general conservatism in libraries toward changing the vocabulary used in headings and by complicated subject heading formation and filling sequences. Such practices, which result in a lack of flexibility, are all but dictated by necessity in card catalogues; however, they were also carried over generally intact to offline versions of computerized catalogues as well. Given the capabilities of computers and the elimination of the need for manual filing, there is no strictly technological reason for some of these practices to have been retained so uniformly.

Additional access points, such as by keywords appearing anywhere in titles or assigned subject headings, could have bee provided with little or no appreciable increase in human labor. Similarly, duplicate listings under variant forms of names could have been supplied in the catalogue. These expansions would have required greater sophistication in indexing and would have resulted in a far greater number of entries, and thus larger catalogues, but whether for economic reasons, ties to tradition, or something else, expansions of this type wee never characteristic of offline computerized catalogues. Only with the introduction of online catalogues have such expansions taken firm hold, and they are changing the very concept of access to records in the library catalogue.

Some OPACs adhere quite closely to other forms of the catalogue in the ways in which access to records may be gained, requiring just as much exactitude and exhibiting just as little flexibility. These are essentially electronic card catalogues. Other OPACs significantly broaden, and even fundamentally change, the traditional concept of access. An over few of several techniques by which this is accomplished is presented in the following pages. One technique that many OPACs use to allow greater flexibility of access to records in the catalogue is keyword, or term, searching. This feature enables a user to retrieve records on the basis of single terms or combinations of terms appearing anywhere within specific fields of a bibliographic record, such as author, title or subject heading. In finding an item by title, for example, a user can retrieve a record simply by entering one or more words in the title, regardless of sequence or position.

A user can find a record for The Peoples of the Soviet Far East, for instance, by entering the title-search terms. "Soviet," "East," and "Peoples." The record can also be retrieved simply by entering the term "Peoples." "People," or any other single terms or combination of terms in the title.

A number of OPACs also allow keyword searching on author fields and on fields containing assigned subject headings, and some permit retrieval on the basis of terms appearing within a variety of other bibliographic fields. Keyword searching has certain advantages over the exact order full-phrase searching required in other forms of the library catalogue.

In corporate author searches, the keyword capability means that the user does not have to know the exact hierarchy and order in which a corporate author name appears in the records. For title searches, the user does not have to know the full and exact wording of the title to be able to find it in the catalogue. A key work search capability expands, and actually alters, the traditional concept of locating an item for which, in cutter's terms, "the author or title is know."

In searches for single title or single names, although the entry of selected keyword is certainly less precise than a full title or authors, name and can rest in retrieving extraneous records, among those retrieved will be the desired items. Key word capabilities are particularly useful in subject searching. When a catalogue permits retrieval of terms appearing any where within assigned subject headings, the user dos not have to know the full and precise working and filling sequences of assigned subject headings and sub-divisions as they appear in the records themselves. Many OPACS allow a broadened view of the subject elements in a bibliographic record; for instance, by allowing keyword searching on title fields.

Given the usually high level of correlation between the subject content of works and the terms appearing in their titles, a keyword title search composed of one or two terms can be a viable from of subject searching in online catalogues. Some OPACs, in fact, automatically retrieve from title fields when subject searches are initiated. When the user carries out a subject search, records are retrieved for items in which the search terms appear either in assigned subject headings or in the title field of a record. Whether or not this combination is provided automatically by the system, the ability to search assigned subject headings by keyword, supplemented with term searching on other fields of the bibliographic record, makes subject access generally far more expensive in and OPAC than in other forms of the library catalogue.

Some OPACs allow a use to truncate, or abbreviate, search terms. For example, many online catalogues allow retrieval of records with an author's surname and first initial. Even through the full forename may be stored on the bibliographic records, the use of an initial is sufficient for retrieval. In addition to truncation or even omission of forenames and middle names some OPACs permit retrieval on truncated forms of surnames. Others allow truncation of keywords in titles and assigned subject headings.

Entry of the term "prehist" in a title search, for example, will retrieve records containing the terms "prehist" in a title search, for example, will retrieve records containing the terms "prehistoric," "prehistory," or any other derivative in the title. This facility often applies to phrase as well, especially in the case of searching on assigned subject heading fields. Entry of the phrase "Moving Pictures," for example, will retrieve records assigned subject headings "Moving Pictures, Talking," or "Moving Picture—History," and so on. In a search on assigned subject headings, truncation on most OPACs requires an explicit expression by the user. A special character must be keyed to indicated that a term or phrase is being entered in truncated rather than in complete form.

In title searches, some OPACs require the user to supply a special truncation designator; others provide an implicit form of truncation whereby the system automatically truncates a search term or phrase for retrieval according to an internally prescribed number of characters or words, regardless of how many the user has entered.

Boolean Operators

In most OPACs, a Boolean "and" is assumed when two or more terms are entered in a search statement, especially if the search is conducted of a single field or type of information such as author, title, or subject. Only records containing all specified search terms will be returned. In the earlier example of entering the terms "Soviet," "East," and "Peoples" in a title search, one records for work containing all three works in the title would be retrieved.

Some OPACs allow the combination of terms from different fields or serving different functions, such as an author's surname and a title word, in which case the user is generally required to enter a economic code preceding each term indicating the field or function to which it applies and then linking the terms with an explicitly stated "and." OPACs with fuller Boolean capabilities allow the user to construct search statements with other operators as well as the most common being "or" and "not."

Depending on which operator is used, the result of Boolean search capabilities is to allow a user to other broaden or narrow the set of records retrieved. Capabilities such as keyword searching expand access to records through traditional avenues like author, title, and subject. Some OPACs index other fields of bibliographic description as well. In a few OPACs, virtually every tern in every field of a bibliographic record are replaced by an all-encompassing concept of access by "bibliographic description" the more specific elements of author, title, and subject headings become simply qualifiers for refining the scope of a search.

OPACs generally have not taken quite this broad an approach, although some have indexed certain additional elements, such as names of publishers, for retrieval on tern searches that act upon several different fields simultaneously. A number of OPACs offer a more restricted idea of nontraditional access points in the form of bibliographic qualifiers that the user can employ to limit the results of a search.

The two most common are language and data of publication. By including a language code or publication data or range of dates in a specified manner as part of a search statement, a user can block the retrieval of records for items that would otherwise qualify but are considered too old or too new to be useful or are in languages that the user does not read. Other bibliographic elements could be incorporated into OPACs for purposes of qualifying search statements. The possibilities depend largely on the types of information discretely identified and consistently entered into records in the bibliographic database. For libraries with records in the MARC format, one likely source of qualifiers is from the elements constituting the fixed fields. Based on these elements, an OPAC could provide the ability to limit retrieval according to government publication, conference publication, fiction, juvenile literature, and a host of other categories.

Few existing OPACs however, currently offer a range of qualifiers beyond the elements of language ad data of publication. In a somewhat different but not unrelated category, OPACs have attempted to address traditional limitations of access in library catalogues in the treatment of alternative forms of name headings and subject terminology.

The most frequent method used by card and offline catalogues has been to provide cross-references guiding the user from variants in the form of a name or subject term to the authorized, library-established, heading under which full bibliographic entries are listed. This technique is not altogether service-effective, since cross-reference cards can be "buried" within long lists of entries or complex headings.

Online catalogues generally fall into two categories in attempting to deal with likely alternatives in the terminology through which users might seek access. One technique essentially mirrors the approach commonly used in card catalogues, namely, by cross-references guiding the user to the authorized terminology. When an online cross-reference is displayed in response to a search, the user must then key in or otherwise instruct the system to search under the authorized term or phrase. Although this approach is similar to that used in most other forms of the library catalogue, the presentation is usually more distinctive because the cross-reference message will be displayed prominently on a single screen instead of being buried among other information. Other OPACs have taken a different approach with respect to cross-references by essentially dispensing with them from the user's point of view, using instead a recognition of equivalent terms as valid for retrieval.

If the library has assigned "Women" and "Females" as equivalent subject terms in an online authority file, for example, the user will retrieve the same full listing of records in a search on assigned subject headings regardless of which of these two terms is entered in the search statement. This approach still requires the creation and use of an authority file, but the linking of terms is strictly internal and visible to the user. Other features, such as the use of word proximity in term searching, have been incorporated into some OPACs father expand the accessibility to records in the catalogue, but those described here are the most common, and they significantly broaden the ways in which library users can approach catalogue. Now of these feature is new to online information retrieval systems used in the library environment in general; they have been standard in such systems as DIALOG and BRS for many years. What is new is their incorporation into the public catalogue librarians have long assumed that systems such as DIALOG and BRS require special expertise and training for effective use. What is most challenging about OPACs is that at least some of these same sophisticated features are intended for people without formal training and with only limited need to use them.

Taking these factors into account is perhaps the most crucial element in the successful design of online public-access catalogues and their implementation in the library environment. Because they are interactive and can offer far border approaches to access, OPACs are a fundamentally different from of catalogue than their predecessors. The overall difference can result in greater value for the library user, but not without costs in human terms. Interaction with computerized systems and the use of such techniques as keyword searching, truncation. Boolean combinations involve skills that many users do not have, especially within the context of application in a library catalogue. For many lack of familiarity with computers and retrieval techniques extends well beyond use in an Online library catalogue. There are still many library users for whom interaction with a compute for any purpose remains an alien experience. This situation is changing rapidly as more and more of the population become educated in computer use, but for some time to come, unfamiliarity is a condition that must be taken into account in the design of online catalogues.

User/System/Catalouge Interaction

As an online computerised system, an OPAC incorporates certain rules that dictage how a user must entr commands and how the system will react to them. In the library catalogue function, certain aspects of interaction will be governed primarily by rules and conventions adopted by the library regarding descriptived cataloguing, summation of subject content, and so on. Rather than distinguishing between an OPAC as a library catalogue and as the mechanical means of conveyance, some discussions blend the two functions together. However, it is important to recognise such a distinction on at least a conceptual level, for each purpose has characteristic that can independently contribute to success or failure in using an OPAC. Some patrons may be well versed in the use of computerized systems and their retrieval techniques, but may be almost totally unfamiliar with the library's cataloguing and other bibliographic practices that do, in fact, influence the degree of success in using the system. Other patrons may have a fairly comprehensive understanding of the structure and organisation of library catalogues, even in online form, but may be unskilled in the mechanics of using computerised systems and unfamiliar with retrieval techniques. Any advantages gained by introducing clarity, case of use, and greater flexibility at one of these levels can be offset by undue complexity or lack of clarity at the other.

By taking advantage of the power of the computer, an OPAC can be more flexible than conventional catalogue forms, but it must be so in a way that allows these new methods to be easily learned and understood. Although the rules that govern the behaviour of an OPAC as a system and as a catalogue can be fairly mechanical and consistent, the rules that govern the behaviour of the library user are not. First and always, "the library user" is an elusive entity. Human factors that influence online catalogue use, such as level of knowledge, skill and motivation, vary widely from one user to another, and even within the same user at different times. Complicating matters is the user's perception of how an OPAC works. It is one thing to say that an online system performs a certain way or that certain rules govern the structure and organisation of a library catalogue, but the more important consideration is the user's own perception about how the system works or how the catalogue structured and organised. The design features of an OPAC can either facilitate or inhibit interaction between user and system.

Libraries are not always able to provide the desired level of guidance and assistance when making as significant a change as introducing sophisticated online public-access catalog. Therefore, an OPAC must be designed to minimise the need for offline guidance, taking on some of the instructional responsibilities and burden of assistance itself. An OPAC must be easy to use and its features easy to learn, and it must be a free as possible from the type language, confusing conventions, and complex rules that are meaningful only to the system.

The term "user friendly" may be ambiguous and trite, but the concepts it represents are perhaps the most crucial criteria for evaluating systems designed to handle the interaction between a computer, a library catalogue, and a diverse group of library users. There are certain similarities from one online catalogue to another in terms of the sequence of stages in which dialogue occurs.

For most OPACs that are not entirely menu-driven, dialogue between a user and the online catalogue generally conforms to the following:

USER: Enters a command to begin session.

OPCA: Acknowledges user's command.

USER: Enters a search statement.

OPAC: Provides "first-level retrieval" of records conforming to the user's statement.

USER: Manipulates and refines results of first-level retrieval in order eventually display record(s) desired.

OPCA: Responds accordingly to manipulation and refinement until the user terminates the session or enters a new search statement.

USER: Enters command to terminate session.

OPAC: Acknowledged user's command.

Many OPACs do not require the user to instruct the system that a new search session is about to begin or to explicitly select the catalogue file. Instead, the OPAC is constantly set for a bibliographic search, enabling the user to begin searching immediately on arrial at the terminal. Many OPACs do not require the user to explicitly information system when a session is completed. The user terminates the session simply by walking away from the terminal, and the display remains on the screen until a new search statement is entered. Even when specific begin-session or end-session procedures are required or available, their execution is normally simple and straight forward.

The real substance of interaction occurs between the time a user enters as search statement and the time at which he or she feels the search is completed. The end of a search may be the display of a single bibliographic record for an item, a list of abbreviated bibliographic records containing one or more of the desired items, or a response or display that leads the user to conclude that the item or items are not in the catalogue. The dialogue from entry of a search statement though final resolution may require any number of user-initiated actions and system responses.

In terms of the general nature of the user interface, it is important here to moment on two of the stages in particular.

The first involves entry of a valid search statement and the initial system retrieval of appropriate records. In some OPACs this stage consists of a single step by the user and a single response by the system. In other, there are two or more interactive steps involved. For example, the use may first be required to indicate the type of search being conducted—author, title, subject, whatever—to which the system responds by acknowledging the type and issuing instructions to enter search terms. The user then keys in the appropriate term or terms, and the system responds by providing first-level retrieval of all records in the database matching the two-step search statement.

The second major stage of interaction involves the manipulation and refinement of the search results provided by the system at the first level of retrieval. If the search is satisfied at the first level, this will be unnecessary. In many cases, however, the search is not satisfied at first stage, and final resolution may require several steps in manipulating and refining the initial results.

These two crucial stages of interaction—entry of a search statement and manipulation and refinement of first-level results—are in fact, part of a continuum in interaction worth an online catalogue. The distinction between them is made partly on the basis of convenience for purpose of discussion, but also partly on the basis of the crucial role that first-level retrieval plays in establishing the content for subsequent interaction. There are few areas in OPAC design that exhibit as much diversity as does presentation of the initial system response to a search statement.

First-level retrieval in some OPACs involves simply an indication of the number of records retrieved, even if there is only. The user must then enter another command to actually see any bibliographic information at all. Another approach indicates the number of records retrieved, but immediately displays bibliographic information only one record is retrieved. Other. OPACs display at least some bibliographic detail at the first level, even if a number of records as retrieved. The way in which this is done, however, can very considerably. For searches where very large numbers of records are retrieved, some OPACs group individual records at a general level if necessary so that everything can be summarised on a single screen display. In others, the first level consists of brief bibliographic information about each item, regardless of the number retrieved or the number of screens required for brief display, so long as a system limit is not exceeded.

In some OPACs the system automatically scrolls through the entire list of enters until the user initiates some action to free the display. In other, a single "page" of entries is fixed and the user must then enter a command in order to see subsequent pages of information, one at a time. A variable in this approach is the criterion used for arranging individual entitles in the list. The basis for arrangement of record in such a listing can vary from one OPAC to another. Entries are displayed in so online catalogues alphabetically according to author, title; or subject heading. The primary basis in other is reverse chronological order by datas of publication. In others, the basis is by some principle strictly internal to the system or something that may not be immediately apparent to the user, such as sequentially by system-supplied bibliographic record control number. These examples underscore the diversity among OPACs at this crucial stage of interaction. Whatever method is employed, the first level of retrieval is the starting point form which interaction between user and onliné catalogue will progress. For any of the stage of dialogue outlined previously, there are specific issues that have a direct bearing on the degree to which an OPAC can clarify and assist interaction between a user and the catalogue.

User-Assistance Features

An OPAC will understand only certain instruction expressed in a prescribed way, and often only at certain points within the course of the dialogue. A command that is valid at one step in the dialogue may not be valid at another. Thus, the range of commands available, the manner in which the must be expressed, and the timing with which they may be used are all strictly defined by the system. For meaningful dialogue to occur, the burden of adjusting to all those limits is on the user. It is the user who must learn, understand, and confirm to the syntax and semantics of the system, not the other way around.

Despite occasional protests to the contrary by some OPAC designers, the rules of operation and conventions of dialogue are not self-evident in most OPACs. A user does not simply intuit the available commands or how and when they are to be entered. They must either be learned obviously presented to the user on a step-by-step basis during each search session. In response to these needs, OPAC designers have tried to build in various online mechanisms to assist a use in carrying out his or her portion of the dialogue.

Some of these address short-term and very specific needs, informing the user at any particular moment in a dialogue about the options available at that point and how they mat be exercised. Others are more general or long term. The form in which, and the extent to which, such features are provided very tremendously among OPACs, but they can be grouped into six general catalogues:

- General explanatory messages.
- Search history: messages indicating what has been done at a previous step or steps during a search.
- Options and prompts: messages indicating what options are available for the user's next action and how they may be exercised.
- Error detection: messages displayed in response to an invalid command entered by the user.
- HELP screens.
- Online tutorials.

User assistance features do not, always fall distinctly into one and only one of these categories. For example, a message explaining a user error might also outline the options available for the user's next action; a message in response to a valid command that outlines the options available at that point might also explain what was just done.

More often than not however, these different types of messages and the user-assistance features they signify are independently identifiable, even when two or more are represented on a single screen display. Most OPACs provide message outlining the general limits of using the system. Frequently, these messages are concentrated on an introductory screen displayed at the beginning of a search session.

They commonly carry the following types of information:

- Generally library data: name of library, hours the system is available and so on.
- Files available on the system.

- Scope of coverage of the bibliographic database.
- List of commands or features that may be used during a search session.
- Options available for searching.
- How to enter a search statement.
- How to retrieve detailed online HELP screens.
- Where to obtain offline assistance.

No existing OPAC can provide all of these types of information on a single screen display, and some types are less commonly included than others. A list of files available on the system, for example, is necessary only on multipurpose system in which the user must select the library catalogue file as opposed to some other.

Although general explanatory messages are usually emphasised on introductory displays or outline in fuller detail on separate HELP screens, some may be included on displays at stages of the dialogue as well. This is most often in the form of message reminding the user of the major options available for searching, the procedures required to enter a new search statement, or the command required to retrieve a HELP screen either general in content or specific to the step that has been reached in the dialogue. An example of this type is shown in. Some OPACs can keep track and inform the user of dialogue that has occurred up through any given point in a search. Few, however, have this capability beyond repeating, as part of a system response, the single most recent command entered by the user; for an example.

A number of OPACs, in fact, do not even go so far as to repeat the most recent command; instead, they simply display a response without repeating the command or terms that led to that response. Not surprisingly this can lead to confusion, especially if the user has made an error in entering a search term. If the search term was not repeated as part of the system response, the user would probably surmise either that he or she misspelled the term or that the library did not own any materials by an author whose surname was Commoner. One cannot assume that the user would conclude the former over the latter.

Even in OPACs that so repeat the user's previous command as part of the response, there is always the possibility that the user will not read the screen thoroughly enough to realize that a term was misspelled or that a command was entered in appropriately, nut such a feature at lest attempts to give clearer explanations of system response to user commands. Along with each response to a valid user command, some OPACs display messages that can assist in selecting and executing the next step in the dialogue. In some cases, these messages only inform the user of which options may be exercised at that point. In others, the actual procedures required to exercise each option are also explicitly stated.

The types of messages that provide either or both levels of assistance generally fall into one of three major categories:

- Questions prompting the user to answer yes or so.
- Lists of alternative actions that can be taken at that point. Sometimes including how to exercise each.
- Textual or other prompts that indicate where a command is to be entered.

When unfamiliarity with computerised systems in general, and online catalogues in particular, is combined with the stringency of rules and conventions required for dialogue with an OPAC, one result is that there is bound to be a certain amount of miscommunication and misunderstanding between the user and the system. The ways in which a user contributes to a breakdown in dialogue vary in degree and kind. So do the ways in which the system responds. In terms of system response, the primary distinction is whether the system can detect that the user has made a mistake. If not, the request will be processed as though correct; for instance, when a user simply misspells a search term. If the command itself was structured correctly, an OPAC cannot tell that the search term was misspelled, and it will attempt to retrieve records and display a response on the basis of the misspelled term.

For certain types of mistakes, however, the system may be able to recognise that the user has made an error. This usually occurs when a user has misspelled the command name itself, has tried to use a particular command at a point in the dialogue where it is not allowed, or has entered more search terms than are permitted in a single statement. These and other possibilities have common source. The user has made a request that the system recognizes as contradictory to the basis set of rules and conventions required for dialogue. The system does not full understand what the user is trying to do. It cannot process the request into normal fashion, but it can detect the fact that miscommunication has occurred.

The exact forms of system response under such circumstances vary, but they generally fall somewhere within the following four leaves.

1. The system recognises that an error has been made and responds in a prescribed manner;
2. The system responds by including an explicit acknowledgement an error had been detected;
3. The system attempts to explain why it considers the user's request to have been an error;
4. The system suggests what corrective action should be taken.

Relationship among these levels is usually hierarchical. It would be possible, of course, for an OPAC to respond to an error only by suggesting corrective action, without explicitly stating that an error had been made and without any attempt to explain why the user's action was considered an error, but this is unusual. Assistance to online users in response to errors is not well developed in OPACs.

A number of OPACs do not interact at even the second level of response. One OPAC, for example, merely displays the "begin-session" screen when an error is detected, regardless of the point to which the search has progressed, and without any explicit statement that an progressed, and without any explicit statement that an error has been made. Others respond simply by redisplaying whatever was on the screen at the time that the erroneous command was entered, again without explicit statement that an error has been made. Others respond simply by redisplaying whatever was on the screen at the time that the erroneous command was entered, again without explicit acknowledgement of an error or statement explaining why the system responded in that manner.

However, most OPACs, do respond at least at the second level of error detection, displaying a new screen that includes an explicit statement noting an input error. Some stop at this level, with no further elaboration about why the command was in error or how it could be corrected, thus giving the user only minimal assistance. The language in which the acknowledgement is stated is often cryptic if not downright unsettling for an inexperienced user. Messages such as "Error Type 23" or "You have entered an Illegal Command" are likely to be discouraging two the novice, whose level of confidence in approaching the catalogue may not have been very high in the first place.

Efforts are being made in OPAC design to provide error messages that are meaningful in content and positive in tone, explaining the nature of an error or indicating why the system is unable to process a command, and in some cases even suggesting what corrective action should be taken. Most OPACs provided some degree of online assistance in the form of special HELP screen, which contain information describing various aspects of using the system. Their function is not unlike that sometimes provided on general "begin-session" displays or in informative error messages, but these screens are usually displayed in response to a specific, user-initiated request for aid.

The available number of HELP screen ranges from only one or a few on some OPACs, to 30 to 40 on others, to more than 150 on the University of California's MELVYL system. On OPACs that provide comparatively few, the instructional data are usually quite general and related to major stages of a dialogue. On OPACs with a greater number of HELP screen, explanation is usually offered on several levels ranging from the very general to the more specific. The more specific levels of detail may provide guidance related to the use of particular commands, access points, or system features such as Boolean searching or truncation, and they sometimes pertain to specific points that have been reached in a dialogue.

The HELP screen repeats the entered subject term and suggests possible reasons why no records were retrieved. If the user concludes that the first reasons was the source of the problem he or she might take the OPAC's advice and enter the command "s" to see a more complete explanation about subject searching for materials in the main library. Of all existing OPACs the MELVYL system on the University of California campuses has the most extensive array of HELP screens. Many pertain to specific circumstances and are most relevant after certain prints of progress in a dialogue. When requested in reaction to a system-supplied error message, the data on some HELP screens are somewhat diagnostic.

If, for example, a list of six entries has been retrieved and the user requests fuller bibliographic information about a seventh record, the following error message is shown:

1. You have asked to display record numbers that do not exist.
2. If the user then enters a HELP command, the system's response it.
3. You have asked for a display of record number 7, nut your search result contains only 6 records.
4. You, may not ask for a display of a record number greater than 6. To read more about the DISPLAY command, type HELP DISPLAY.

After display of either a user-requested HELP screen or a system-initiated error message, the point of progression a dialogue is not lost. The user should be able either to return immediately to the point in the dialogue reached before a HELP screen or error message was displayed, or even to proceed from the HELP or error display directly to the next logical step. Although this capability is fairly common to OPACs in some a request for HELP or system-detected error will mean that the user has to begin the search all over again. Probably the most elaborate from of online assistance that OPAC can offer is programmed tutorial instruction. Rather than begin problem-or situation-specific, an online tutorial is more a teaching facility than a "moment-of-need" reminder. Few existing OPACs currently provide a fully developed online instructional package. Although such a feature might be useful, it does presume two conditions. First, it implies that the rules and conventions required for dialogue are too complex, or at least not self-evident enough for effective communication without formal instruction. Second, its value would ultimately depend on the inclination of users to take advantage of it. Both of those condition run counter to trends detected in most OPAC-use studies.

Users generally prefer to be led through a dialogue on a step-by-step basis, getting point-of-progress assistance only when necessary. They do not want to spend a great deal of time and energy reading about how to use the system and memorizing rules and conventions. Some users might indeed welcome such features and would be glad to use them, but OPAC designers should never view online tutorials as a substitute for clarity and completeness provided as part of routine system response during interactive dialogue. Such a shifting of priories would ultimately detract from the overall suitability of an online catalogue.

An online tutorial can be of value, but only if intended as additional to, not in lieu of, other types of online user assistance. Each of the system features already described can play a crucial role in determining the ease with which a user can carryout a dialogue with an online catalog. But merely incorporating any or all of these features, into an OPAC does not ensure their usefulness. The manner in which they are presented in equally important, and one of the most critical elements in this is language; the terminology used to convey message, to prompt commands, to explain options, and so on.

The difference between a feature itself and its mode of expression can be illustrated by an example cited earlier. An error message was displayed informing the user that he or she had attempted to change the TYPRUN OPTION, whose value was fixed and could not altered. The user probably had not the faintest idea of what a TYPRUN OPTION was, much less wanting to change it From the message displayed, the user may have been able to surmise that the intended command had been entered incorrectly, but that conclusion was not part of the actual language used in the error message. That example may be extreme, but in fact most OPACs so use a great deal of specialized system and other jargon. Generally the language carries a certain degree of ambivalence in basis approach. There is a commitment to employ "natural-language" vocabulary, both expressed by the OPAC and required of the user, that as closely as possible resembles everyday conversational language. At the same time, there is also a strong and visible reliance on language that is not natural in any common conversational sense. It is, rather, "inside" language, specific either to the OPAC itself or in some cases to computerized systems or library catalogues in general.

To understand inside language, the user must be familiar with it or clever enough to figure it out. In either case, at some point the user must learn new vocabulary that may have little or no application outside the specific context of the OPAC itself. The specialised meanings of natural-language terminology in OPACs apply not only to "system" vocabulary, but also to the vocabulary of librarianship. Phrases such as main entry," "copy number," "full bibliographic record," Library of Congress Subject Heading," and many others displayed on OPACs all use fairly common terminology, but he way in which the words are combined probably not obvious to most users.

In OPACs with the traditional distinctions of author, title, and subject for searching, for example, a user who wishes to see a list of books about rather than by an author must treat the author's name as a subject term rather than as the name of an author. This may be an easy distinction for librarians, but it may to be self-evident to all OPCA users. In judging the appropriateness of terminology for presentation in OPACs, librarians should not only be wary of vocabulary that seems somewhat "computers," but should take not account the effects of using their own jargon as well. The language used in some OPACs draws appreciably on non-alphabetic characters, both in the presentation of information and in the command structure used in dialogue. In searching an online catalogue users may have to treat certain characters differently from the method that is usual in searching other forms of library catalogues.

Most online systems, for example, recognise some non-alphabetic characters, particularly numerals also, as valid in themselves. Thus, in searching of the title 50 Houses of Charleston, South Carolina, users of some OPACs may have to enter the first word as 50, not fifty. This runs exactly counter to the standard procedure in searching in card catalogues. Punctuation within search terms can be another problem, and some OPACs have strict rules governing its use.

In dealing with words, phrases, or abbreviations such as O'Hara, Al-Hardalo, I/O, or I. W.W. as search terms some OPACs retrieve records only when the punctuation within the term has been entered in the search statement exactly as it appears in the appropriate field of the machine-stored bibliographic record or records. This places something of a burden on the user; he or she may not know the exact punctuation, and is certainly unlikely to know how it appears in the record until the record is actually retrieved. In contrast, some OPACs do not allow any punctuation within search terms, even though the punctuation will be displayed on the retrieved records. Still others are flexible, retrieving records whether the user includes or omits the appropriate punctuation within search terms. Some OPACs rely heavily on the use of punctuation to separate major elements of information in search statements and bibliographic displays.

Users frequently must separate elements of a search statement—for example, the command name or functional qualified from the actual search terms—by some form of punctuation, most commonly a diagonal slash (/) or equals sign (=). In OPACs that permit Boolean searching, special provisions—some times in the form of punctuation—must be made for the user to differentiate between the function of certain words as Boolean operators and as normal search term, he or she must place quotation marks around the world in the search statement (as "and"). In some OPACs, forms of punctuation are used to separate elements in bibliographic displays. In one OPAC, for example, imprint data are enclosed between a less-than sign (<) and a greater-than sign (>), and subject heading are separated by a diagonal slash followed by a number sign (/#). Although this practice tends to clutter the display with nondescriptive characters when used in excess, this use of punctuation does separate desecrate pieces of information and is not really a problem unless the user infers that the characters signify something more than simply demarcation.

Most OPACs attempt to use natural, easy-to-understand language in explanatory messages, descriptions of options, bibliographic displays, and so on, but they have not broken entirely free of cryptic codes, computers and technical library jargon. In fact, it is doubtful that they could, or should even try to, free themselves entirely of specialised language. Terms such as enter, entry, exit, record, index, and so on, will always have different meaning in that context asks no more of catalogue users than might be required when applying the terms in other contexts. Clear and understandable language should be part of the pursuit of user-friendly OPACs, but individuals will always have to learn certain precise meanings to carry on dialogue with an OPAC. This is not to say that OPAC languages should not be refined; on the contrary there is still a great deal of room for improvement.

The language used in OPACs must be balanced between the need for precision in a specialised context on the one hand, and the case with which it can be learned, understood, and applied on the other. Many of the features already described relate to the clarity with which an OPAC can assist a user in progressing from one point in a dialogue to another. A related but some what broader question concerns the ease and speed with which a user may more around among various points or change the direction of a dialogue. OPACs Impose fairly stringent limitations on the number of directions that a dialogue may take from a given point. At any juncture, the user will usually have two or more immediate options, but these will not necessarily include all the options that a user might see as the next logical step for his or her own purposes. The user will always be able to move the dialogue to a point where that desired option may be exercised, but it may require several separate steps to do so.

For instance, an OPAC may contain the holdings of several different libraries. A user may complete an author search in one library's catalogue, but find no records under the author's name. If the user wishes to search the same author in one of the library's catalogues, several steps might be required just to get to the point where the same name can be searched in the other catalogue. The speed and case with which an OPAC allows a user to mover in various directions during a dialogue are dictated by design. In the example just given, greater complexity in progression is caused in part by the fact that the OPAC is multi-institutional, containing the catalogues of several different libraries. In a multi-institutional, containing the catalogues of several different libraries.

In a multi-institutional OPAC in which so many steps are required to execute the same search in different libraries' catalogues, design assumption would have to had been made that a user was much more likely on want to search a single library's catalogue for different items than different libraries' catalogues for the same item. But even in OPACs where dialogue does not have to take into account such factors as switching from one library's catalogue to another's the progression through which dialogue must occur is usually rather inflexible and often requires several steps if the user wishes to change directions or otherwise exercise an option that is not immediately available at a given point of progress. One of the more common circumstances is when a user has begun or completed one search and decides to begin a new one.

In a number of OPACs, three separate steps are required to enter the new search statement under these circumstances. First, the user must return to the main menu. He or she must then select the type of search desired: author, title, subject, and so on. When the OPAC acknowledges this second step, the user enters the search term or terms, the third step. The limitation of options at any given juncture in a dialogue and the segmenting of dialogue into separate and distinct steps can actually be quite helpful for novice OPAC users, minimizing ambiguity and reducing the risk of a user's becoming overwhelmed and confused by a plethora of alternatives and different rules and conventions. Such actions emphasise simple and logical progression, proceeding one step at a time. For users who have little or no experience with computerized retrieval systems, who are unfamiliar with library catalogues, or who have very straightforward needs, such an approach can help them understand what is happening and gain greater confidence and skill in the user of an OPAC. For the user who has greater experience or more complex needs in using an online catalogue, the degree to which an OPAC tends to segment the progression of a dialogue can be something of a nuisance. The necessity of carrying out two or three or even more interactive step to get to a logical nearby point in a dialogue can come to be seen as overly rigid, simplistic, and time consuming, leading to impatience and frustration on the part of the user.

Thus, OPAC design is faced with the formidable task of attempting to accommodate both novice and experienced users, and both simpler and sophisticated needs. Some OPACs have tried to minimise this problem by building in at least a few optional capabilities that allow dialogue to be expedited, or more sophisticated features to be used, without compromising the availability of the simpler actions for those who are less experiences or who have less complex searching needs. Among some of the features designed to expedite dialogue, one is allow the user to "stack" commands, that is, to enter two or more commands in a single statement.

For example, in an OPAC that normally requires two separate steps to enter search terms in a combined author/title search there might also be an optional procedure that enables the user to construct a single search statement containing both elements.

Another example of stacking commands, this one pertaining to commands fro displaying bibliographic records, van be drawn from the MSUS/PALS online catalogue. Like many OPACs, MSUS/ PALS can display individual records in several different formats, each containing a different amount and arrangement of information about the same item. Although there is a "default" from that normally displays, a user also has the option of requesting a longer, more detailed version.

When a search statement has retrieved several records, the user can select any one of them to display in the default format by entering the command DI 3 for the third record in the set. When the default format display, the user can then enter another command to display the long version of the record. But there is also an option for these two steps to be combined in a single statement, DI 3 L, which will immediately display the third record in a set in its longer format.

Although stacking commands enables a user to expedite dialogue by combining two or more steps that may otherwise be carried out separately, there are other, usually less powerful features available in many OPACs that can also reduce the amount of time and effort required of the user.

The most common is simply to allow a user to abbreviate some of the language required in entering commands. For example, one OPAC allows the command name FIND to be entered in either its complete from or abbreviated as F. A number of OPACs offer similar options; they do not really affect the course of progression, but they do give a user the opportunity to reduce the amount of keying effort required. The realised and potential ways in which OPACs can accommodate both novice and experienced users, frequent and infrequent users, and simple and complex needs all at the same time are important, but greatly complicated by two additional factors.

First, the user population does not include simply novice and experienced users, or simply frequent and infrequent users. The overwhelming majority of OPAC users are occasional users who defy the simplistic dichotomy of novel versus experienced in any matter pertaining to OPAC use whether it is familiarity with computerised systems, knowledge about library catalogues, or the complexity of their needs.

A second and related factor is that these limits cannot always be stated even with respect to a single user. Each user will have his or her own mix of expertise and levels of retention when it comes to specific features and rules and conventions, and one person's strengths can be another's weaknesses.

The complexity and non-uniformity of the library-user population pose a tremendous challenge in the development and refinement of online catalogues. It not a condition, however, that is unique of new to online versions of the library catalogue. The same diversity influences catalogue uses whether one is dealing with card, COM, or online catalogue. The latter certainly brings in new elements in the form of computer terminals, interactive dialogue, and the possibility of more flexible retrieval techniques, but it also provides the opportunity to introduce mechanisms that can at least begin to address the question of diversity by enabling a single catalogue to accommodate different levels of expertise, knowledge and need without prejudice award one group of users. Other forms of the library catalogue have never been about to make this claim.

OPACs have only just begun to address this issue, and there is no way of knowing how far it will be possible or desirable to go in developing hierarchically structured features that accommodate different levels of user need and even tale into account such matter as increasing familiarity on the part of individual users. Assisting patrons and conducting formal instruction in the use of library catalogues are recognized functions of public service libraries. If carefully designed, the library catalogue in its online form can assume some of these responsibilities, but it is unlikely that online user-assistance features will ever altogether obviate the librarians' role in providing aid and instruction in the use of the catalogue.

As Anne Lipow has noted with regard to online catalogue use, "If there is a way to make a mistake, to misinterpret instructions, there will be a large number of users who find that way." There is a growing and already sizable oral history of miscommunication between OPACs and their users. The range of incidents is itself staggering, nut two examples can illustrate a common type of misinterpretation and miscommunication.

In describing online catalogue use in four different libraries, Carole Weiss Moore noted that a common experience was for users, realizing that they had made a spelling or other error before transmitting a command, to try to delete the command from the screen by depressing seemingly logical keys marked "Clear," "Erase," "Rub Out," and so on—the results were never those desired, and such attempts often threw a search into near total collapse. Lipow relates another experience at the University of California at Berkeley, also having to do with the use of the terminal keyboard; "I found a man the other day typing 'return' because my catalogue instructs you to press return after keying your side of the transaction. He was indeed pressing R-E-T-U-R-N; he didn't realise there was a return key."

Some such problems could perhaps be at least partially alleviated through better system design and more user-friendly equipment or instructions. Especially in the first case, it is difficult to fault novice users for depressing inappropriate keys when the language on them seems to express exactly the action that they want at their point. But there is only so far that care in design can be expected to go in solving the multitude of problems that some users experience with online catalogues. In the second example, the misinterpretation might have been avoided if an instruction had elaborately informed the user to "depress the blue RETURN" key located on the right-hand side of the keyboard" or some such statement. For each situation for which the more detailed message would add clarity, however, it would probably lead to confusion in another. Especially given the contemporary environment into which online catalogues are being introduced, there will always be users, inexperienced with computerized retrieval systems or library catalogues or both, whose problems would not be avoided regardless of the clarity of instructions, the explicitness of error messages, or the number of HELP screens available. Explicitness and clarity of explanation should be guiding principles in the design of OPACs, but they are still not likely to eliminate the need for offline guidance materials and human assistance.

If anything, the present state of OPAC design and the current environment in which online catalogues are being introduced argue for more, not less, offline assistance and formal instruction in the use of the library catalogue. The development of cataloguing, systems has roughly followed the development of acquisition systems, and this holds true in the progress from off-line to online systems. In the case of cataloguing systems, however, the end products are normally produced off-line in a "batch" mode—that is, all at one time, rather than as the data are entered—and only the functions of inputting data and searching the data files are performed on-line and in 'real time'. With rare exceptions, this tends to be true whether the products are catalogue cards, book catalogues, or both.

Typewriters and typewriter-like devices have been used as terminals connected to the computer, as well as visual display (cathode-ray tube) units, the advantage of the latter being principally the increased speed with which the information is displayed. The capability of contains interaction with the computer is particularly valuable in cataloguing systems because of the nature of cataloguing. There is a greater need for precision and typographical accuracy in catalogue in records as opposed to acquisitions records, so the ability to perform editing on line and see the results of the editing action immediately is helpful. Further the riles to be searched in cataloguing are much larger, so the ability to perform editing on-line and see the results of the editing action immediately is helpful. Further the riles to be searched in cataloguing are much larger, so the ability to modify search strategies as one sees the results of the search is also highly advantageous.

Perhaps the earliest on-line cataloguing systems used routinely for production of catalogue cards began in 1970 at the Shawnee Mission Public School system in suburban Kansas City. IMB 2740 and 2741 type-writer terminals were used to input bibliographic data, and an IBM 360 Model 40 computer to do the processing and print catalogue cards.

A generalized package of programmes called FASTER was obtained from IBM, thus avoiding a much of the programming effort such a system normally requires. Unit costs to create and key data, print cards and labels, and prepare items for delivery were estimate at $2.50 per time, based on an estimate 1,00,000 items to be processed in 1971. In 1972 the cost of cards and labels was calculated at $2.25 per item, or $2.53 if the various listings, reports and other printed products were included. The development of the system write that "the librarians are satisfied that direct access to master library disk files is an efficient, accurate, and economical method of creating and updating bibliographic can holdings information. The public schools of Oregon were also early user of an on-line system using the same terminals. A large, generalized computer system located in Eugene was already available. This systems, called OTIMS (for Oregon Total Information System), utilized an IBM 360 Model 50 computer with 77 keyboard terminals located in various buildings around the state. Three of these terminals were placed in the Springfield School District's Library Processing Center, and approximately 43,000 titles, representing the complete holding of the district's libraries, were then entered and edited on-line. 4 By 1971 catalogue cards were being supplied for several other libraries.

University systems also began to be implemented in 1971. At Northwestern University, 2470s were connected to a small IBM 370 Model 135 computer in the Administrative Data Processing centre. The system as implemented is a "total" system in what it provides information or titles in press as well as those catalogued, plus bibliographic and holdings information for approximately 35,000 serial titles. The machine-readable files were originally on a data cell, but when this became operationally inconvenient the records were transferred to portable disk packs. Lack of tape drives in the Data Processing Centre created another inconvenience, necessitating; tape drives were later added for this reason. The most serious equipment limitation, however, was the "display" rate of the typewriter terminals which is only 14 characters per second, "far from ideal when long bibliographic records are involved." This difficulty in communication has been the chief reason for the use in later on-line systems of cathode-ray tube terminals with their much faster and often almost instantaneous response.

Georgia Tech, whose work on other methods of catalogue card and book catalogue production, began inputting data in 1971 with Model 33ASR teletype terminals on line to their Univac 1108, 8 and the University of Toronto began the same Year, using Model 1 KSR37 teletype terminals on line to a Xerox Sigma 7 computer. The toronto teletypes were modified to include a large number of characters—seven more, in fact, than the MARC character set. The toronto system also users a Xerox Graphic Printer which provides upper and lower case type fonts and various type sizes, thus allowing more characters to be placed on a single card and reducing the number of second cards needed. Several hundred thousand records have been input at Toronto using the on-line system, and another 700,000 by a separate keypunch activity.

OCLC

The Ohio College Library centre in Columbus, Ohio, know universally as OCLC—also began its on-line operations in 1971. Perhaps no other system has had as much effect on library practice in this country; indeed, if the development of MARC is the most significant accomplishment to date library automation the development and operation of the Ohio College Library Centre is probably the second most significant. This is not primarily because of the technological expertise employed in the development of the system but because it is the largest and most efficient shared cataloguing system yet implemented. OCLC produces catalogue cards economically, as do many of the other systems already described, but its important lies in the fact that it provides a common cataloguing data case for searching and consolation by almost 350 libraries The margin of savings achievable by any system of catalogue card production is small in relation to the total budget of most libraries, but the cost of performing the intellectual task of original cataloguing is much larger; the OCLC system provides significant savings because both MARC records and the cataloguing records prepared by all member libraries can be displayed of the terminal screens in any one member's library, thus obviating the need for any library but the first to catalogue it. Catalogue cards can then be ordered from Columbus and arrive in a few days, formatted to a member library's specifications and arranged in rough filing sequence.

The Centre was founded by the Ohio College Association in 1967 with over fifty members "to operate a computerised, regional library centre to serve the academic libraries of Ohio." 10 From the beginning, it was agreed that records compatible with the MARC II format would be used in the Centre's cataloguing system so that the Center could play a part in any future national systems. By 1970, the first OCLC operation, an off-linecard production system was functioning. Members sumitted IBM punched cards containing the LC card umbers of books for which they wished catalogue cards, along with their own call numbers if they were unwilling to accept LC's and OCLC then ran these requests against the MARC II data base. If the titles were in MARC, catalogue cards were then produced on computers at Ohio State University using programmes modified from the Yale project described earlier. Two technical developments associated with this effort should be noted in particular. Visual display terminals were abundantly available by 1971, but most of them were unsatisfactory for library use; typically only uppercase characters could be displayed, and the number of characters that could be displayed at any one time on the screen was far too low. After beginning with Spiras LTE terminals the Centre contracted for production of a visual display terminals specifically designed for the OCLC application, manufactured by Beehive Medical Electronics, In., Called the "OCLC 100" the terminal has been enthusiastically received in those libraries employing it. The second development of interest is the designs of an efficient searching mechanism. OCLC files could be accessed from the beginning by a Library of Congress card umber, but a method was also needed to allow searching by authors and titles. After some interesting experiments at OCLC and elsewhere, a search "key" technique was devised which requires the terminal operator to input only six characters: either the first three characters of the author and the first three letters of the first word of the title not an article and the first letter of the next three words. This technique and the programmes written to accommodate it reportedly retrieve five or fewer titles 99 percent of the time or 80 percent of the member libraries; additional standardized procedures reduce the number of replies in the remaining one percent to less than eighteen with very few exceptions. Approximately half of the tilts were from MARC records, the other half from participating libraries. And the number of participating libraries was growing rapidly, following a decision in 1973 to allow other regional network to connect to the system. The Pittsburgh Regional Library Center. For many of these customer as for Ohio members, the economic justification for a participation in the system is more than the saving on cataloguing costs.

As the price of library materials has risen, the need to share regional library resources has become increasingly urgent, and the OCLC system provides a convenient and effective means of doing so; precise statistics are difficult to come by, but it is clear that more and more participating libraries are using the OCLC system to find and request a copy of a book owned by another library, rather that to catalogue a copy already owned.

Indeed, the implications of the system for resource sharing have often been felt to be as significant as the implications for savings in cataloguing costs. Most importantly, the library wanted to improve communication with the system through the use of visual display terminals, which would al-low catalogue card information to be displayed on the screen and edited before being printed. One problem that plagued the old system may still be a problem with the new, although the library appears to be taking steps to avoid it.

In the old system, the computer used was changed from a 360 Model 30 to a 40, then to a Model 50, then to a Model 65, and somewhat later to the present 370 Model 168, all with inevitable delays. Significantly the new system is also designed so that eventually it can support other user, whereas the old system supported only the University of Chicago library.

Perhaps ironically, the part of the system that makes it accessible to multiple user is called CHASM, 28 symbolizing the wide gap between a single-library system and a cooperative one. Whether Chicago will bridge this chasm in time to attract users away from such established and growing cooperative projects as OCLC remains an important question.

Perhaps the most sophisticate technical processing system presently in operation is the system at Stanford University. Development of the system began in 1967, but its first portion operations did not occur until 1972, when the capability of searching the MARC data base and using it to produce catalogue cards become operational. A large IBM 360 Model 67 computer is used with a small PDP 11 computer as an intermediary and a number of Sanders 804 programmable display terminals. The searching capabilities of the system, developed for the most part under another programme called SPIRES (for Standard Physics Information Retrieval System) are its most impressive feature with many fields and indexes on-line and numerous automatic promptings and suggestions from the computer to the terminal user as a search proceeds.

For cataloguing, the user consults one of eleven terminals located in a single area shared by Acquisitions and Cataloguing, and following the instructions displayed progressively on the screen calls up the bibliographic information generate in the acquisition process, makes any necessary changes, and adds copy numbers and shelving locations symbols.

The end of this process signals production of cataloguing products, including not only catalogue cards and necessary cross-references sequence, but also two kinds of labels, produced on an IBM 2741 terminal with a Se-Lin labeling device attached. One label is for the spine, the other for the inside of the book in connection with circulation use. If the record used in acquisitions was not derived from MARC, the cataloguing department may also search the on-line BALLOTS/MARC files to see if a MARC record is now available. If so, the user may substitute the MARC record for the preliminary acquisition record and add information as needed.

If no MARC record is available, original cataloguing does not necessarily have to be performed at this point, because the system is designed to continue searching for MARC records automatically, at least in categories for which MARC data are expected. If the system later finds a MARC record, the library is notified automatically; in one is found within a specified period of time (up to eight months), the search is terminated and original cataloguing is then performed. In the event that no MARC record is found either on receipt of the item or after the automatic search period, the terminal presents a pretagged from to facilitate input. Editing of the input may be done directly on the terminal or a "catalogue data sheet" which the cataloguing personnel use for making handwritten changes that clerical staff the enter via the terminals. The catalogue data sheet may appear redundant, but it has the advantages of providing a portable version of the proposed catalogue or other sources of information for checking.

In this respect, the BALLOTS system has overcome a disadvantage noted for the OCLC system: the physical problem of checking information retrieved on a visual display terminal against information located elsewhere. Foundation support for the project has been used solely for development and Stanford has paid the operating costs, so when the grant funds eventually disappear the operation of the systems presumably can continue. Nevertheless, certain operational aspects of the system are expensive, and Stanford shares with Chicago the danger of having a glorious white elephant on its hand unless these costs can be spread over a broader base—presumable by supporting the technical processing activities of other libraries as well.

In Stanford's case, work along this line is well advanced. With a new grant from the Council on Library Resources of almost

$3,50,000 announced in early 1975. Stanford will alter the system's software to develop BALLOTS as a California library automation network, and in-cidentally enable it to handle all of the diacritics in the MARC character set. The California State Library has also arranged with Stanford to make BALLOTS available to seven public libraries as the first step toward a California Public Library Automation Network (PLAN). Commercial firms have also become interested in the possibilities of on-line systems. The System Development Corporation began development of a project called LISTS (for Library Information System Time-Sharing), which would allow libraries connected to the system to perform a variety of technical processing tasks, including not only production of catalogue cards but also printing of orders and acquisition reports, maintaining outstanding order and in-process files, and even circulation control. The system began in 1968 with seven libraries (two public and four academic, plus the SDC library) connected by ASR33 teletype terminals to a 360 Model 67 located at SDC headquarters in Santa Monica, California, but it has never been seriously marketed. The Information Dynamics Corporation announced a service called BIBNET, which uses Datapoint 2200 or Hazeltine 2000 terminal connected via regular telephone lines (though Tymshare's TymNet service) to a computer owned by System Development Corporation. The Datapoint terminals have not only a keyboard and a cathode-ray tube but also a small computer memory and provision for insertion of two magnetic tape cassettes containing programmes or data; in effect, therefore, they are minicomputers themselves. When a desired record or information is located by searching. It can be stored on one of the cassettes and then called up on the screen at a later time and edited without typing up expensive telephone lines. GE Terminet printer terminals are also available, with rated speeds of either 30 or 120 characters per second. The printers can be used for production of catalogue cards, or printing of proof sheets to be checked against an existing card catalogue. Searching may be done by the LC card number the International Standard Book Number, by author, by title, or by use of a "Ruecking algorithm."

In early 1975, company was still in the process of leading

MARC record into the system, but brief "index" entries for many records were already available, providing the full author, titles and imprint, as well as LC card number and ISBN, If the full bibliographic record is desired, a key on the terminal can be depressed to ask personnel at IDC headquarters to search manually for the full record, convert it to machine-readable form, and send it back, several days later. The New Mexico State Library has used the systems and a Hazeltine terminal to add holding codes for eighteen libraries in the state, and then search for locations on request from interlibrary loan librarians around the state. SDC's ORBIT programme is used for the searching operation. The costs, in addition to cost of the terminal and its installation, are $45 per hour, plus 20 cents per location added and 90 cents per location retrieved.

All of the systems described above use on-line input and searching techniques in connection with the production of catalogue cards; one other large on-line system, however, has book catalogues as its final product instead. This is the New York Public Library system, perhaps the best and certainly the biggest book catalogue system, in existence at this time. NYPL is really two libraries in one-a large research library, and pubic library with eighty six branches—so two book catalogs are produce, each containing records added since February 1927. The catalogues are produced on a schedule of so-called "continuous re-accumulation." This means that in order to locate a particular titles the user must consult only the cumulation for that portion of the alphabet, plus the cumulative supplement, plus the old card catalogue of entries prior to February 1972. To reduce printing costs, all added entries are condensed, omitting "title page extension," publisher and bibliographic notes, "the assumption being that the user who is interested in such data that will take the trouble to refer to the main entry" Input to the system is off-line but three 2740 terminals are used for inquiry. An IBM 370 model 145 computer is used processing, and production of the book catalogue pages in done by an RCA Videocomp photocomposer. In 1972, the cost of production was about $1,00,000 per year for 550 to 600 copies of the branchlibraries, catalog, and about $90,000 per year for 200 copies of the research Libraries, catalogues, of which about forty are sold. The costs of development for the system have been estimated at anywhere from $2 million to $4 million, and the annual computer bill is around $360,000; of this latter amount however approximately $200,000 is paid of by renting out time to private industry. The project traces its origins to the work of a Columbia University doctoral candidate who found that at NYPL approximately 20 percent of its nine million cards showed substantial deterioration. This study led to a fuller report, which recommended that the library cease adding to the card catalogue cards for new titles using automated techniques.

By 1968, plan had been developed for new card catalogs which would grow for five years and then be converted to book form; by 1969 however, the idea of using catalogue cards had been dropped, and a decision was reached to use book catalogues exclusively. The largest programme in the system and its strong feature is its authority file control; a single machine-readable file includes all subjects, series titles, and names used in the system and every new record is checked against this file before being entered in the system. This provides valuable assistance to the cataloguers and avoids the problem of variant forms of entry, a problem that has plagued other similar systems, notably OCLC. This feature also makes it possible to change outdated terminology for new, readily and efficiently, both in catalogue headings and in the cross-reference structure. Other products of the system include processing information lists, cataloguing work sheets and two shelflist cards for each book which are sent to the branches or divisions. Several other book catalogs, including one of the Dance Collection of the Research Library of the Performing Arts, have also been published. At least two systems have been designed to produce both catalogue cards and book catalogs fro on-line input. The Western Kentucky University library in Bowling green originally began its project as a means of reclassifying from Dewey to the Library of Congress classifying from Dewey to the trminals were installed in 1971 on-line to an IBM 360 Model 40 computer and temporary workers were used to enter data. The computer printed out proofsheets of the data daily, and these were then proofread and edited by cataloguers, reinforced as needed by librarians from other parts of the library. Labels, pockets and book cards were produced of reprocessing of some 250,000items, and both catalogue cards for a divided card catalogue and book catalogs were then printed. Since the reclassification project, catalogue cards and book catalogs continue to be produced on a regular basis.

The UCLA Biomedical Library's cataloguing application differs from most other in that it makes no attempt to use MARC records, and is designed to accommodate only "original' cataloguing. The majority of the records acquired by the Biomedical Library are not available on MARC in any case, since the Library of congress by policy avoids adding works in clinical medicine or other areas covered by its sister institution the National Library of Medicine. The cataloguer for the Biomedical Library types information on a "cataloguing coding sheet" which a clerk then rekeys on a terminal, the redundant keyboarding action apparently necessitated by the objection of the cataloguer to using the terminal.

The terminal itself is a Delta Data Systems device with a cassette section added; the information is recorded on the cassette, and periodically the computer reads the information from the cassette into disk storage. A prooflisting is printed periodically, and is used by the cataloger to make editing changes. Corrections are then input by the typist. Catalogue cards are produced once a week on a 360 Model 20, prearranged in filing sequence, and a list of new accessions is produced once a month. The same programmes that arrange the cards are also used for the book catalogue, which is produced primarily or regional interlibrary loan purpose. A three years, $40,000 grant provided funds for development of the system, and operating costs are estimated at $1,000 per month. A few libraries have taken what some regard as the ultimate step and devised systems that use on-line terminals not only for input and searching but also for regular conciliations of the catalogue file, thereby eliminating the use of catalogue cards and book catalogues altogether.

Perhaps the first such system was the Experimental Library Management System (ELMS) at the IBM Advanced System development Division Library in Los Gatos, California, parts of which have been in operation since 1965. Catalogue information is input via IBM 2741 terminals and is consulted by both library staff and patrons using IBM 2260 display terminals. There are four of these—two in the processing area, one at the reference desk, and one in a carrel. Public use appears to be successful but since this is a small, specialised library it is difficult to estimate the problems that might result if the same techniques were used in a large research library.

Before the on-line reference function was implemented, the system produced nine separate book catalogs or listings, and apparently this capability is still used. Spine labels and book pocket labels are produced. On-line reference to machine-readable catalogue files was also the subject of much intensive study during Project Intrex at the Massachusetts Institute of Technology. Intrex was a multimillion dollar research project, which began in 1965 and was finally terminated in 1973. On idea that received much experimental study during the lie of the project was the concept an "augmented catalogue", which would be consulted on-line and would contain not only the usual bibliographical information, but such additional data as the "author's purpose," the "level of approach," excerpts from the text, all except the author being what the project staff referred to as "content-indicating" fields.

CHAPTER 4

Functions of Collection Management of Serials

For a variety of reasons (e.g., a subscription was not begun until several volumes had already been published, a subscription was canceled and later reinstated, etc.), a library may have incomplete holdings of a particular periodical's backruns. This section focuses on the collection management decision of whether a gap should be completed, with the processing aspects covered in chapter 8. The concept of completing gaps should be differentiated from filling in missing issues at the time of building.

This issue has not received much attention in the literature, so formal guidelines and theoretical discussion are sparse. Filling in the gap decisions are usually made on a micro (title-by-title) basis. The decision criteria include the journal's intrinsic importance, the length and age of the gap, usage patterns in the library, interlibrary loan (ILL) or document delivery requests for the missing volumes, the journal's cited half-life in the Journal Citation Reports (JCR), the availability of the missing volumes in nearby libraries, the cost of completing the gap, and whether the library has a current subscription.

The cited half-life, available for thousands of journals in the JCR, indicates the extent to which older urns are still being cited by researchers and thus has potential application to gap-filling decision making. For a technical explanation of the Institute for

Scientific Information's (ISI) calculation of cited half-life, see chapter 5. One doubts whether a great number of librarians consults the JCR while reaching decisions about periodical gaps, yet the potentially useful data contained in this source should be brought to their attention.

Treatment of Unbound Issues

Traditional print periodicals are generally received as single, unbound issues. The old Horizon and American heritage magazines are rare examples of periodicals with hardbound single issues. Thus when the unbound issues accumulate to a certain point, typically a bibliographical volume, a decision must be made about their permanent preservation. Generally, five options are theoretically possible:

1. Discard
2. Binding
3. Microformat in lieu of binding
4. Permanent maintenance in an unbound form
5. Digitization or electronic preservation

Each of these is discussed below. A survey of college and small university library directors found that, on average, 65.6 percent of periodical titles in their libraries were bound, 16.9 percent maintained on microfilm, and 12.2 percent on microfiche.[1]

Discard

Unbound issues can be discarded if the library does not wish to permanently maintain them in the collection. Obvious candidates for discard would be issues that are superseded by a cumulative volume (e.g., indexing or abstracting services such as Library Literature). Periodicals whose content is of ephemeral value, for example, providing current awareness, would be strong candidates for discard. Many newsletters would fall into this category. Gift periodicals are often discarded because the library does not wish to commit funds for binding. When the discard option is adopted, a decision should be made to keep issues for a set time period, such as six months, one year, two years, and so forth. Whether a periodical is of temporary or enduring value often requires a subject specialist's judgement.

Binding

Binding is the preferred and most frequently used method for dealing with unbound periodicals. This option reduces the loss of individual issues. A significant portion of library budgets is devoted to periodical binding, but it is a worthwhile expenditure because it more or less adequately protects the library's substantial investment in serial subscriptions.

P.G. Peacock has published a decision table on which periodicals to bind. A scale of one to three is applied to four variables:

Physical condition: good = 1; average = 2; poor = 3

Number of parts issued per year: less than 4 = 1; 5 to 12 = 2; more than 13 = 3

Frequency of use: low = 1; average = 2; high = 3

Value in terms of price, rarity, academic or local interest; low = 1; average = 2; high = 3.

Peacock states that, generally, a title scoring several threes will be sound, but those rating several ones will be left unbound.[2] Unfortunately, he does not precisely outline the definitions for high, average, and low physical condition, use, and value.

Microformat in Lieu of Binding

Use of microform instead of binding saves shelf space, offers protection against mutilation and theft, and is particularly appropriate for serials, which do not lend themselves well to binding because of their size, frequency, and sometimes poor paper quality. Several disadvantages are associated with this option. Both print and microfilm formats must be paid for certain periodicals, such as those in which illustrations area a major feature, are unsuitable for microformat. Many readers feel uncomfortable with the microformat (e.g., browings is difficult); and although there are four ways to put it into the machine, three of them are wrong!

Moreover, the microformat requires expensive equipment and storage cabinets, and there is a danger of obsolescence in the format itself or the equipment that runs it. If the microformat option is adopted, there is often a choice between microfilm or microfiche. Factors in determining whether a title should be preserved in microform are outlined below, but not in priority order:

- *Condition of paper holdings*. If many missing or multilated issues are in the current holdings, microformat would be preferable to binding, all other factors being equal.
- *Use*. Highly used titles normally should not be preserved in microform because of user resistance to the format.
- *Language*. Foreign language periodicals are often strong candidates for microform because they are less likely to be heavily used.
- *Cost*. There is conflicting evidence in the literature whether binding or microformat is less expensive, but the cost-effectiveness of the two formats should be separately calculated for each periodical under consideration because it will vary among titles.
- *Indexing*. Indexed titles are better candidates for microformat preservation than un indexed ones because microforms are hard to browse and indexing helps users locate needed articles.
- *Illustrations*. Periodicals in which illustrative matter is a major feature are not good candidates for microform.
- *Type of periodical*. Technical titles that contain numerous graphs, maps, scientific illustrations, or statistical tables; quasi-reference journals that emphasize book reviews or other features that would not be indexed; and poetry or short story magazines whose format is part of their "charm' are not good candidates for themicroformt.[3] Microform is the recommended preservation method for daily newspapers. Weekly news magazines, such as *Time, Newsweek* or the *Economist*, are more problematic because their physical size is compatible with binding but several volumes would

be required for single year's run.

- *Article length.* Most authorities contend that periodicals with short articles are more appropriate for microform than those with long articles because the reader will be less inconvenienced. Taking a contrarian position, Helen M. Grochmal argues that whether long-article or short-article periodicals are best suited to micro-form will depend on user preference and the availability of copy machines.[4]
- *Availability in microformat.* It titles are not commercially available in microformat, the expense of in-house production or non-demand commercial production would probably be prohibitive.

Microform in lieu of binding is a distinct concept form microform conversion, which entails substituting the microformat for periodical runs that are already bound. Nonetheless, the criteria outlined above would apply to both situations.

Permanent Maintenance in an Unbound Form

Theoretically, periodicals could be maintained indefinitely without binding, such as by storing them in a Princeton file—a container especially designed for periodicals. Indeed cogent arguments have been made against binding periodicals. As summarized by Peacock, money is saved; a volume's separate parts can be simultaneously used by more than one patron; volumes are not missing form the shelves wile at the bindery; and unbound issues are easier to photocopy.[5] Fortunately, most libraries reject this option. The cost of binding or microformat can reasonably be viewed as a means of protecting the library's already substantial investment in serials.

Digitization of Electronic Preservation

One can easily imagine that at some future point electronic archiving or digitization will be used for the permanent preservation of print periodicals, but this is presently not a feasible solution for most libraries. The Library of Congress's (LC) National Digital Library Programme for preserving valuable resources through digitization is focusing on formats other than serials. The JSTOR project is experimenting with digitization of print journal backruns.

Multiple Copy Decisions

Determining the number of copies for a particular title is a basic collection management decision that applies to both monographs and periodicals. In the past libraries have held multiple subscriptions for a variety of reasons, including high usage, the need for the same title indifferent branches, and the desirability of extra copies for staff use. One presumes, given the current environment, that libraries now seldom place additional periodical subscriptions. In fact, duplicate subscriptions are frequently among the first to be canceled.

Location Decisions

Multi-branch libraries, especially university libraries with subject-based branches, often question which branch should house a particular periodical title. Key questions include

> Which location should place an initial subscription?
>
> For locations with duplicate subscriptions or holdings, which one should cancel or weed a title?
>
> Should a particular title be transferred from one location to another?

Location decisions, about which very little has been published, are undoubtedly assuming greater importance as libraries cancel duplicate subscriptions in response to the current serials crunch. The obvious decision criteria would be patron need, a periodical's relevance to a location's subject emphasis, and actual or estimated usage. A collection development policy might help resolve conflicts by explicitly assigning subject responsibilities to the different locations within a library system. However, this tactic will not work for periodicals that legitimately fall within the domain of more than one subject areas or whose focus is difficult to ascertain. The issue is complicated by the interdisciplinary nature of modern scholarship as demonstrated by innumerably citation and circulation studies.

Serials Decision Models

Many criteria affect serials collection management decisions. Obvious questions concern what weight should be assigned to various factors and how they can be combined to reach a decision. This section reviews some explicit journal decisions models that have been proposed in the literature and analyses the major issues regarding these models.

A decision model may be viewed as a complex journal ranking method. Unlike the standard journal ranking methods, which are usually based on a single dimension such as citation data or expert perception, or the cost-per-use methodologies (mentioned in chapter 6), which in corporate the two criteria of cost and use, a decision model combines numerous variables. Generally, some type of mathematical formula is used to calculated a numerical score or rating for each journal in the set under evaluation. These ratings are then used to construct a hierarchical rank ordering of the complete set so that all journals can be listed from the most valuable through the least valuable. If the results are used for selection, one could presumably begin with the highest ranking title and work down the list until the budget's limit has been reached. In contrast, one would begin at the bottom for cancellation decisions.

More than a dozen published serials decision models are listed in this chapter's "further Reading" section. To illustrate the structure and nature of these models, a small number are examined below.

In 1980 S.M. Dhawan, S.K. Phull, and S.P. Jain published a model based on a journal's use, citation record, and coverage by abstracts, Data from the Science Citation Index (SCI) JCR, Physics Abstracts, and usage in several libraries were used to test the mode on a set of 400 physics journals. By combining the three variables noted above, the authors advocated journal acquisition according to five hierarchical categories;

1. Journals that are cited abstracted, and used.
2. Journals that are abstracted, used, but not cited.

3. Journals that are cited, used, but not abstracted.
4. Journals that are used but neither abstracted nor cited. Journals that are abstracted cited, but not used.[6]

Logical analysis of this hierarchy indicates that Dhawan, Phull, and Jain place the highest value on use, followed by abstract coverage, then citedness.

At the American society for information science (ASIS) 1981 annual conference, Gilda maria braga and Cecila Alves Oberhofer presented a model , developed at the Brazalian institute for information in science and technology , for decisions making about scientific and technical journals published in developing countries and summarized in table 4.1 . A five point rating system (1=low; 5=high)m was applied to numerous variables grouped under seven broad heading: standardization, duration, frequency of appearance , indexing , dissemination, collaboration and contents division, and authority. Examination of table 4.1 which represents their scoring system, indicates some problems. The assumption that more–frequently is issued periodically are more desirable than less- frequently issued ones is highly questionable. Determining whether the editorial board is composed of "experts of well-established competence" may be difficult. A unique characteristic of this model is that the authors offer a method for interpreting a journal's score, unlike most models, which rank order a journal set. An appended "Valuation Scale" states that 0 to 30 points are "very bad"; 31 to 55, "bad"; 56 to 80, "good"; and 80 plus points, "verygood,"[7] Although interesting from a theoretical perspective and serving as a good illustrative example, this model would seem to have little practical value for most North American libraries.

Judith A. Segal described a relatively simple deselection model that was used in a cancellation project for behavioral sciences and education journals at Ben Gurion University of the Negev, Israel, in 1984. Her model focused on six variables: completeness of holdings, cost, JCR impact factor, indexing, listing in the Katzes's Magazines for Libraries, and relevance to curriculum. It awarded five points for each of the following: complete holdings, a cost at or below average for the discipline, an impact factor at or above average in the discipline, and inclusion in the Katzes's Magazines for Libraries. Five points were also granted if, during three of the preceding four years, the journal directly related to at least one course taught at the university. One point was received for each of the discipline's top five indexes that covered the journal. If no impact factor was available because the journal was not covered in the JCR, this variable was eliminated from consideration. Thus, the maximum point total would be 25 or 30, depending upon whether five or six variables were included. The actual points received were then converted to a percentage of the maximum potential points. Then Segan added five points for journals identified as "top priority" in a faculty questionnaire and subtracted five points for journals that were not used during a brief survey. This is obviously a crude model. For many variables, either five points or nothing is awarded without any intermediate scores. The author does not claim it can be applied in other libraries.[8]

Table 4.2 illustrates a journal decision model developed at the University of Evansville and published in 1986 by Ruth H. Miller and Marvin C. Guilfoyle. This model incorporates seven variables: indexing; ILL data; reviews in core lists or bibliographies; demand; programme support; cost; and miscellaneous factors. From 0 to 10 points can be assigned in each category, and the weight attached to each ranges from 0.5 for miscellaneous factors to 2 for programme support. The indexing category helps illustrate the model's application. A title covered in a major index receives 8 points; if included in a second index, the title gains an additional 2 points for "multiple indexing," resulting in a score of 10. Titles covered in a less-important secondary indeed receive 5 points (or points if in two or more secondary indexes), whereas unindexed titles receive no points. Examination of the "miscellaneous factors" category clearly indicates that the model requires considerable subjective judgment (e.g., is the "format appropriate" or the "publisher reputation sound"?). However, as stated by Miller and Guilfoyle, the system turns "subjective judgements into numerical scores."[9]

Edward P. Miller and Ann L. O'Neill proposed in 1990 a model for calculating a journal's "effectiveness factor" to be used for deselection purposes. This model is unique in its flexibility. The library using the model can decide which variables (Miller and O'Neill use the term element) to include as well as the weight assigned to each, ranging from 1 to 10. Miller and O'Neill suggest numerous possible variables: "use, curriculum, indexing, ILL availability, holdings, binding/check-in costs, publishers reputation, format, paper quality, claiming problems, Language, micro film "and JCR impact factor. THEY also present an instrument for surveying users about their assessments on 1- 10 scale of such factors as author prestige, article quality, overall journal rating, and "level of embrasement to admit ignorance of the journal rating, and "level of embrasement to admit ignorance of the journal." A library can use some or all of these variables as well as add others. The author do not explain, except in a few instances, how the variables can be converted to numerical point scales. In fact, it is the library's prerogative to set the numerical scale for each variable. Although this feature may contribute to the model's flexibility, it might also present some practical difficulties. The author state that the effectiveness factor should be calculated only for candidates for cancilation.

Dawn Bick and Rita Sinha, in 1991 published a sophisticated model that was developed at a Houston academy of medicine-Texas medical center library. Twenty factors were used as a evaluation criteria, including indexing; impact factor; and holdings in the library, Houston area, or region. An evaluation matrix was then used to determine the importance of the evaluation criteria by comparing all criteria with ach other on a one-to one basis. For example, impact factor would be compared in importance with the indexing, using a 3-point scale: "3 for a major difference in importance, 2 for a medium difference, and 1 for a minor difference." The weights are then added to obtain a "score" for each journal under evaluation. Predicated on the assumption that a journal's benefit increases with its use, the journal score is multiplied by the number of uses to obtain a "BNENFIT" factor. The BENEFIT

Table 4.1: Braga and Oberhofer'sModel Evaluating Scientific and Technical Journals

Criterion	*Variable*	*Condition*	*Number of Points*
1. Standardisation	1.1 Journal in the whole	• to be explicit in the journal	4
	(standard for submitting papers)	• to be explicit in the journal and following national standards	5
	1.2 Journal issues		4
	1.2.1 Table of contents	• existence	1
	1.2.2 Bibliographical strip	• existence	2
	1.3 Joural articles		
	1.3.1 Author affiliation	• indication	3
	1.3.2 Abstracts only in the local language (ifnot English)	• existence	2
	1.3.3 Abstracts only in English	• existence	2
	1.3.4 Billingual abstracts	• existence	4
	1.3.5 Descriptors of key-words	• existence	2
2. Duration	2.1 continuous time of existence	• each 2 (two) years of life	1

	3.1 Regular frequenc of issues	• 2 times per year	1
3. Frequency of Appearance		• 3 times per year	2
		• 4 times per year	3
		• 6 times per year	4
		• 12 times per year	5
	4.1 Coverage by abstracting and indexing services	• for each national indexing or abstracting service	2
		• for each foreign and/or abstrating service	5
	5.1 Circulation (number of copies per issue)	• for each national indexing or abstracting service	2
4. Indexing		• for each foreign and/or international indexing or abstrating service	2
		• for each foreign and/or international indexing or abstracting service	5
	5.1 Circulation (number of copies per issue)	• between 1,000 and 2,999	1
		• betwene 3,000 and 4,999	2
		• 5,000 and above	3
5. Dissemination			
	5.2 Existence of reasonably complete collections (at leat 75%	• for each library	1

	in local libraries)	• explicit availability	1
	6.1 Authorship	• Inclusion of about 20% papers from foreign authors	3
		• inclusion of papers from authors of different regions of the country	5
6. Collaboration and Contents Division	6.2 Communication of on-gong research	• to be a regular section	4
	6.3 Letters	• to be a regular section	2
	6.4 Book Reviews	• to be a regular section	2
	6.5 Review Articles	•regular inclusion	5
7. Authority	7.1 Editorial Board	• to be formed by experts of well-established competence	5
		• to be interinstitutional	3

Reprinted with permission of the American Society for Information Science from Gilda Maria Braga and Cecilia Alves Oberhofer, "A Model for Evaluating Scientific and Technical Journals from Developing Countries," in The Information Community: An Alliance for Progress: Proceeding of the 44th ASIS Annual Meeting, Washington, D.C., October 25-30, 1981, vol. 18, ed. By Lois F. Lunin, Madeline Henderson, and Harold Wooster (White Plains, N.Y.: publshed for the Americna Society for Informatio Science by Knowledge Industry Publications, 1981), 53.

factor is then divided by cost to rank the library's current journals by a cost-benefit ratio.[11]

Additional published descriptions of journal decision models were developed at various libraries, including California State University at Dominguez Hills, by Jeffrey Broude;[12] the Lawrence Livermore National Laboratory Biomedical Library, by Richard K. Hunt;[13] the University of Nijmegen Faculty of Medical Sciences (in the Netherlands), by Rikie Deurenderg;[14] and the University Of Maryland at College Park, by Natalie Schoch and Eileen g. Abels[15] Other models based on theory (without explicitly stating they had been used at a specific library) have been advanced by Eeanor D. Dym. And Donald L. Shirey,[16] Donald H. Kraft and Richard A. Polacsek,[17] Roy Rada and others,[18] and Victor A. Trioloand Dachun Bao.[19] Andrew Peters reported use of a modified version of the Kraft and Polacsek model at the Central state University library in Oklahoma.[20]

In summary, the major issues in design of a serials evaluation model concern.

1. the number of variables included;
2. which variables are included;
3. the numerical scale;
4. the weight or hierarchical value attached to each variable;
5. the difficulty of implementing the model;
6. the degree of flexibility allowed the implementing library;
7. whether the model is based on theory or actual library practice; and
8. the model's explicit purpose (e.g., selection, cancellation, etc.).

Some concerns about journal decision models should be noted. One might question whether a model developed in the context of a single discipline or library can validly be transported to other disciplines or libraries. Moreover, most models are intended to be used in a cross-disciplinary sense—often for all journals

Table 4.2: Miller and Guilfoyle's Journal Subscription Model Developed at the University of Evansville

---

I. **Indexing (8/5/2 Points)** Weight: 1.5

1. Primary indexing; ASTI/BPI/CIJE/CINAHL/CLI/EDIHUMI/ PsYCH/ SSI/USPSD/
2. Secondary indexing available at U.E.
3. Multiple indexing

II. **Interlibrary loan (5/10 Points)** Weight: 1.0

1. 5-8 requests in last year from multipel requestors
2. >8 requests in last year form multiple requestors

III. **Review/Core List/Bibliography (4/3/3 Points)** Weight: 1.5

1. Strong review
2. Indication of appropriatenes for U.E.
3. Currency or review or list

IV. **Demand (4/4/2 Points)** Weight : 1.0

1. Faculty
2. Librarian
3. Student or other patron

V. **Programme Support (4/3/3 Points)** Weight: 2.0

1. Substantial number of students or courses/programmes supported
2. Periodical use by these courses/programmes is high
3. Relative strength of current periodical holdinds for these courses/programmes is low

VI. **Cost (4/0/3/3 Points)** Weight : 1.0

1. <$75
2. $75 +
3. Amount spentfor all subscriptions for this department or area (versus other areas) is low in relation to need and use
4. Amount spent for subscriptions (versus books) for this department or area is low in relation to need and use

VII. **Miscellaneous Factors (3/3/1/3 Points)** Weight : 5

1. Format appropriate
2. Not available locally
3. Publisher reputation sound
4. Published longer than one year (an acceptable risk)

Reprinted with permission of Haworth Press from Ruth H. Miller and Marvin C. Guilfoyle, "Computer Assisted Periodicals Selection: Structuring the Subjective" *Serials Librarian* 10 (spring 1986): 13.

sub-scribed to by the implementing library. For some variables, cross-disciplinary comparison may be like comparing apples and oranges, as citation and price patterns vary from discipline to discipline. There may be a strong subjective factor in the selection of variables and the weight assigned to them. The conversion of data about a specific journal to a numerical scale could sometimes be problematic. Most models appear to have been developed for academic institutions and may not be applicable to other types of libraries.

Journal decision models are of considerable theoretical importance for serials collection management. Unfortunately, there is little evidence, based on surveying the appropriate literature and listervs, that these models have actually been used to any appreciable extent in libraries other than the library where a particular model was developed. Ironically, many libraries implementing serials cancellation projects often reach their own decision rules for combining journal evaluation variables even though a formal, explicit journal decision model is never published.

Core Lists of Serials

The so-called core collection has long been a major concept in collection development thought. The word core refers to the most important materials that should form the core or heart of the collection. Such terms as essential or indispensable have been used to describe core material. The concept has been applied to subjects, formats, and library types as well as combinations of these categories. Specific examples of the core concept include the core books for a college library (e.g., Books for College Libraries) or, more relevant to this text, the core periodicals for a type of library or in a particular discipline.

The most frequently used methods for determining the core are inclusion on recommended lists, subjective judgement, use, and citation data, but overlapping holdings among libraries, indexing, and complex multivariable approaches have also been used. Some of the reported methodologies for identifying core periodicals are described below. Standard lists of recommended journals or magazines are often considered to constitute the core. The best-known list of this type, first published in 1969, is Magazines for Libraries, by Katz and Katz. The mint edition, issued in 1997, lists and annotates more than 7,300 titles deemed "most useful for the average elementary or secondary school, public, academic, or special library."[21] The second edition of Selma K. Richardson's Magazines for Children: A Guide for Parents, Teachers, and Librarians, published in 1991, recommends and lists more than 110 magazines for children through age 14 and the 8th grade,[22] Since 1965 Afred N. Brandon and Dorothy R. Hill have been publishing biannually in the Bulletin of the Medical Library Association the so-called Brandon-Hilllit of recommended books and serials for small medical libraries. Their April 1997 list contained 141 journals.[23] The Core collection of Medical books and Journals, compiled by Howard Hague,[24] has been identified as the "British Counterpart" to the Brandon-Hill list but with an international focus. The 1994 edition lists 249 journal titles.[25]

Although identification of the core was not their primary intention, Tim LaBorie, Michael Halperin, and Howard D. White's study could be used to determine core journals in library and information science. They analysed overlapping coverage of Library and Information Science (LIS) journals in ten indexing and abstracting services: Four from the discipline itself (Abstract Journal: Informatics, Information Science Abstracts, Library and Information Science Abstracts, and Library Literature) and six outside the discipline, such as the Social Sciences Citation Index (SSCI) and The Current Index to Journals in Education. LaBorie, Halperin, and White then identified the 59 titles covered in five or more of these indexing services as the "defactor core journals of library and information science."[26]

James C. Baughman's structural analysis of sociology, based on more than 10,000 citations in 446 articles listed in the 1970-1971 Social Science sand Humanities Index, included an identification of the core sociology journals. He raned journals according to the number of their articles that were cited atleast twice and designated the top ten as representing the core. It is noteworthy that five of these were outside the discipline of sociology, thus illustrating the interdisciplinary nature of the social sciences.[27]

At the University of Delaware library Linda Lawrence Stein identified 27 core "fashion, textile, and apparel merchandising/ manufacturing periodicals by accessing on the Internet the online public access catalogs (OPACS) of eight other major university libraries known to possess strong collections in that specialty. Titles held by a majority of the other libraries (five of eight) were considered the core.[28] Stein's methodology is particularly interesting because it combines the Internet and traditional collection management approach—analysis of overlapping library holdings. A possible flaw in this method is that the analysis was limited to the 55 titles already held by the University of Delaware library. Thus, a title meeting the decision criterion to be considered core (appearing in five of the eight OPACs accessed on the Internet) would have been overlooked if it were not initially in the University of Delaware collection.

The core concept has obvious relevance to serials management. In selecting periodicals for a new collecting area, one would logically place the highest priority on core titles. A list of core titles can be used as a checklist for collection evaluation. A core title would not normally be a strong candidate for cancellation weeding, or relegation to remote storage. In some cases a multi-branch system might wish to duplicate core periodicals. Core lists can assist budgeting by indicating the cost of subscribing to the core periodicals in a subject area. Moreover, in an age of increasing emphasis on access over ownership, the core concept assumes greater significance. Libraries would presumably wish to subscribe to the core periodicals and rely on access for non-core titles.

Indeed, requests for core lists in various subject areas frequently appear on listervs.

In addition to its practical application in libraries the core serials concept has been used in the research process. Many scholarly investigations have been based on the core journals of a particular subject. For example, Bluma C. Peritz used the citations in 39 core library science journals for her biblioetric analysis of the discipline.[29] Judith Serebnick and Stephen P. Harter used coverage in each of the three major library and information science indexes to identify 39 core LIS journals so they could survey their editors about ethical practices in journal publishing.[30]

Some limitations to the core concept should also be mentioned. A core list does not consider the unique needs of a specific library and its clientele. Each major method for determining core lists (e.g., citation data, subjective judgement, or indexing) may contain its own methodological flaws. Subject-or discipline-oriented core lists will probably not contain interdisciplinary journals.

Major Approaches to the Macroevaluation of Serials

Most of this chapter focuses on micro treatment of individuals serial titles. In the final analysis, the most significant question concerns who well the library is meeting patron needs for serials. Thus, macroevaluation is directed toward the entire collection or the library's performance rather than individual titles. A macro-evaluation project can concentrate exclusively on the serials format, but commonly the focus is on a particular subject areas or the whole collection. In the latter case, serials are usually evaluated as a component of support. This section introduces some fundamental evaluation concepts, the major collection evaluation approaches, and their application to serials.

Approaches to collection evaluation have been characterized as quantitative versus qualitative or collection centered versus client centered. A quantitative approach concentrates on the number of items held, whereas a qualitative method is concerned with the quality of the holdings. A collection-centered method focuses on the collection itself or compares it with an external standard. In contrast, a client-centered method analyseds how well the collection meets the needs of library patrons.

General evaluation techniques can be characterized according to whether they are objective or subjective, real or simulated, and obtrusive or unobtrusive. An objective method relies on measurable units of analysis, such as the number of current periodical subscriptions; a subjective technique is based on impressionistic perceptions, such as a faculty member's opinion on how well the serials collection is supporting his or her research. A real technique is based on an actual situation (e.g., the proportion of time that serial titles are on the shelf when patrons seek them), whereas a simulated technique is structured on an artificial contrivance for research purposes (checking a list of serial citations that are presumed to be representative of patron information needs). At the risk of over implication, the involved human subjects are aware of an intrusive evaluation, but unaware of an unobtrusive one. In practical terms, a periodical use study could be either obtrusive or unobtrusive depending on whether patrons are informed that the study is taking place.

Three distinctive concepts relating to serials macro-evaluation are ownership, availability, and accessibility. Ownership obviously relates to a library "owning" or holding an item as a permanent part of its collection. *Availability* addresses the question of whether a patron can find an item on the shelf when he or she is seeking it. Accessibility concerns the time required to provide a sought-after document to a patron.

A brief introduction to the major collection evaluation approaches, out-lining the benefits and drawbacks of each, can be found in the American Library Association's (ALA) Guide to the evaluation of library Collections. Practical step-by-step instructions about implementing the leading techniques are provided in Blaine H. Hall's collection Assessment Manual for *College and University Libraries*. Finally, the academic library collection evaluation literature from 1980 to 1991 is surveyed in Thomas E. Nisonger's Collection Evaluation in Academic Libraries: A Literature Guide and Annotated bibliography.[31] The traditional collection evaluation approaches and their relationship to serials are discussed below.

The Checklist Approach

The checklist method represents the oldest and most traditional approach to collection evaluation. Many other methods, such as availability studies or document delivery tests, are simply more sophisticated modifications of the checklist technique. As implied by the term checklist, a list of items is checked against the collection and the percentage of items held is then tabulated. The larger the proportion of items held, the better the collection is presumed to be. This is a collection-centered, qualitative technique. (Although the checklist method contains a quanticentered qualitative technique. (Although the checklist method contains a quantitative aspect in that the number of held items is calculated, it is usually considered a qualitative technique because the list is assumed to represent high-quality. items.)

A major issue concerns which list to check of the ALA Guide to the evaluation of Library Collections lists 15 possibilities, including bibliographies; recommended lists; items, items cited in faculty publications, Ph.D. dissertations or course reading lists; or titles listed by subject in the JCR.[32]

The unit to be checked against the library's holdings can be either a periodical title or a specific article. The list's for at—whether it lists citations to articles or simply titles—might determine the checking strategy used. In article-level checking, the criterion for determining a hit would be whether the specific citation is actually contained in the collection, whereas in title-level checking, one presumes the criterion would be whether the library maintains a current subscription. Checking at the article-level probably provides a more meaningful indication of the serial holdings' depth but it would tend to overestimate collection strength in libraries that have recently canceled many current periodical subscriptions. In some evaluation studies, one might tabulate the findings by both article and title. Note that a checklist can consist exclusively of serial items or include serials entries with other formats. In the latter, the data can nevertheless be tabulated separately for serials.

Many uses of list checking to evaluate periodical holdings have been reported. For example, the University of California at Berkeley Environmental Design Library checked its periodicals against seven major indexes.[33]

Expert Opinion

This subjective, qualitative, collection-centered approach is often termed "direct examination" or "impressionistic judgment." A presumed expert examines the collection and reaches an impressionistic assessment of its quality. This approach would normally be used for a specific subject rather than the whole collection. In assessing a subject's serial holdings, the expert should consider whether the major titles are included, balance among sub areas, currently, language, completeness of holdings, and alternate means of access. This method requires considerable subject expertise.

Compiling Holding Statistics

Compiling statistics on the size and growth of the collection represents one of the older, more-traditional, quantitative, collection-centered approaches to evaluation. For serials the most crucial data are totals of current subscriptions, volumes held, ad expenditures. The statistics can be compiled for the complete collection or specific subject areas. In some instances, the number of periodical subscriptions per student or pupil is used as an evaluative measure. Statistical data are especially valuable when placed in a comparative context with other libraries or used for longitudinal comparisons of the same library. Serials data for large U.S. university libraries can be found in the annual Association of research Libraries (ARL) statistical series. (For details on various statistical sources, see appendix 1.) A major issue, unresolved in the mid-1990s, concerns counting such "virtual holdings' as electronic journals—which are accessible but not owned in the traditional sense—in holding statistics. In light of the increasing emphasis on access rather than ownership, it is probable that holdings data will, in the future, become less significant as a periodicals evaluation measure.

Standards

A standard is typically promulgated by an authoritative organisation and covers numerous components of library support such as budgets, staffing, facilities, and collections. The collection section usually addresses periodicals. Although traditionally a collection-centered approach, standards can be quantitative, qualitative, or sometimes both. A quantitative standard specifies as set number of items to be held in the collection or acquired within a year; qualitative standards provide prescriptive statements outlining adequacy or excellence without specifying numbers.

Standards date back more than three quarters of a century. In 1920 the ALA published the National Education Association's standards for senior and junior high school libraries,[34] and standards for junior college libraries were first issued by the American Council on Education and the American Association of Junior Colleges in the early 1930s; for college libraries, by the Association of College and Research Libraries (ACRL) in 1959; and for university libraries, by the ACRL and ARL in 1979.[35] Because many standards have been adopted for practically every type of library, a comprehensive review is beyond this chapter's scope.

The current ACRL, ALA, and Association for Educational Communications and technology (AECT) standards for junior and community college libraries serve as an example of the quantitative approach.[36] This document contains a table (labeled table E, which is partially preproduced here as table 4.3, on page 108), prescribing a given number of current serial subscriptions for 10 categories of student body size in both a "minimum" and an "excellent" collection on a single campus. The recommended number of current serial subscriptions for a "minimum collection" ranges from 230 when there are fewer than 1,000 full time equivalent (FTE) students to 1,8000 for 17,000 to 19,000 FTE students. In contrast, the stipulated numbers for an "excellent collection" range from 400 for fewer than 1,000 FTE students to 2,400 for 17,000 to 19,000 FTE students. Although not illustrated in table 4.3, numbers for volumes; film and video; such "other" items as microforms, maps, etc.; and total collection size are also specified.

Table 4.3: Number of Recommended Serial Subscriptions from Table E of ACRL-ALA-AECT Standards for community Junior, and Technical College Learning Resources Programmes

Minimum Collection	
FTE Students	Current Serial Subscriptions
Under 1,000	230
1,000-2,999	300
3,000-4,999	500
5,000-6,999	700
7,000-8,999	850
9,000-10,999	900
11,000-12,999	1,000
13,000-14,999	1,200
15,000-16,999	1,500
17,000-19,000	1,800
Excellent Collection	
FTE Students	Current Serial subscriptions
Under 1,000	400
1,000-2,999	600
3,000-4,999	800
5,000-6,999	1,000
7,000-8,999	1,200
9,000-10,999	1,400
11,000-12,999	1,600
13,000-14,999	1,800
15,000-16,999	2,100
17,000-19,000	2,400

Information Power (the AASL-AECT standard for school library media centers, discussed in chapter 3) presents data on the number of serials held and the number of current serial subscriptions per 100 pupils at the 75th and 95th percentile levels in seven categories of school libraries—to be used as quantitative national guidelines. As of the end of 1985, a high school wit more than 1,000 students "held" 145 serials at the 75th percentile level, 198 at the 90th percentile, and 231 at the 95th. (Although not explicitly stated, one presumes these numbers refer to current subscriptions.) Total subscriptions per 100 students were reported as 10 at the 75th percentile, 14 at the 90th, and 15 at the 95th.[37] See Information Power's appendix A for corresponding data on other school sizes and levels.

The qualitative approach is used in the ACRL guidelines for university undergraduate libraries, which states, "Reference collections in undergraduate libraries should concentrate on the more standard and interdisciplinary indexes and sources. Periodical collections should emphasize the titles covered by these indexes."[38] The 1995 ACRL standards for college libraries asset that "Institutional needs for periodical holdings vary widely," but, as previously mentioned, they suggest a library consider subscribing to any title needed more than five times per eyar.[39]

Standards are somewhat controversial. Some critics claim that qualitative standards represent meaningless verbiage that cannot easily be applied in practice; others asset that quantitative standards place too much emphasis on numbers at the expense of quality. Moreover, most standards adhere to the traditional ownership paradigm and fail to adequately address electronic journals.

Formulas

Another traditional collection evaluation method is the use of a formula—an objective, quantitative, collection-centered approach. Most formulas being with a base number of volumes and add additional volumes for such variables as the number of FTE faculty and the number of degree programmes to calculate the total volumes a library should contain for hypothetical minimum-level collection adequacy. The best-known and most frequently used example is the Clapp-Jordan in 1965 and reprinted as a classic paper in 1989.[40] (A faculty member once told the author that this formula reminded him of a venereal disease.)

The Clapp-Jordan Formula contains separate components for books, periodicals, and documents. To calculate the required number of periodicals for a senior college or university library, begin with 250 subscriptions and 3,750 volumes, which are asserted to be the appropriate figures for a basic undergraduate collection. To this base, add 1 subscription and 15 titles for each FTE faculty member, 1 volume for each FTE graduate and undergraduate student, 3 subscriptions and 45 volumes for each subject major available to undergraduates, 10 subscriptions and 150 volumes for every master's filed, and 100 subscriptions and 1,500 volumes for each doctoral programme. As would be expected, lower numbers are stipulated for a junior or community college library: 125 periodical subscriptions and 1,875 volumes for the basic collection plus 1 subscription and 15 volumes for each FTE faculty member, 1 volume for each FTE student, and 3 subscriptions and 45 volumes for each field of study. Note that the ratio of subscriptions to volumes is consistently 1:15.

Clapp and Jordan justified the figure of 250 periodical subscriptions for a basic under-graduate collection by noting that it represented half of the 500 periodicals listed in three standard indexes: readers' *Guide to Periodical Literature, International Index*, and *Applied Science and Technology Index*.

Some lesser-known formulas should be briefly mentioned. The California State Formula is structured on a similar principle to the Clapp-Jordan Formula but uses a different base number among with a different set of weights and variables. Likewise, the Clapp-Jordan formula itself has been modified by slightly changing the variables and their assigned weights (e.g., the Washington State Formula or the Texas version of the Clapp-Jordan Formula). Finally, the ACRL Standards for College Libraries are modeled on the Clapp-Jordan Formula.

Formulas have been used primarily for evaluating the entire collection by calculating whether it contains the requisite number of volumes. Formulas with a separate periodicals component, such as the Clapp-Jordan Formula, could potentially be used to evaluate the size of a library's whole periodical collection. In contrast, most formulas are not intended to evaluate specific subject areas. The Claspp-Jordan Formula's stipulation of an additional 100 subscriptions and 1,500 periodical volumes per doctoral area represents an average figure and should not be interpreted as applying equally to all subjects. The number of periodicals required to support PH.D.-level study varies from one subject to another, depending upon the subject's scope and the number of journals published in its area.

Formulas do not consider quality or relevance to user need and may discorage weeding in order to "pad the numbers." Furthermore, like many traditional macro-evaluation methods, most formulas are not well suited to the newly emerging paradigm of librarianship because they fail to address virtual holdings, which can be accessed but are to owned.

Availability Studies

The term availability studies can be applied to a genre of closely related client centered techniques, which may also be called "shelf availability studies" "frustration studies," or "failure studies." In essence, these studies focus on the level of user success in locating items on the shelf. (Technically, an availability study on the causes of nonsuccess.) Patrons are normally asked to complete forms listing which items they were and were not able to locate, and the library staff does follow-up analysis to determine whey the latter were not available.

"The branching technique." Developed by Paul Kantor during the 1970s and probably the best-known availability study method, examines four branches:

1. Acquisition—the item must have been acquired by the library
2. Circulation—the item must not be checked out
3. Library operations—the item must not be lost or in processing
4. The user—who must e able to successfully locate the item

For the patron to locate the item on the shelf, success must be achieved in all four branches. Lack of success in any single branch leads to overall failure. Most availability studies conducted in libraries have focused on books. Nevertheless, the method generally lends itself well to serials, except that the circulation branch would not be a factor in libraries where serials do not circulate. It is possible that an OPAC that one can dial in to form home using a modem might skew an availability study's results—patrons might not even come to the library if the item they wanted was to listed in the online catalog. For a detailed description, including flowcharts, of the successful application of Kantor's technique to measure serials availability at the University of New Mexico library, see the study by Jan Bachmann-Derthick and Sandra Spurlock. Output Measures for Public Libraries: a Manual of Standardized Procedures, second edition, by Nancy A. Van House and others, contains instructions for a "Materials Availability Survey," which includes serials along with other formats.

Neal K. Kaske argues that the traditional availability study is no longer relevant in the present environment, where a large proportion of patron needs are met by resources external to the library. Instead, he proposes that a modified availability study could be used to evaluate patron access to Internet resources. One can easily envison this techniques' application to electronic journals on the Internet. If a patron were unable to access to networked electronic journal, was it because a file server was down? A password was required? The maximum allowable number of simultaneous users were already logged on? Or the patron did not know how to use the system?

Surveying User Opinion

As previously discussed, user input, a subjective, client-centered approach, can be an important microevaluation criterion, but it is likewise an established approach to macroevaluation. JohnBudd and Mike DiCarlos method, tested at the Northeast Lousiana University and the South-eastern Lousiana University libraries, is an example of a user survey. Faculty and students were asked to complete a survey instrument using a 1-to-6 scale to rate the library's performance in 20 different areas as well as each area's perceived importance. Three of the 20 related to serials—local newspapers, out-of-town newspapers, and "journals and magazines meeting your needs." Alain Bessn and Ian Sheriff later used Budd and DiCarlo's method to evaluate the journal collection at the University of London's medical college libraries.

Unlike many of the traditional methods, surveying user opinion could be used to measure the effectiveness of document delivery programmes and patron access to electronic journals. For instance, Tina E. Chrzastowski and Mary A. Anthes report a survey of user satisfaction with serials document delivery at the University of Illinois at Urbana-Champaign chemistry Library.

Document Delivery Tests

A document delivery test (DDT) measures a library's speed in providing documents, that is, accessibility, regardless of whether the documents are obtained from the collection or an external source. The best-known DDT was developed by Richard H. Orr and colleagues during the late 1960s for evaluating the performance of medical libraries, and subsequent research by Rudolf Jacob Penner found Orr's technique appropriate for other types of libraries. To implement the test, one calculates the amount of time required to obtain each of 300 periodical citations presumed to correspond to user information needs. Orr proposed a "Capability Index," ranging from 0 (none of the 300 items in obtained within a week or less) to 100 (every item is procured in 10 minutes or less).

More recently, a DDT was included in Output Measures for Public Libraries, a manual of standardized procedures for evaluating the performance of small and medium-sized public libraries. In contast to Orr's use of citations, Output Measures for Public Libraries' DDT is based on items actually wanted by patrons. Beginning with a sample of sought-after items that were not immediately available, one calculates the percentage that were provided in 7 days, 14 days, and 30 days. Although developed for all materials, this measure can be separately calculated for periodicals.

A DDT would be considered an objective, qualitative, client-centered approach. It sees probable that this technique will be more frequently used in the future because it tests access rather than ownership.

The Conspectus

Developed by the Research Libraries Group (RLG) beginning in the 1970s, the conspectus, although quite controversial, has emerged as an internationally recognized collection evaluation instrument. It has been used in evaluation, cooperative collection development, policy-making, budgeting, preservation, and grant applications. Two different versions—by RLG and Western Library Network (WLN)—are now available. The RLG conspectus is organized into 22 divisions corresponding to broad areas of knowledge such as art and architecture" or "library and information science" and 8,139 specific subject headings. The subject breakdown generally corresponds to segments of the LC classification system. The WLN Conspectus is divided into 24 divisions, 500 categories (somewhat similar to the North American Title Count, which uses approximately 500 segments of the Library of Congress classification system to report library holdings), and approximately 5,000 specific subjects. Libraries applying the WLN Conspectus have the option of using the 500 categories, 5,000 specific subjects, or some combination of both. Accordingly, some observers believe the WLN Conspectus is more appropriate for medium-sized or small libraries and nonacademic institutions. The original RLG Conspectus applied to the Subject breakdown a 0 to 5 rating system (0 = "Out of Scope," 1 = "Minimal Level," 2 = "Basic Information Level," 3 = "Study or Instructional Support Level," 4 = "research Level," and 5 = "Comprehensive Level") for the current collecting activity and existing collection strength. The WLN version introduced a 10-pont scale by dividing level one into two categories (even and unevenminimal coverage), level two into introductory and advanced categories, and level three into three divisions (basic, intermediate, and advanced instructional support). WLN gives libraries the option of using either the 6- or 10-point scales, which are applied to three collection aspects: the "collection leave," meaning accumulated strength: the "acquisitions commitment," that is, the current collecting intensity or activity; ad the 'goal level," or desired collecting intensity. Finally, the WLN Conspectus is available in two different versions; one corresponding to the LC classification system, the other to the Dewey decimal classification (DDC).

This qualitative, collection-centered tool has been used in Australia, New Zealand, Canada, the United Kingdom, and continental Europe. The second edition of the ALA's Guide for Written collection Policy Statements recommends use of the Conspectus codes in collection development policies to promote standardization among different libraries. Tools available to assist with implementing the Conspectus include Using the Conspectus Method: A Collection Assessment Handbook, by Mary Bushing, Burns Davis, and Nancy Powwell, and the manual for the North American inventory of Research Library Collections, prepared by Jutta Reed-Scott.

The Conspectus must be mentioned because it is a major collection evaluation method even though it does not evaluate serials as a separate format. Instead it considers serial holdings as a component in reaching an overall assessment for specific subject categories. The segments of the WLN Conspectus collecting code definitions pertinent to serials, as reported in the Guide for Written Collection Policy Statements, are extracted below, A separate set of language codes describes the English and non-English makeup of the collection, but they do not address serials.

Level 2, the Basic Information Level—a few major periodicals

Level 2b "Basic Information Level, Advanced"—"a broader selection of basic...periodicals and indexes the serve to introduce and define a subject"

Level 2c "Basic Information Level, Introductory"—"selective major periodicals"

Level 3 "Study or Instructional support level"—"a selection of representative journals"

Level 3a "Study or Instructional Support Level"—"a selection of representative journals"

Level 3a "Basic Study or Instructional Support level"—"a selection of basic representative journals/periodicals, and subject-based indexes"

Level 3b "Intermediate Study or Instructional Support Level"—"all journals on primary topics, selected journals...on secondary topics"

Level 3c "Advanced Study or Instructional Support Level"—"a significant number of...journals on the primary and secondary topics in the field."

Level 4 "Research Level"—"is intended into include...a very extensive collect of journals and major indexing and abstracting services in the field."

A revised set of Conspectus collecting definitions to address remote-access electronic resources was introduced at the 1997 ALA Midwinter Meeting. Drafted by an international committee of 30 to 40 librarians who work with the conspectus, the revised definitions state that an electronic journals' is equivalent to a print journal if three conditions are met: access to it equals or surpasses access to print journals, the library provides a sufficient number of terminals and there is not additional cost to the patron. The revised definitions also state that delayed availability through document delivery is not the equivalent of immediate on-site or electronic access.

The Conspectus offers the benefit of a uniform standard for describing collection strength that can be used for collection evaluation, collection development policies, preservation decisions, budgeting, and cooperative collection development. Common criticisms of the Conspectus approach include the subjective nature of the collecting levels assessments, the questionable ability of libraries to apply it consistently, and its possible unsuitability for medium-sized and nonacademic libraries. Many feel that the benefits derived from the Conspectus have not been significant enough to justify the extensive time and effort libraries extended in its implementation. Some have questioned the Conspectus's usefulness for evaluating some subject areas, such as the sciences, where serials form a substantial portion of the support.

Citation Studies

The use of citation data is considered a major approach to collection evaluation. Citation analysis can be collection-centered if citations are used as a checklist or client-centered if citation studies are used as evidence of patron need. Chapter 5 is devoted to citation analysis's application to journal collection management.

Use Studies

Analysis of use has been a long-standing, client-centered approach to collection evaluation. Use is also a major factor in periodical evaluation at both the micro level (a single periodical) and the macro level (a single periodical) and the macro level (see patterns for the whole collection). Use studies can consider circulation or in-house use or both, although most periodical use studies focus on in-house use. Because periodical use studies receive detailed coverage in chapter 6, there is no need for further discussion here.

The most appropriate method for a particular evaluation project will vary depending on numerous factors such as the projects purpose, the type of library, the available time and resources, and the evaluating librarian's level of subject expertise.

Many experts recommend the use of different approaches in a single project to lend greater credibility to the results. With the exception of DDTs, user opinion surveys, and possibly availability studies, the standard collection evaluation techniques are generally tied to the ownership paradigm and do not address the effects of electronic technology.

REFERENCES

1. Jamie Webster Hastreiter, Larry Hardesty, and David Henderns, comps., Periodicals in College Libraries, CLIP Note 8 (Chicago: Association of College and Research Libraries, 1987), 9.

2. P.G. Peacock, "The selection of periodicals for Binding," Aslib

Proceedings 33 (June 1981): 258. Peacock states his work is based on a decision table for assessing conservation priorities developed by Nicolas Barker of the British Library.

3. Helen M. Grochmal, "Selection Criteria for Periodicals in Microform," *Serials Librarian* 5 (spring 1981); 16.

4. *Ibid.*

5. Peacock, "The Selection of Periodicals for Bindig," 259.

6. S.M. Dhawan, S.K. Phll, and S.P. Jain, "selection of Scientific Journals: A Model," *Journal of Documentation* 36 (March 1980): 24-32.

7. Gilda Maria Braga and Cecilia Alves Oberhofer, "A Model for Evaluating Scientific and Technical Journals from Developing Countries," In the Information Community: An Alliance for Progress; Proceedings of the 44th ASIS Annual Meeting, Washington, D.C., October 25-30, 1981, vol. 18, ed. Lois F. Lunin, Modeline Henderson, and Harold Wooster (White Plains, N.Y.: published for the American society for information Science by Knowledge Industry Publications, 1981), 51-54.

8. Juith A Segal, "Journal Deselecton: a Literature Review and an Application," *Science and Technology Libraries* 6 (spring 1986): 25-42.

9. Ruth H. Miller and Marvin C. Guilfoyle, "Computer Assisted Periodicals Selection: Structuring the subjective", *Serials Librarian* 10 (sprint 1986: 9-22.

10. Edward P. Miller an Ann L. O'Neill, "Journal Deselection and costing," *Library Acquisitions: Practice and Theory* 14, No. 2 (1990): 173-78.

11. Dawn Bick and Reeta Sinha, "Maintaining a High-Quality, cost-Effective Journal Collection," *College and Research Libraries News* 52 (September 1991): 485-90.

12. Jeffrey Broude, "Journal deselection in an Academic Environment: a comparison of Faculty and Librarian Choices," *Serials Librarian* 3 (winter 1978): 147-66.

13. Richard K. Hunt, "Journal Deselection in a Biomedical Research Library: A Mediated Mathematical Approach," *Bulletin of the medical Library Association* 78 (January 1990): 45-48. The work was performed

under contract from the U.S. Department of energy.

14. Rikie Deurenberg, "Journal Deselection in a Medical University Library by ranking Periodicals Based on Multiple Factors," *Bulletin of the Medical Library Association* 81 (July 1993): 316-19.

15. Natalie Schoch and Eileen G. Abels, "Using a Valuative Instrument for Decision Making in the Cancellation of Science Journals in a University Setting," In ASIS '94: Proceedings of the 57th ASIS Annual Meeting; Alexandria, Va., October 17-20

16. Eleanor D. Dym and Donald L. Shirey, "A statistical Decision Model for Periodical Selection for a Specialised Information Centre," Journal of the American Society for Information science 24 (March-April 1973): 110-19. This model was developed at the University of Pittsburgh's Knowledge Availability Systems Center under contract for the National Library of medicines' Toxicology Information Programme

17. Donald H. Kraft and Richard A. Journal-Worth Measure for a Journal-Selection Decision Model," *Collection Management* 2 (summer 1978): 129-39.

18. Roy Rada and others, "Computerized Guides to Journal Selection," *Information Technology and Libraries* 6 (September 1987): 173-84

19. Veictor a. Triolo and Dachun Bao, "A Decision Model for Techncal Journal Deselection with an Experiment in Biomedical Communications," *Journal of the American Society for Information Science* 44 (April 1993): 148-60.

20. Andrew Peters, "Evaluating Periodicals," *College and Research Libraries* 43 (March 1982): 149-51.

CHAPTER 5

Digital Serials Management

They often prefer the electronic version, especially for indexing and abstracting capabilities. One advantage of the electronic index is the capability to perform complex searches quickly, such as a Boolean search. Another advantage is the ease of printing or down-loading the search results. Most of the serials that are currently digitized fall into one of five of Machlup's categories journals magazines, newspapers, newsletters, and loose-leaf services. Just as there are several terms for paper-based serials, so there are for the digital format; electronic journals, online journals, digital journals, and the more all-embracing electronic resources. According to Thomas Nisonger, there is no standard accepted definition of an electronic jurnal/serial.1 E-Journal is a reasonably short term and the one we will use, simply to save space.

Producers take three broad approaches with-journals: an electronic-only version of a new title, an electronic-only version of a title converted from a paper version, and both an electronic and paper version. In the past decade or so, libraries and producers have struggled with how to migrate from a print-only world to one that is a mix of paper and electronic resources. The electronic side is becoming more and more dominant and will continue to do so in the future, at least in some serial categories. One of the first forays into the digital world that is still widely used is the CD-ROM product. Those first seen in libraries were primarily DOS-based, and have since evolved to a Windows environment. Starting principally with indexing and abstracting services, the

CD-ROM products quickly became popular in reference departments. Proprietary software and differing search engines created and continue to create challenges for the library's public service staff. Sand-alone systems were satisfactory at first, but it was not long before there was significant pressure to "network" the stations and allow users to select from a number of products from any station. Making CD "jukeboxes," network software, servers, and user computers all work together is a continuing challenge for libraries.

When the producers moved into full-text products, the issues of compatibility became even more complex. Naturally, more and more people wanted more and more access and variations in computer platforms and equipment became increasingly complex. Full-text products were created by scanning printed pages. Producers then converted the scanned data into bit-mapped images, put them on optical discs, and manufactured and distributed the CD-ROMs. Early scanners had fairly high error rates, so a step had to be interposed between scanning and creating the bitmap images, namely, comparing the scan results against the original. All these steps took time, resulting in products that were electronic in character, but appeared some weeks or even on this after their paper-based counterparts. (One still encounters this problem, at the beginning of the third millennium, with some Web-based products from e-journal aggregators.) Essentially, the CD-ROM products complement traditional paper-based ones, even if end users seem to have a misplaced faith that electronic products are always the most current and complete. What CD-ROMs are best at is solving the problem of misplaced, misshelved, and multilated journals, as well as "at the bindery" issues.

Another, somewhat later, approach was to have libraries load tapes on their local computer system. This basically transferred a number of producer/publisher problems and costs to the libraries. Libraries quickly found that this approach took up ever-growing amounts of staff time an created demands for more an more computer memory. Neither CD-ROMs nor local tape loads completely solved the problem of users having remote access to e-resources when the individuals had different computer platforms (PCs and Macs). Most libraries struggled, and some still do, with how to provide equal access for each group. "Black boxes" of various types were produced that were supposed to emulated one or the other system—most often to emulate the PC. Very few of these systems really provide complete equality in access, and one often heard (and still hears) complaints form Mac users that their needs are ignored.

Today the move to Internet/Web-based products has helped to bring a balanced to the access issues. Up to a point, any "authorized" user who has access to the Web will have the same access to a product, regardless of the computer platform. The "up to a point" assumes that all users have equivalent computer systems, which is of course not true except perhaps in a special library situation where all employees have the same equipment. In the rest of the world, libraries have a few users with the very latest high –end configurations, many with the current "average" setup, and a fairly large number with rather old, slow machines. Nevertheless, Web-based e-journals and indexing/abstracting services do provide much more equal access for end users. Where the next stage in the migration will come from and take us to is impossible to predict with any degree of assurance. What we do know is that print is still with us, and it is likely to be for some time to come.

Hazel Woodward and her colleagues[2] outlined what they called 15 myths about electronic journals. Although they based their article on research they conducted in the United Kingdom (primarily at Lought borough University), we believe the myths they discuss are universal in nature. These myths are:

1. Electronic journals will productive better access to journal articles.
2. Academics and researchers read journals at their office desks.
3. Readers want electronic journals.
4. Electronic journals are quick and convenient to access.

5. Readers know and care who publishes a journal.
6. Readers want page integrity.
7. Electronic journals will bypass libraries and make them redundant.
8. Electronic journals will save libraries money.
9. Storage and dissemination of electronic journals is inexpensive or free.
10. Electronic journals will save paper.
11. Publishers care about readers.
12. Electronic journals will save publishers money.
13. Electronic journals will make subscription agents redundant.
14. Only recent issues of journals are required.
15. All scholarly journals will be available electronically in a few years.

To that extensive list we would add several more "myths":

- Electronic journals are always more current than their print counter-parts.
- Electronic journals provide all graphic materials of their print counterparts.
- Electronic journals are always accessible.
- All readers have equal access to required computers at anytime.
- Electronic journals will save library staff time and effort in handing serials.

We point out these myths not to suggest that electronic serials are unimportant, but rather to note that they are not the final answer to the issues of providing readers with access to the most current and accurate information in the most timely manner. They certainly are important and are the next step in the process, but they are not the ultimate solution as they now exist. Many of the myths exist because the popular press and somewhat overenthusiastic technology people promote the concept beyond its current actual capabilities.

Academic and special librarians have, all too often, encountered a chief financial officer who believes at least one of the myths—that electronic journals will save the library money. We have not found that e-serials save the library money; in fact, they add to the cost of operations, as they are almost always add-ons rather than replacements. Several years ago the senior author's library tried to cover the cost of an aggregator's product, which offered the full text of a large number of journals online, by canceling the paper subscriptions to the titles that would be available electronically. After one year the library reinstated all but five of the paper subscriptions.

A number of reasons (the aforementioned myths) caused this to happen. First of all, full text means just that: full text, but not necessarily including graphics. Some products claim to include tables and charts, but in this particular a case data was too difficult for users to interpret, so a number of paper subscriptions were quickly restarted. The library had not even thought about ending paper subscriptions for journals that are highly dependent on graphics. (Even in the future, when graphics are consistently available electronically, the library will probably continue the paper subscriptions, as many of the users who want and have remote access to the material do not have computers that can effectively handle graphics.) Another reason was the staff's discovery that a surprising number of the electronic titles were a month or more behind the paper versions. That proved unacceptable to several academic departments as well as individual users. Yet another factor was network issues, both on the off campus. Because users were accustomed to finding certain titles on the library's shelves, they still expected the materials to be there when the networks were slow or down. Finally, the volume of printing from the library's public-access printers skyrocketed, even after installation of network printers and charging as much per printed page (without any volume discount) as for the photocopy machines. (Clearly users were not reading the material on the computer screens.)

What the product did accomplish was to give PC and Mac users equal access to the material, as well as providing easier remote access as long the networks were operating properly.

There are a number of issues to ponder in the interplay between digitized and paper-based serials. One issue is how to provide access. Digital serials, in theory, are accessible anywhere, anytime, as long as there is a connection between a computer and the database continuing the desired material. Many customers and technology supporters see this as the ideal future: anywhere at anytime. Library literature generally approaches this issue in terms of ownership versus access.

When a library subscribes to a paper journal, the library owns the copies of those titles, for which it paid the appropriate fee. Electronic formats are often a different matter. Producers of electronic material usually include a license agreement that limits the library's ability to use the material and normally states that the library has access rights only so long as the annual see is current. In essence, the library only leases the data. If a library has any responsibility for long-term retention of information, leasing is a problematic policy even if the producer says it will archive the files and gives the library the right to access the fields for the years for which it paid a lease fee.

Other aspects of serials are the issues of "just-in-case" and "jsut0in-tie." Long-term preservant is, in a sense, "just-in-case." That is, someone at some time will require the information. "Just-in-time" is locating the desired material at the time the user needs it, most often from somewhere other than the home library collection. Digitized data makes just-in-time delivery work well, but one cannot help but wonder (as we did in chapter 6), about how far profit-oriented producers will go to maintain backfiles, or, for that matter, who will still be in business 20 years in the future. There are serious concerns about who, how, and for how long electronic data will be available (archived).

Without a doubt, digitized serials are a mixed blessing. They are very popular, they provide more flexibility n searching than their paper-based counterparts, and remote access at anytime is a possibility. Although they do not reduce library operating costs, they do present new challenges for public service staff. Electronic systems can fail, as do power supplies, causing customer and staff frustration. Also, as anyone who has spend much time with Internet-based services knows, "electronic" does not always translate into "fast." One the one hand, waiting for files to download, waiting to have a server "accept" you query, or being abruptly cutoff in mid-session are source of frustration that do not exist with paper-based serials. On the other hand, torn-out articles, misshelved or missing volumes, or holiday library closers are not problems with the electronic serials (provided offsite access to the required systems is available): Without question, e-serials will be increasingly important in any overall collection development plan for any type of library. Thus, one must understand their benefits as well as their limitations.

E-Serials Selection

The process of selecting e-serials different from that that followed for print serials? The answer is no, not really; however, there are some additional steps. (Note: One good source for identifying electronic serials is *Books and Periodicals Online: 1997*,[3]) We believe that all the factors that apply to selecting paper titles also apply to e-journals. One factor that differs is that often, at least in the case of journal aggregator services, the purchasing decision is made for a package of titles rather than title by title. (We return to this issue later in the section on aggregators.) That in turn means that the cost being considered is substantially higher than for any single typical library paper subscription. Thus, one adds factors of new costs, vendor support, and a "package" of titles.

Another factor complicating the decision is that electronic resource decisions involve more staff than is typically for paper-based selection decisions. If nothing else, there are questions about technology requirements and capabilities that systems staff must answer. In addition, ore of the public service staff are involved in supporting users of electronic resources. Few users need assistance in opening a paper journal, but many may need it when locating and using an electronic title. Packages from either producers or other vendors often employ different search engines; this requires staff to remember which database operates in which manner. Thus, public service staff often want a voice in deciding what, if any, new electronic products to add to the service programme.

- Economics
- Ease of use/User flexibility
- Archival implications
- Future accessibility
- Access
- Licensing, copyright, and distribution restrictions
- Single or multiple publisher
- Print vs. electronic comparisons.
- User support
- If a package, is it "all or nothing"?
- Planned enhancements.

To her list e would add cost per user, technological issues, and aggregators.

We have mentioned the two typical methods for securing e-serials: direct from the publishers/producers or from so-called aggregators. An aggregator is an organisation that develops "packages" of electronic serials. The aggregator enters into contracts with a number of publishers/producers to offer their titles as a group. Producers again by not having to invest as much in marketing, programming, and technology. Then the aggregator adds value to the package by providing a consistent search engine for searching all the titles. Naturally, aggregators then add a charge for their services on top of what the cost was from the producers, often in the 30 to 40 percent range. Some of the large aggregators are OCLC, Bell & Howell Information and Learning Company, Lexis/ Nexis, and EBSCO.

Deciding on aggregator packages usually entails accepting a number—sometimes a substantial number—of titles one would never subscribe to in print. Few of the aggregators allow a library to take only the titles of interest. Naturally, that means the library pays for titles it does not want. Thus, one question to consider is if the overall cost is really appropriate for the number of titles the library does want. One interesting effort in 1999 was the California Stage University System's issuance of a Request for Proposal (RFP) to aggregators to supply access to a list of 1,279 journals on what the System calls the "Journal Access Core Collection."[5] The titles on the list are those in highest demand in the Systems 23 libraries. At the time we prepared this edition, there was no indication of how successful the RFP would be in providing access to just the titles desired rather than titles to which the aggregators have easy access.

One system for evaluating aggregator as well as publisher/producer titles is the weighted system developed by the California State University Libraries (CSUL) for deciding on system-wise purchases. CSUL has a committee of 12 members, representing the 23 campuses of the system, who each serve for two years. Evaluations are made independently by each committee member, using the weighted system, during a two-week trial period. Results of their evaluations are available on the system's Web page (http:/ /ww.co.calstage.edu/irt/seir/).

The form used by the CSU system, which is submitted online, contains the elements shown in figures 7.1, pages 187-89 and 7.2, pages 190-94. (The figures were slightly reformatted for this book; this original for mass are available online.)

Figure 7.2 is an example of the type of evaluation that the system produces and posts for all staff to read. Keep in mind that what the figures shows is only an example stating the assessment as of the date shown. Databases can and do change over time; sometimes changes are due to critical reviews. This example is for JSTOR (Journal STORage).

Most of the basic issues to be considered when selecting e-serials were visible in the JSTOR example. Financial concerns are high, and it is highly improbable that a library will save any money by subscribing to electronic serials. Thus, the real question becomes; how much value/benefit does the library gain as a result of the expenditure? How does that benefit compare to benefits from spending the same amount on something else? Pricing models vary widely from vendor to vendor. (When one looks at both single-institution and consortial purchasing, on e ca identify more than 50 variations in pricing models. A cynical person might think the producer has an amount needed in mind and will work up any model the library wants—but the final price will always be the same.)

Staff and customer comfort leave with a chosen product is important. Outstanding content in a product that is complex or difficult to use, even if the cost is relatively modest, may not be the most cost-effective purchase. An unused resource is a waste of funds.

Technical issues of network capability stability and compliance with general standards are all key factors. Also, how much support is available from the vendor, and during what hours/ If required, how is authentication handled? Domain access—recognizing IP ranges—is a low cost motion for the library; however, remote users with private Internet service providers will not have access without special arrangements such as a proxy server.

Content concerns relate to the usual subject issues and also to how complete the material is, assuming there is a print counterpart. Another concern should be whether there are "additions" to the product, and whether they are necessary or beneficial. Some vendors/producers add some form of multimedia—sound or video clips—to their material. Often this is of the "gee whiz, look what technology allows us to do" variety at her than being a true added value. Such additions create hardware and software compatibility problems for some library owned and certainly for some remote users' Machines.

Another issue to consider is what the library can or cannot

do with the electronic material. Some vendors place restrictions on who can use the material, even is a public access setting. Such restrictions create problems for the public service staff—how to identify user types and monitoring what is being used. For example, Academic Universe® from Lexis/Nexis is contractually limited to the students, staff, and faculty of the purchasing institution. Individuals not affiliated with the institution are not permitted to use the service. What happens if the purchase was through a consortium and a person is visiting another campus that is part of the consortium? Can the visitor user the service without violating the license agreement, since the home institution also has the service? Logically, one would think that such use would be acceptable; however, useless the consortium's agreement so indicates, there is a chance that such use would be a violation. Another concern is that all contracts call for the purchaser to be responsible for copyright violations. The whole question of license agreements is complex, and we will discuss these matters more fully in chapter 18 on legal issues.

Finally, long-term access to and preservation of material is usually a concern. Who will archive the material? How will it be archived, and for how long? These are questions one needs to consider at the point of making a selection decision. Programmes operated by libraries, such as JSTOR, are more likely to provide the electronic long-term archiving that both librarians and scholars expect with print materials. Commercial ventures are profit-driven and are unlikely to maintain a service that loses money for very long. Although the current purpose of JSTOR—a not-for-profit organisation-is the selective digital conversion of retrospective files of print journals of scholarly interest, it seems likely that it, or a similar organization, will being archiving e-serials.

Handling E-Serials

Handling e-serials? What does that mean? Unlike a print subscription, after the appropriate record keeping files are in place, e-serials require more set-up steps. Generally a new print subscription merely goes into its appropriate pale with the other current issues of the print journals.

In the case of e-serials, as we mentioned in the section on selection, someone must assure that the technical issues have been addressed before the service is implemented. If the access is Web-based and domain in nature, providing IP ranges is fairly straightforward. However, password verification is still a requirement of some systems, and libraries must decide who will have access to these passwords. Will patrons be logged on individually, or will certain patrons (such as faculty members) be given the password to use as needed? There must be testing to determine compatibility with other services (changes in hardware or software configurations, for example). Libraries must also consider what, if anything, will appear in the library's OPA about the product. If a package of, say, 1,000 full-text journals is purchased, will the library add a note to the holdings statements for titles the library also has in a print format? What about entries for the "new" titles, even those a that may not be important to the library's customer base? Will the OPAC reflect just title, electronic address only, or both? Will there be a "hot link" in the OPAC or on the library Website? It images are included in the package, does the library need "helper" applications (such as Adobe's Acrobat Reader) installed ion it public machines?

Every library using electronic materials needs one person or office that handles and maintains a file of license agreements. Someone must review the agreement and notify staff of any new requirements.

Public services staff will need time for familiarization and training in using the new product. Vendor support telephone numbers and/or Internet addresses should be available to staff. End users may also need assistance, especially if they want to print, e-mail, or download an article from the product for the first or second tie. If the journals are accessible from off site, whether through a proxy server or other means, when support exists in the library and at the institution for offsite patrons who have trouble using the resource? A good article outlining all the steps and issues in implementing a new e-serial is Cindy Stewart

Kaag's "Collection Development for Online Serials."[6]

In 1998, Janet Hughes and Catherine Lee published an interesting article[7] that can serve as a case study of the process of selecting, acquiring and implementing a full-text journal package. Part of what makes this article interesting is that it addresses issues related to multiple service points. The authors described the process used a Pennsylvania State University and its statewide 23-campus system. They concluded by stating, "Overall, although the experience of implementing the first networked full-text databases at Pen State was a positive one, its success depended upon careful planning and dedicated inter-departmental and campus cooperation. These qualities will be needed to make future for as into full text equallysuccessful."[8]

Up until this point, our discussion of print and electronic serials has focused upon some of the more standard entries: scholarly journals, magazines newspapers, and the like.. There is a type of literature that does not receive much discussion, the so-called grey literatre. In the past, some research and special libraries made an effort to collect this type of material. Today, with electronic "publishing on the Internet a fact of life, grey literature takes on a new meaning. Grey literature was and is primarily of scholarly interest, particularly in the sciences, and tends to be the output of the "invisible college." A widely accepted definition of grey literature has yet to be formulated. *Harrod's Librarians' Glossary* defines these items as "semi-published material, for example reports, internal documents, theses, etc. not formally published or available commercially, and consequently difficult to trace bibliographically."[9] Julia Gelfand stated, "the definition of grey literature has changed rather drastically since the First International Conference, held in Amsterdam, four years ago [1993]."10 One of the reasons for the changing nature of the concept of grey literature is electronic publishing.

To some degree, what we now call the Internet was developed so that scientists and scholars could more quickly share results (grey literature) and work together from different physical locations (the invisible college). Today, technology and the Internet are creating new types of grey literature, not just online preprint services and technical report access. Perhaps the most striking change is the ability to describe phenomena is other than textual terms—modeling online, movement, sound, and true interactive collaborative work. Julia Gelfand suggested,

> Learning about this new grey literature is in itself a non-traditional role for librarians and scholars...Training and bibliographic familiarity in this age is indeed quite different, because one does not follow a curriculum or set of readers or textbooks, but instead studies by doing, engaging in online time, discovering what the digital literati in different fields contribute as resources for good, appropriate, critical, sought after information. Usually, a strong needs assessment for the information, coupled with this new facility in making it readily available without enhanced packaging, encourages its use.[11]

It grey literature a serial? As it tends to be ongoing in nature, one can consider it at least a semi-serial. To what degree the library tries to provide access to such material is very much a matter of local need and close collaboration between the library and its users.

Document Delivery

We debated where to put this discussion, as it could fit into several chapters. We first touched on this issue in chapter 6, and finally settled on this chapter as the place for this section because many of the services draw on electronic serials to provide the "document." In the past, traditional inter-library loan (ILL) services often provided the only access to materials not owned, especially to grey literature. Today libraries have a choice in how to provide customers with needed but unowned materials.

There are at least seven broad types of document delivery services in addition to the traditional ILL: general commercial services, specialized commercial services, direct from publisher/producer, aggregator services, national library collections, information brokers, and fee-based services in a large research library.

Why are libraries turning to this approach, and how does it relate to collection development? The answer to the relationship question resides in how a given library decides to address the issues of access or ownership. The more material a library knows it must own, the greater the work for the collection development officers. Even when employing document delivery to provide "just in time" access to very low-use materials, there is a need for collection development staff to coordinate their activities with those of document delivery. Essentially, there must be ongoing planning and coordination of both activities.

The answer to why use services other than traditional ILL is more complex. Certainly a major factor is the escalating costs of serials, which far outpace inflation in other areas of the economy and library budgets that are hard-pressed to do more than maintain constant collection levels, much less increase their size. Almost every library of any size has had to implement at least one journal reduction exercise some time in the last 15 years. Many libraries have had to undertake several such cutting efforts in the recent past. The first such programme is relatively easy, as there are usually a number of titles that were acquired of the "just-in-case" need and show little or no use over time. Depending upon the size of the necessary reduction, perhaps the first time will only have to "hit" very low-use titles; in those cases, depending on Ill to fulfill the rare request may be an adequate alternative.

Unfortunately, most of the reductions is serials collections have cut more deeply, which required thinking about how to supply to wanted material more quickly than traditional ILL. Also an issue is how much of an increase in ILL requests tne existing staff can handle. If there are alternatives that allow the requestor to have direct access to the document-supplying service, there will be little or no increase in the ILL workload.

Another factor, at least for a few libraries, relates to space and money. Libraries have had difficult maintaining their operating budges; when it comes to securing funding for additional space to house the every growing collections, the track record is even bleaker. One way to a in space in an existing facility is to look a t long back runs of journals, especially those that have very little usage. Withdrawing the physical volumes will provide shelving space. The question then becomes how to provide access to the withdrawn titles. Certainly, buying microfiche/film versions is one option; however, microfilm storage cabinets take up space, and the cost of the microforms an the equipment to use them must be considered. Going with a document delivery option saves space and the cost of requested materials may never equal the cost of the microforms.

Gale Etschmaier and Marifran Bustion discussed the pro and cons of such services in an article about the experience of Gelman Library at George Washington University implementing a document delivery service. The situation they described was a major journal cancellation project in which the library cancelled 1,031 journal titles in 1993-1994. One of their interesting findings was that, as of early 1997, only 35 of those titles (roughly 3 percent) had been the subject of any requests for articles,[12] They concluded by stating," The data gathered through monitoring direct requests through document delivery and interlibrary loan services can be monitored and analyzed as an aid to collection development."[13]

When evaluating possible document delivery services, one should use most of the factors one employs to assess any vendor. The additional elements to consider are similar to those for choosing an e-journal vendor:

- Type of access provided
- Quality/content of the database
- Ordering options (user, library)
- Costs and what is covered (copyright fees)
- Delivery options (fax, e-mail, overnight mail)
- Reliability (does the service meet advertised delivery times?)
- Payment options (credit card, invoices, prepaid deposit)
- Customer service availability (end users, staff only)

As Suzanne Ward stated in her article evaluating delivery services, "The only certainties in document delivery today are that the number of requests will increase exponentially and that tomorrow there will be even more suppliers and methods for ordering from them."[14]

Pricing

As we note din the myths section, e-serials do not save either the producer or the library money. Perhaps at some point in the past there was a reasonable expectation of such savings. However, by tehmid-1990s it was clear to both vendors and libraries that this would not be the case. For example, as Robert marks noted, the American Chemical Society estimated that its CD-Rom journal cost 25 to 33 percent more to produce than their print versions. The higher cost was attributed to the need to provide and maintain a searchengine.[15] In another article, Tom Abate reported the American Institute of Physics estimate that providing both a print and electronic copy of a title cost between 10 and 15 percent more than just offering a print version of the same title.[16] Conversations with publishers of electronic-only serials indicate that they see no difference in costs; they claim it costs just as much for an e-only version as it does for print-only. Jant Fischer of MIT Press indicated that the reason producers of e-only. Janet Fischer of Mit Press indicated that the reason producers of e-only serials see costs as equal was not so much a function of production costs as it was an overall loss of revenue—no back-issue sales, no renting of subscriber mailing lists, and, perhaps most importantly, the loss of advertising income.[17]

The dual pricing one found and still finds with many scholarly print serials (that is, one price for individuals and a higher price institutions) continues in the electronic environment, if in a slightly different guise. Individuals do to face the same licensing issues as libraries and do not pay for more than one user, nor are they asked about number of potential users in the household or office. Libraries usually have to pay extra fees, rather substantial at times, for more than one simultaneous user license. Different producers use different increments, such as 1 to 4 users at one rate, 5 to 9 another rate, and so on to a rate for unlimited access.

Another pricing mechanism is by size of the service population, frequently based upon the number of full-time students or staff (full-time equivalent or FTE) at an institution. This is probably one of the most costly approaches for libraries when it comes to specialized serials and products. For example, say a fictitious university (we call it ICU) has an anthropology department with 10 faculty, 68 graduate students, and 129 undergraduate majors, and its course offerings each year enroll a total of 1,400 different students. The library considers subscribing to an electronic version of a print product in the field of anthropology that has a record of modest use. The producer, using the FTE pricing model, sets the price at 50 cents per FTE. Unfortunately, typically the vendor calculates the cost on the basis of the institutional ETC, not that of the department or even a realistic estimate of the potential users. Thus, if the institutional FTE (staff/faculty/students is the typical request) is 12,000, then the cost become s$6,000 for a product that has had only modest use in the print format. Certainly there is the prospect that the electronic version will have greater use, assuming the product comes with a reasonably good search engine, but there is no reasonable expectation that every person at the institution will access the database at some point during the year.

Transaction-based fees are another pricing mechanism that can drive up the cost of electronic serials for a library (this is the model that OCLC was using for First Search in the late 1990s). In some ways, this approach is less costly than the FTE model, as actual usage determines the price. One drawback of this model is that the library is never certain what its costs will be until after the fact. With First Search, OCLC (at least with consortinums0 sets an annual fee that includes a fixed number of searches. The fee is paid in advance, and at the end of the year there may be additional charges if the search limit was exceeded. The amount may be something of a shock for the library, if it has not been carefully monitoring usage. (The Loyola Marymount University library belongs to a consortium that purchased access to First Search, and members discussed what databases they could "turn off" to control the year-end charges. Somehow it seems strange to buy access to a database and then have to discuss which ones we should strict public access to in order to a save money.) Pat of the problem with the transaction-based approach is that every search counts, even those in which the searcher has misspelled a word or does not understand how to search the database. It is difficult to know how much value for money expended one actually receive from this model. At least with paper formats user and staff mistakes do not cost the library additional money.

When buying a package from an aggregator, the library knows it will be paying an extra fee for the "added value" of having a single source and search engine for journals from a variety of producers. However, on e often is buying access to titles or little or no interest to the library's service population, because a package truly is all or nothing. This effectively drives up the cost of the title s that are of interest to the library users.

Some publishers/producers, at least in 1999, have not decided which model to follow. As a result, some offer free access to an electronic version of a title if the library has a subscription to the print format. Others offer such access for a modest fee (10 to 15 percent} above the print subscription cost.

Where the pricing will go is difficult to predict beyond the fact that pries will continue to escalate. As Bill Robnett stated, "The complexities of online serials pricing may increase as more publishers enter the electronic publishing market...One consideration is that serials budgets will be redefined as libraries purchase access in units of articles, an open-ended concept quite different from the now prevalent subcription."[18]

Electronic serials are probably the "wave of the future," but perhaps a more distant future than technology enthusiasts would have us believes. Despite the advantages of having materials available in such formats, it appears that there is little prospect of either producers or libraries realizing any cost savings as a result of migrating to an electronic environment.

REFERENCES

1. Thomas Nisonger, "Electronic Journal Collection Development Issues,"

Collection Building 16, no. 2 (1997): 58.

2. Hazel Woodward et al., "Electronic Journals: Myths and Realities," *OCLC Systems and Services* 13, no. 4 (1997): 144-51.
3. Nuchine Nobari, Books and Periodicals Online: 1997 (Washington, D.C.: *Library Technology Alliance*, 1997).
4. Mary Jean Pavelsek, "Guidelines for evaluating E-Journal Providers," *Advances in Librarianship* 22 (1998): 39-58.
5. Michael Rogers, "Cal State Proposes New E-Journal Buying Model," *Library Journal* 124 (February 15, 1999): 107
6. Cindy Stewart Kaag, "Collection Development for Online Serials: Who Needs to Do What, and Why, and When" *Serials Librarian* 33, nos. ½ (1998): 107-22.
7. Janet Hughes and Catherine Lee, "giving Patrons What They Want: The Promise, the Process, and the Pitfalls of providing Full-Text Access to Journals," *Collection Building* 17, no.4 (1998): 148-58.
8. *Ibid.,* 153.
9. R. Prytherch, Comp., *Harrod's Librarians' Glossary* (Aldershot, U.K.: Gower, 1995): 285.
10. Julia Gelfand, "Teaching and Exposing Grey Literature," *Collection Building* 17, no. 4 (1998): 159.
11. *Ibid.,* 160-61.
12. Gale Etschmaier and Marifran Bustion, "Document Delivery and Collection Development: an Evolving Relationship," *Serials Librarian* 31, no. 3 (1997): 24.
13. *Ibid.,* 26
14. Suzanne M. Ward, "Document Delivery: Evaluating the Options," *Computers in Libraries* 17 (October 1997): 26.
15. Robert Marks, "The Economic Challenges of Publishing Electronic Journals," *Serials Review* 21 (Spring 1995): 85-88.
16. Tom Abate, "Publishing Scientific Journals Online," *Bioscience* 47 (March 1997): 175-79.
17. Janet Fischer, "True Cots of an Electronic Journal," *Serials Review* 21 (Spring 1995): 88-90.
18. Bill Robett, "Online Journal Pricing," *Serials Librarian* 33, nos. ½ (1998), 68.

CHAPTER 6

Serials Management of Collection

Collection management is now frequently used to describe the specialty previously called collection development, although both terms are still used, sometimes almost interchangeably, wit their precise meanings and connotations varying among authorities. *Collection management* was chosen for the chapter title because it implies the management of scarce financial resources to obtain—through a variety of means—information resources that meet patron information needs. The focus of serials collection management has shifted over the last several decades. During the 1960s, the profession devoted much attention to selection for collection building and imicroform conversion.

Beginning sometime in the 1970s or early 1980s, deselection and budgeting strategies to meet exploding serials costs became major issues. In the late 1990s, the management of electonic journals, the implications of the World Wide Web (WWW), and the effective use of document delivery services are the dominant topics. Ironically, even though new issues rise to the forefront of professional attention, most of the earlier issues must still be confronted. Collection management is probably both the most important and the most challenging serials function, although this statement might reflect the author's personal bias as a collection development specialist. Undoubtedly, interest in serials collection management has increased in recent years because of continuously escalating serials cross in tandem wit stagnant library budgets, the emergence of new electronic formats, and an increased emphasis on access rather than ownership.

Collection management takes place in both a micro and a macro sense. Micro refers to a title-by-title approach, whereas macro refers to broad, cross-the-board decisions or the entire collection. The micro and macro concepts can be applied to evolution, criteria, and decision making. This distinction may be somewhat artificial in regard to serials because the whole serials collection is often evaluated on a title-by-title basis, but it offers a useful framework for discussion.

This chapter emphasizes serials micro-evaluation criteria and the basic serials collection management functions: selection; de-selection (i.e., cancellation), weeding, and relegation to remote storage; document delivery; the concept of access versus ownership; and budgeting for serials. Chapter 4 addresses such serials collection management functions as filling gaps in backruns, treatment of unbound issues, and multiple copy and location decisions; serials decision models; core lists of serials; and serials macro-evolution methods. See also chapter 5, which addresses the application of citation analysis to journal collection management; chapter 6, which is devoted to periodical use studies; chapter 7, which covers journal ranking methods; chapter 8's section about copyright law's implications for serials management; and chapter 9, which contains analysis of electronic journal management.

Serials Microevaluation Criteria

All the crucial serials collection management decisions require evaluative judgements about specific serial titles—in other words, microevaluation. The criteria for making these judgments are outlined and discussed below. This section does not distinguish between strictly evaluative criteria relating to a particular title's intrinsic merits and selection or deselection criteria (or both) on a title's appropriateness for a particular library. The criteria are listed in a alphabetical rather than priority order.

Alternate Format availability

An increasing number of journals are published in both print and electronic format. This situation creates a complex set of options, as the library faces four choices for such titles; a print subscription only; an electronic subscription only; simultaneous print and electronic subscriptions; or no subscription—presumably relying on a document delivery service or interlibrary loan (ILL) to meet user needs. Similarly, a title's availability as part of a full-text collection the library subscribes to or is considering, such as EBSCO's *MasterFile* Full Text series (described in chapter 9), might influence decisions regarding the print version.

Authors

The stature of authors can be useful for assessing a journal's scholarly quality. Author names can be obtained from the table of contents, and institutional affiliation is usually indicated in the bylines for specific articles. Use of this criterion presupposes some level of knowledge concerning the leading scholars in the journal's discipline. However, the title, rank, and institutional affiliation of authors can offer helpful clues concerning their stature. In some disciplines (e.g., library and information science), the institutional affiliation of authors will also help indicate whether the journals is oriented toward scholars or practitioners. The extent of international authorship can also serve as a significant indicator of a journal's basic character, if not quality. A caveat should be noted: New titles may artificially recruit big-name scholars for initial issues, creating an artificial illusion of the authors' stature.

Citation Record

Citation analysis is predicated on the assumption that citation of an item by a researcher indicates that it has been used in the research process. Accordingly, citation data, although controversial, can provide clues about a journal's usefulness to researchers. This criterion is primarily applicable to academic and research libraries because support of the research process is a major component of their mission. Basic citation data (i.e., total citations received, impact factor, and comparison to other journals in the same discipline) are readily available for thousands of journals if a library has access to the Science Citation Index (SCI) or Social Science Citation Index (SSCI) Journal Citation Reports (JCR). Also, the Institute for Scientific Information (ISI), the JCR's publisher, can provide customized reports about faculty citation patterns at a particular university.

Collecting Priorities

A library's collecting priorities regarding a title's subject, audience, purpose, and so forth are undoubtedly some of the most important criteria. Serials collecting priorities should be outlined in the library's collection development policy, assuming it has one. In cases where no written collection policy exists, staff with collection management responsibilities usually possess an informal perception of collecting priorities, although informal perceptions are so unstable they may have little practical value—hence, the desirability of a written policy. Margaret Hawthorn's 1990 survey of mor ethan 200 North American academic librarie serevealed tht 51 percent of large and 48 percent of small academic libraries have unwritten politics on serils selection and cancellation,whereas onyly 14 percent of large and 25 percnet of small academic libraries have written policies.[1]

Collecting priorities often take the form of an across-the-board macro-decision. For example, G. Edward Evan's textbook, Developing Library and Information Centre Collections, outlines but not necessarily endorses a number of such decisions for serial selection; subscribe to all journals users request if in a collected subject area, any journal requested on ILL more than X times, and all core titles; do not subscribe to unindexed periodicals or unrefereed journals.[2]

Core Recommended Lists

Whether a particular title is listed on a core or recommended periodical list, such as Magazines for Libraries, can, in many instances, be a significant factor in collection management decision making. A detailed discussion of the use of these tools, along with an explanation of the core concept.

Cost-Effectiveness

Two other basic criteria, use and subscription cost, can be combined to determine a periodical's cost-per-use or, in other terms, cost-effectiveness. Cost-per-use data are most valuable when used to rank groups of journals—by subject, library location, or possibly the library's complete list (although comparing the cost-effectiveness of journals from different subject areas may result in methodological flaws). Because usage data are required, this criterion would normally be used in cancellation rather than selection decisions. The library would presumably wish to retain the most cost-effective titles and target the least cost-effective ones for review. This is a more valid criterion than cost alone because the most expensive titles can be highly used and thus be more cost-effective than many less expensive periodicals. Most libraries have cost records readily available, but usage data usually require a separate study. For a lengthier discussion, see "Cost Per Use" in chapter 6.

Editor and Editorial Board Membership

This criterion is significant primarily for scholarly journals—most of which have editorial boards. The appropriate names along with their institutional affiliation can usually be obtained from a journals' masthead. The earlier discussion concerning author's stature and affiliation as evaluative criteria would also apply to the editor and editorial board members.

Geographical Area Availability

This factor frequently affects serials collection management decision making. For example, a serial with one or more other subscriptions within the same library, library system, consortium, or geographical are a may, by virtue of this fact, become a more likely candidate for cancellation than a unique subscription that is not available nearby. On the other hand, a title might be selected for subscription because it is not available elsewhere. Finally, many libraries, during their first round of serials cancellations, focus on duplicate copies within the library or system for cancellation.

Grade-level and Age-Level

These criteria, of course, are limited to children's or young adult magazines and would be of interest only to only to public, school, or academic libraries supporting education programmes that collect for these audiences. Publisher-reported age-and grade-levels for numerous children's magazines can be found in Selma K. Richardson's Magazines for Children: A Guide for Parents, Teachers, and Librarians. However, she cautions readers to consider "age-and grade-level designations as rough estimates or general indicators of the reading differently."[3]

Indexing

Whether a periodical is indexed is a long-standing evaluation criterion. Yet Hawthorn found that only 19 percent of large libraries and 24 percent of small libraries considered indexing during the selection process. (Large libraries were defined as having more than 5,000 current periodical subscriptions, and small libraries had between 1,5000 and 4,999.)[4] In contrast, an informal survey reported on SERIALST in 1997 revealed that 76 per cent of the responding libraries consider indexing a "very important" factor in serials collection management.[5] the conventional wisdom states that an indexed journal is preferable to an unindexed one and that a journal's stature increases with the number of indexes covering it (although a simple count of index coverage would give an unfair advantage to interdisciplinary journals). The validity of index in and abstracting coverage as a criterion is predicated on two assumptions; The title's selection for coverage testifies to its perceived caliber; and patron demand for the periodical will increase because they will locate citations to it, assuming the coverage is by an index to which the library subscribes or provides access. This criterion penalizes new journals that have not had an opportunity to be picked up by an indexing service.

Ironically, the indexing criterion was once a dual-edged sword. If a library did not hold an unindexed journal in its collection, patron access through ILL would be inhibited because it would be impossible, except through footnotes and bibliographies, to locate citations to specific articles in order to a generate ILL requests. Currently, however, citations to a journal not covered by the standard indexes in a library's collection might well be found through CARL's UnCover, accessible for free on the Internet, or a table of contents service.

Interlibrary Loan and Document Delivery Statistics

Because copyright requirements mandate that libraries record serial titles requested on ILL (see "Additional Copyright Issues" in chapter 8), useful evaluation data are provided. As stated in the American Library Association's (ALA) Guide to the Evaluation of Library Collections, ILL "loan requests are generally acknowledged to be indicators of unmet research demand on the part of the library's users. These analyses may be used...to identify specific current or retrospective journal titles to be purchased."[6] ILL and document delivery data are obviously more useful for selection decisions than for identifying candidates for cancellation. Hawthorn's 1990 survey found that 71 percent of large libraries and 61 percent of small ones incorporated ILL data into selection decisions.[7] Theoretically, there should be no Ill or document delivery requests for a title if a library currently subscribes to it and owns the complete beckruns. In such an instance, ILL and document delivery statistics could clearly not be used in cancellation decisions. However, if gaps exist in a library's holdings, ILL and document delivery requests for the missing years would be pertinent to a cancellation decision. Also, ILL and document delivery data can be used for export facto monitoring of cancellation decisions.

Language

A journal's language is often no considered a major evaluation criterion because it is such a self-evident factor. For many smaller libraries, language is a criterion only by default, as the collecting emphasis concentrates on english-language periodicals. However, if a significant segment of a public or school library's clientele are monnative speakers of English, magazines should be collected in the appropriate non-English language. The recent emphasis on multiculturalism in library services and collectiosn implies an increasing need for non-English language periodicals in public and school libraries. Large academic libraries have traditionally collected a substantial number of foreign language periodicals to support research, specially in area studies. The extent to which an academic library should collect foreign language serial publications to support the personal needs of international students is a debatable issue.

Patron Needs

On the surface this seems like a rather simple, straightforward criterion, as meeting client information needs is a fundamental collection development principle. Indeed, many have argued that this should be the most important periodical selection criterion. Beneath the surface, the concept of patron need covers a complex set of issues, including type of need (i.e., research versus teaching); category of patron (e.g., adult versus juvenile or community resident versus nonresident); and the question of need versus demand—a long-standing controversy in collection management thought.

A major, practical question is, How does one determine a particular periodicals' relevance to patron needs? A precise scientific approach does not necessarily exist. Most of the other criteria outlined here would be incorporated in reaching the judgement. Helpful strategies include gaining guidance from the collection development policy, informally consulting key patrons, directly examining the periodical in question, reading reviews, and using such tool as *Magazines for Libraries*, by Bill Katz and Linda Sternberg Katz.[8] Often the question boils down to a librarian's professional judgement concerning the match between a periodical and his or her patron's' needs. As Bill Katz stated in 1971, "Selection of any material for the library presupposes some type of judgment."9 although the statement is a collection development truism, one can not overemphasize the importance of knowledge concerning the user community and their information needs. Other criteria listed here—use, citation, and ILL and document delivery data—can provide objective indicators of patron demand.

Physical Makeup and Illustrative Material

Public and school libraries attach much greater importance to the physical construction of popularly oriented magazines than academic libraries do for scholarly journals. Major issues relating to physical composition include size, shape, paper quality, binding, typography, and the quantity and quality of illustrative material. These criteria are often mentioned in reviews or can be ascertained through direct examination.

The nature of illustrative matter can be a particularly significant criterion for some serial categories, such as popular magazines, periodicals for a juvenile audience, or art magazines or journals. For example, Phyllis J. Van Orden lists "pertinent and adequately reproduced' illustrations as one of six newspaper and periodical selection criteria for school libraries.[10]

Place of Publications

Place of publication is generally not thought of as a major criterion in serials evaluation and selection. Nevertheless, most libraries tend to emphasize periodicals published in their own country. Moreover, place of publication can be especially important in certain circumstances of for some types of serials.

Locally published periodicals. For public libraries, the fact that a magazine, newspaper, or newsletter was published in its local community or service area would be an important consideration. Likewise, an academic library might place a high priority on journals published or edited at its institution.

Periodicals pertaining to area studies. Academic libraries supporting area study programmes clearly need to collect historical, literary, economic and political periodicals and newspapers published in the appropriate areas.

Newspapers. The place of a newspaper's publication can be critical for libraries seeking geographical balance in their newspaper coverage or wishing to give either representation or emphasis to particular cities, states, or countries. For example, a library could decide to emphasize newspapers published in its own state or region and selection only a single newspaper (presumpably the most prestigious) to represent other regions or foreign countries.

Political implications associated with place of publication. Often the place of publication can have political implications (i.e., the knowledge that a periodical is published in a communist regime, a Third World nation, or a military dictatorship would be a valuable indicator of its political stance). For a cogent discussion of the role publication place plays in the selection process, see Ross Atkinson's article "The Citation As Intertext; Toward a Theory of the Selection Proess."11 This factor may now be less significant than in the past, considering the Soviet Union's dissolution in 1991 and the end of the cold war, but neverthless, it can still be a consideration for some periodicals.

Finally, given fluctuations in international currency exchange rates, the country of publication can have profound implications for a periodical's cost.

Present Holdings

This criterion would obviously apply to cancellation, weeding, and relegation to remote storage but not subscription decisions. Many serials collection managers seem to assume that a long, complete run of a title is positive, whereas a short or incomplete run is negative. Although this premise has some validity, such factors as use, relevance to user need, and the library's collecting priorities should take precedence over the extend of holdings. For cancelled titles, the fat that holdings are incomplete and scattered would be a good reason for weeding.

Price

Subscription price is clearly important yet more complex than might be assumed. Some serial titles are deemed so important that librarians feel they must subscribe to them regardless of the price. AHawthorn's research reveled that subscription cost was a much more important criterion in cancellation decisions (with 70 percent of large and 92 percent of small libraries listing it as a factor) than in selecting a new serial subscription, where only

12 percent of large libraries and 9 percent of small ones responded t was a consideration.[12]

Publisher

The publisher's name, a basic evaluative criterion, is readily obtainable by examining the serial and normally included in reviews and advertisements. There are two dimensions to this criterion: the specific publisher's reputation and publisher type-commercial, university press, or society or association. Collection management experience in a subject usually leads to knowledge concerning the reputation of the area's major publishers. Research suggests that periodicals from nonprofit publishers may be more cost-effective than those from commercial ones (see Bernard M. Fry and Herbert S. White,[13] Sandra R. Moline,[14] and others).

Refereed Status

Whether a journal is refereed is an important factor in judging its scholarly quality. For collection management purposes, this criterion would be most important to academic libraries. Apart from libraries, a journal's refereeing status is critical in author's manuscript submission decisions and in evaluating a scholar's publication record during the promotion and tenure process. Usually (but not always) one can ascertain if a journal is refereed by reading the masthead or the instructions to authors section. Other methods include consulting such standard sources as EBSCO's Serials Directory, Ulrich's, or Magazines for Libraries or telephoning the editor.[15]

Requestor

When a title is under review for cancellation, the name of the individual who originally requested it can be quite useful, especially in an academic setting, where collections have commonly been built in response to faculty demands. For example, a cancellation decision can be much easier if the faculty requestor has left the institution. Obviously, the requestor's name will be available only if the library has maintained a record, which is not always the case. Likewise, when considering titles for subscription, the requestor's status can be significant, with a dean's request carrying more clout than a faculty member's and a faculty member's more than a student's. Based on the author's professional experience in collection management, the requestor's status can sometimes be more critical than the intrinsic merit of the item being requested. Surely political considerations are important in serials collection management, yet there is an ethical dimension to favouring one user over another—raising important and complex issues beyond this discussion's scope.

Subject Focus

A periodical's subject content is obviously one of the most important considerations affecting any collection management decision, especially when placed in the context of the library's collecting priorities and user needs. For academic libraries, the critical factor is the subject's relevance to the curriculum and faculty research interests. Subject focus can normally be ascertained from direct inspection or reading reviews. However, remember that for some periodicals, the subject focus is not readily apparent and, in any case, a title's subject content can change over time.

Subjective Judgement Based on Direct Examination

This criterion differs from most of the others discussed here because it is a technique instead of an intrinsic characteristic of a periodical or library. Nevertheless, a great deal can be learned about a periodical title and many of the other evaluation criteria outlined here can be accessed simply by examining one or more recent issues. Direct examination can verify such basic factual information as the publisher, place of publication, language, and frequency. A quick perusal should reveal the title's subject content and audience (i.e., scholarly journal or popular magazine). For journals, examining the table of contents, scope statement, masthead, and instructions to contributors should indicate whether the journal is refereed, whether there is an editorial board, and the qualifications of authors and editorial board members—thus providing clues to the journal's scholarly quality.For magazines, observe the writing style and physical format as well as the type and quality of illustrative material. Through such perusal, an impressionistic judgement can be made concerning the periodical's scope, intended audience, overall quality, relevance to client information needs, and consistency with the library's collecting priorities.

For cancellation, weeding, and relegation to remote storage purposes, journal issues will obviously be available for examination. Publishers or serial subscription agents frequently provide sample issues to libraries that are considering a title for subscription. With increasing frequency, sample issues can also be examined electronically, such as through the Electronic Newsstand as well as a publisher or journal page on he WWW.

Use

A serial's use record is one of the most decisive criteria, as actual usage is crucial evidence of relevance to patron need. This criterion clearly cannot be used for subscription decisions, unless a duplicate is being considered (which is rather unlikely in he present financial environment). Nevertheless, a collection manager's estimation of usage level might affect a selection decision, and actual use is a major consideration in cancellation and weeding decisions. Because of its importance.

User Input

Although a technique instead of a serial or library characteristic, user input counts as an important criterion because it can provide useful information on which to base serials collection management decisions. Input from end users can help access a periodical's relevance to their needs and overall quality as well as provide great political advantages to the library—it is harder for constituents to criticize decisions on which they were consulted.

This approach is most frequently used in academic libraries, where faculty input can be a major—and in some instances, the decisive—criterion. Input can be obtained through both informal (i.e., a personal conversation or telephone call) and formal means (such as a survey).

Writing Style

Writing style is a significant criterion for some types of periodicals, such as literary reviews popular magazines, and children's and young adult publications. It is used much more frequently b public and school libraries than academic libraries, which would not normally use this criterion in the assessment of scholarly journals. Although judgments about writing style are somewhat subjective, they can be ascertained through direct inspection, reviews, or annotations in recommended lists. Major stylistic issues include clarity, readability, and appropriateness for the intended audience. Because style can vary from article to article within the same magazine, one should base judgements concerning style on more than a single issue.

A few other possible criteria, not listed above, should be briefly mentioned. A magazine's circulation might be used as a measure of popularity, but it is seldom a critical decision-making criterion. Frequency of publication, although a basic serial characteristic, is usually not a major micro-evaluation criterion. A serial's age is occasion all considered a criterion, based on the assumption that older titles are more established. A journal's acceptance rate—that is, the percentage of submitted articles accepted for publication—is deemed a measure of scholarly prestige. Acceptance rte and perceived scholarly quality display an invere relationship—in other words, the lower the acceptance rate the greater the scholarlyring or attributed to a journal. This criterion, primarily of interest to scholars, is seldom used by librarians in serials decision making, partially because it can be difficult to obtain the data. Curricular relevance and qulity, frequently stated to be major criteria, are not listed here because curricular relevance is covered under the heading "Patron Needs," above, and quality represents numerous criteria that have been analysed under other headings.

Every criteria examined here will not be used in each serials collection management decision. Moreover, their relative importance varies from situation to situation depending upon the type of serial and library and the purpose for which the serial is being evaluated. Methods for combining and assigning relative value to various criteria are discussed in chapter 4, under "Serials Decision Models."

Serials Collection Management Functions

The basic serials collection management functions are

- selection
- cancellation
- weeding
- relegation to remote storage
- filling gaps in backruns
- treatment of unbound single issues
- multiple copy decisions
- location decisions
- subscription versus document delivery decisions
- budgeting

This section covers the most important functions: selection, deselection (cancellation, weeding, and relegation to remote storage), subscription versus document delivery decisions, and budgeting. The remaining functions are addressed in chapter 4.

Selection

Selection of materials for addition to the collection is probably the oldest and most basic collection management function. For this discussion, selection is defined as deciding to place an initial subscription. Although libraries in the present financial environment are more likely to be canceling subscriptions than selecting new ones, some selection is essential to meet new needs of users and to respond to developments in publishing.

Selection can be seen s a three-stage process: identification, evaluation, and selection, *Identification* determines that a periodical actually exists. Evaluation assesses the periodical's intrinsic merit or quality. Selection entails a library's decision to subscribe to a particular periodical. Each stage will be briefly discussed.

Before an item can be considered for selection, its existence must be identified. Identification can take place through reviews, publisher advertising, or inclusion in core lists or standard tools such as Katz and Katz's *Magazine for Libraries*. For a detailed listing of serials identification tools, see Luke Swindler's chapter on collection development in Marcia-Tuttle's *Managing Serials*. He annotates approximately 35 sources for identifying various types of serials, including periodicals, newspapers, and newsletters.[16] Often identification is provided by an individual requesting the subscription. For gifts, identification might take place when he first free issue arrives in the library.

Evaluation focuses on the journal itself and can be either internal or external. In internal evaluation, the collection manager or committee reaches their own assessment of a journal's intrinsic merit. In external evaluation, an evaluation is explicitly supplied by an external third party (e.g., a review of *Magazines for Libraries*). Typical evaluation criteria for a scholarly journal for an academic library would include citation record; indexing; publisher reputation; professional stature of the editor, editorial board members, and contributing authors; and refereed status. In evaluating magazines, a public library would consider writing style, indexing, audience, place of publication, and physical makeup. A school library media centre would place emphasis on such criteria as audience, indexing, age and grade level, as well as format and quality of illustrations.

The decision to select a journal for subscription represents the final step in this three-stage framework. Traditional selection criteria include financial considerations, perceived user needs, availability elsewhere in he geographic vicinity, the library's collecting priorities, and such political considerations as the requestor's status. Remember that evaluation and selection do not necessarily correlate with each other. A periodical could be evaluated highly but not selected because the library can not afford it or is not interested in this subject area. Fr example, a library might decide not to collect the premier dog racing journal because it has not interest in the that topic.

The framework of identification, evaluation, and selection represents an idealized intellectual model. In practice, libraries have (or should have) a written procedure for selection of new periodical subscriptions.

Deselection

Three distinct actions—cancellation, weeding, and relegation to remote storage—are grouped under the term serials deselection. For the following discussion, cancellation is defined as identifying current subscriptions for termination; weeding and relegation to remote storage refers to moving materials from the active collection to a less-accessible physical location, internal or external to the library.

Unfortunately, these terms are not always used consistently. Many authorities, including Loriene Roy in her thorough review of the weeding literature in the Encyclopedia of library and Information Science,[17] have used periodical weeding to encompass all three types of deselection. The American Library Association's *Guide to Review of Library Collections; Preservation, Storage, and Withdrawal* applies the term weeding to both withdrawal and storage.[18] In great Britain, the term relegation is applied to what North Americans call *weeding* or *placement in remote storage*.

In recent years, serials deselection in the majority of libraries tended to concentrate on cancellation rather than weeding or relegation to storage. Most libraries that cancel a current periodical subscription do not immediately weed the backruns from the collection. Periodicals are usually cancelled to save money, but typically they are weeded or relegated to remote storage to save space.

Cancellation

As a consequence of library budgets that do not keep pace with serials inflation rates, serials cancellation has become all-too-frequent in innumerable academic libraries throughout North America. In fact, many libraries have faced repeated rounds of cancellations. Thomas E. Nisonger's *Collection Evaluation in*

Academic Libraries: A Literature Guide and Annotated Bibliography annotates more than 25 serials cancellation case studies published during the 1980s and early 1990s,[19] thus illustrating the fairly substantial literature on the topic.

In a sense, serials cancellation is easier than selection because more information is directly available upon which to base the decision. Recent holdings are available for inspection; the periodical's actual usage in the library can be accessed; and patrons can provide input based on their experience using the title.

Although budgetary pressures have been the driving force behind most academic library serials cancellations in recent years, responsible serials collection considerations. The library's collecting priorities or a journals' quality or focus may change so that a subscription to a specific title is simply no loner needed. Furthermore, one can reasonably anticipate a future trend of canceling print subscriptions and replacing them with electronic subscriptions to the same titles. It could be argued, however, that this action represents a shift from one format to another rather than genuine cancellation.

Cancellation Criteria

Cancellation is the logical opposite of selection—a self-evident observation but one with significant implications for the application of evaluation and selection criteria. The various criteria outlined in this chapter's initial section apply to cancellation as well as selection as well as selection decisions but generally from the opposite direction—that is, a journal ranking high on a criterion would be selected, whereas one with a low ranking would be canceled. Some of the most important cancellation criteria are summarized below.

- *Use.* Use is the most frequently employed cancellation criterion—a fact verified in Judith A. Segal's review of 53 published item about journaldeselection.20 One should focus attention on the least used titles.
- *Foreign language titles.* Foreign language serials have

traditionally been among the first to be canceled.

- *Duplicate subscriptions*. As with foreign language titles, duplicates are traditionally among the first to be deselected.
- *Cost and cost-effectiveness*. Expensive and non-cost-effective titles are usually prime targets for cancellation, with obvious exceptions. Journals that can not be canceled for political reasons, no matter how expensive, are sometimes called "sacred cows."
- *Indexing*. Unindexed titles are major candidates for cancellation.
- *Patron input*. In academic libraries, faculty input is a major, if not decisive, factor.

  Inclusion on core or recommended lists. Inclusion on a credible list would be a compelling reason not to cancel a title. This criterion would be more useful for smaller and medium-sized libraries.

The potential value of citation data as cancellation criteria is somewhat controversial. Robert N. Broadus proposes that instead of conducting an expensive use study, a library could check the citation record of its subscription list in the Journal Citation Reports and review the bottom-ranking 20 percent for possible cancellation.[21] But Marice B. Line argues that citation data for low-ranking "fringe" titles are of citations received can cause a large fluctuation in rank. Line also asserts that national citation data might not reflect actual usage in a local library.[22] Research on these issues is reviewed in chapter 5. In the final analysis, citation data are valid criteria, but they must be used with caution and with other variables.

Tony Stankus, a prolific author on scientific serials, has proposed canceling and weeding journals in the research areas of faculty members who have ceased publishing. How does one known a faculty member has stopped publishing? Stankus concludes, based on analysis of the publication records of 53 Ph.D. –holding chemists, that "when a faculty member exceeds his own longest previous gap without a paper" he or she has probably ceased publication activity.[23] Although Stankus's technique is intriguing, it is not necessarily recommended, as its implementation could create political problems for a library.

The Serials Cancellation Project

It is beyond this chapter's scope to present a comprehensive outline for conduction a serials cancellation project. It is difficult, in any case, to generalize about cancellation projects because each one presents unique problems dependent upon the library's circumstances. Nevertheless, some practical considerations, gleaned from the literature and my own professional experience are listed below.

Be prepared in advance. One cannot overemphasize the importance of advance preparation. Too often serials cancellation projects are carried out in a sense of crisis after unexpected budgetary developments. Have a contingency plan. Keep readily accessible the information you will need, including expenditure records, use studies, collection evaluations, and pertinent correspondence with faculty. Analyze past cancellation projects so that mistakes can be corrected in future projects.

Maintain a database of serial records, ideally in electronic form. The record for each title should, at a minimum contain basic information—the publisher, holdings, frequency, vendor, yearly costs for the past several years, the requestor, and programmes supported by the periodical. Additional information might include circulation, use data, citation data, indexing coverage in recommended lists, and results of user surveys. Sherrie Schmidt, Jane Treadwell, and Gloriana St. Clair describe the use of database management software to create as serials review list at Texas A&M University.[24]

Develop a plan for he project. The plan should address such issues as the project's goal in terms of the dollar amount or percentage to be cut; the set of steps to be completed; a timetable for the completion of each step and a final deadline; the decision-making methodology to use; who is ultimately responsible for final decisions; a mechanism for communicating with library users;

and staff responsibilities.

Consult with faculty, but retain final decision-making authority in the library. Anecdotal evidence form academic librarians indicates that all-too-frequently, decision-making authority is turned over to he institution's faculty. Although this may be politically advantageous, it is also an abdication of professional responsibility. One is tempted to paraphrase the adage "war is too important to be left to the general" with the statement "serials collection management is too important to be left to the faculty."

Be fully aware of the political implications. This is a self-evident but vital point. Communicate why the project is necessary. Place your library's action in the context of national trends (i.e., innumerable libraries throughout the country are canceling (i.e., innumerable libraries throughout the country are canceling serials). Stress that access to canceled titles can be provide by means other than ownership. Devise a mechanism for faculty input concerning which titles are canceled.

Maintain a positive attitude. Maintaining staff morale can be challenging because a serials cancellation project often requires considerable extra work. Remember, however, that serials cancellation is not inevitably bad. Regular review of serial subscriptions may be viewed as part of responsible collection management, which is why cancellation endeavors are sometimes termed "serials review" projects. In the initial round, these projects often identify numerous periodical titles that should be cancelled in any case based on changes in library collection priorities.

Weeding

Weeding refers to removing items form the collection, much as one excises obnoxious weeds from a garden. A fairly voluminous body of literature concerning weeding has been published, and some explicit weeding methodologies have been proposed. Both the theory and practice of weeding have traditionally tended to focus on monographs, although the concept can be applied to any format collected by the library, including periodicals. The two best-known guides to weeding, Stanley J. Slote's Weeding Library

Collections: Library Weeding Methods,[25] issued in four editions and arguably the premier work on the topic, and Joseph P. Segals' Evaluating and Weeding Collection in Small and Medium-Sized Public Libraries: the CREW Method,[26] concentrate almost exclusively on books, with only limited reference to serials weeding.

Slote lists (but does to necessarily endorse) six periodical weeking criteria applicable to various types of libraries, which he "culled" from the published weeding literature: unindex titles; ceased-publication titles that have no cumulative index; incomplete runs; early volumes of long runs, especially of 50 or 60 volumes; "journals in English petroleum libraries after 13 years;" and "in school libraries, keep three to five years; one year if not indexed."[27] In the third edition of his work, Sloe asserted, "For runs of periodicals, remove all before a specific publication date. This date should be established separately for each run."[28] Segal's CREW Method proposes weeding periodicals that are not indexed in the Readers' guide or other major indexing tools owned by the library. He also states that periodicals and newspapers should be clipped "sparing" for the vertical file prior to discard.[29]

Periodical weeding differs from monograph weeding in some key respects. Periodical weeding is easier because fewer titles must be reviewed. It is also more complicated because periodical weeding can occur at two levels: the decision to remove the complete holdings or the decision to remove part of the holdings, presumably those older than a particular date.

Major criteria for weeding periodicals are enumerated below (but not in a priority order). These criteria should normally be applied in combination with each other.

- *Physical condition.* As with all formats, periodicals in deteriorating physical condition are good candidates for weeding.
- *Completeness of holdings.* Short, scattered holdings are better candidates for weeding than long, complete runs.

  Use. Unused or infrequently used periodical runs are obvious targets for weeding. Use in relation to shelf space occupied has also been suggested as a periodical weeding criterion.

- *Age.* Older periodical runs have traditionally been considered prime targets for weeding. However, the critical variable is use rather than age per se. The concept of "literature obsolescence" relates use to age by demonstrating that older periodical holdings are less frequently used. As explained in chapter 5, obsolescence varies among disciplines.
- *Current collecting priorities.* One of the most compelling reasons for weeding is a change in the library's collecting priorities.
- *Availability elsewhere.* Periodical runs that are available in nearby libraries are clearly stronger candidates for weeding than holdings unique within the geographical area. Likewise, duplicate runs within the same library system may be prime weeding targets. Locally published periodicals should not be weeded to ensure their permanent archiving in at lest one library.
- *Cooperative agreements with other libraries and consortiums.* A periodical can be weeded with greater confidence if another library has agreed to maintain the specific title or a strong collection in its subject area.
- *Indexing.* The conventional wisdom assert that unindexed titles are excellent possibilities for weeding, and indexed ones should be maintained. However, it should be stressed that the critical factor is not current indexing but whether the runs under consideration for weeding were indexed.
- *Core or recommended lists.* Most libraries are reluctant to weed titles on core or recommended lists. Some small libraries use a strict policy: Any title not on a recommended list should be weeded.
- *Whether the library currently subscribes to the periodical under examination.* Lack of a current subscription can be

a major factor in deciding to weed the backrun holdings, as they become more obsolete with each passing year.

From a more theretical perspective, John Urguhart argues that the effectiveness of any weeding criterion can be tested y two measurements; the proportion of weeded items subsequently needed for use and the proportion of total use lost by weeding.30 However, very little empirical research on periodical weeding criteria effectiveness has been reported in the literature.

For academic and research libraries, citation data can be especially helpful in decisions about weeding as well as relegation to remote storage. When a journal's backruns are no longer cited or cited infrequently, it is presumed that use by researchers has ceased or tapered off. The 'cited half-life," available for thousands of journals in the ISI's JCR, is a helpful indicator of how long a particular journal's backruns are cited. Detailed explanations of the cited half-life and the JCR may be found in chapter 5.

From a long-term perspective, the development of electronic journals has potentially profound implications for serials weeding strategy. Disposal of print holdings that are easily accessible electronically might be a logical step. However, there is no present guarantee that electronic holdings will be permanently archived. Finally, canceling and weeding electronic journals per se offers a myriad of unresolved issues that librarians have hardly even begun to address.

Weeding is often the most difficult collection management function. It can be expensive in terms of staff time and requires changing cataloging or holdings records. Moreover, weeding is fraught with political risk, as many patrons do not understand why a library would dispose of holdings. Yet, apart from the space-saving issue, a well-weeded periodical collection should be stronger and more effective at meeting client information needs.

Relegation to Remote Storage

The terms remote storage, secondary storage, or simply storage may be considered synonyms. The Association for Library Collections and Technical Services' (ALCTS) Guide to Review of Library Collections defines storage as "the transfer of less-used materials to restricted areas within the library building or to a remote facility."31 In the following discussion, the concept of remote storage refers to a secondary location facility for material that has been processed and added to the collection. A storeroom housing a backlog of unprocessed materials that are inaccessible to library patrons is not considered remote storage.

Relegation to emote storage represents a compromise between full retention in the active collection and weeding. As with weeding, the primary motivation for placement in secondary storage is usually the conservation of shelf space. A typical remote storage area would receive both books and serials. In some instances, a group of libraries may share a single remote storage facility.

The numerous organisational and technical problems involved in administering a remote storage facility (e.g., regular shelves versus compact shelves, the arrangement of material within eh facility, and so on) are beyond this book's scope. The major serials collection management issue concerns determining which titles and runs will be placed in remote storage. Most of the weeding criteria and methods discussed in the preceding section would also be applicable to remote storage decisions and consequently need not be repeated here.

An October 1986 survey of college and small university library directs found that nearly half of their libraries (precisely 49.2 percent) used a "storage or secondary location" for at least some serials titles. In terms of location, 65.6 percent of these facilities were in the library, 25 percent on campus, and 6.3 percent off campus. Moreover, 54.2 percent of those responding to the question indicated periodicals in storage were accessible "within minutes"; 15.3 percent, "within an hour"; 20.3 percent, in 24 hours; and 10.2 percent responded "other"—presumably more than 24 hours, Respondents indicated the following criteria for placement of periodicals in remote storage: a cutoff date, 16.9 percent; use record, 28.8 percent; faculty recommendation or approval, 6.8 percent; and "other' (such as duplicate holdings or items in poor physical condition), 7.6 percent. Moreover, 12.6 percent indicated that canceled journals were placed in storage.[32]

Document Delivery

Traditional collection development postulated that patrons' information needs were to be met by materials owned by and housed in the library. In recent years, a new paradigm emerged, stating that a library's ownership of an item is irrelevant as long as patrons can be provided access to needed documents. The frequently heard but somewhat simplistic slogans "access versus ownership" or "just-in-time versus just-in-case" symbolize this new approach.

The document delivery concept lends itself especially well to journals because individual articles represent distinct units of manageable size that can easily be procured externally. Furthermore, the currently available indexing and abstracting services provide reasonably adequate bibliographical control of the serials literature, thus helping end users identify pertinent articles.

The term document delivery is sometimes used in a broad sense to embrace both traditional ILL and commercial document delivery. However, document delivery using the numerous commercial document delivery services that have become major players on the library scene in recent years is usually viewed as a distinct phenomenon from traditional ILL. Dennis P. Carrigan writes:

> If [document delivery] refers to libraries' efforts to secure for their clients copies of materials not available in the libraries, b turning to suppliers that offer the service for a few. Although the suppliers receiving the most attention are commercial and not-for-profit firms, there are libraries that while continuing to perform their traditional roles, have become document delivery agents in this sense of the term. Depending on one's perspective, document delivery and interlibrary loan are complements or competitors.[33]

Document delivery differs from traditional ILL In several respects:

- An Ill item is obtained from the collection of another library, whereas document deliver is usually provided by a commercial vendor.
- ILL is often, but not always, provided free of charge, but there is invariably a fee for document delivery.
- In traditional ILL, a library staff member act as an intermediary to process the request, but in document delivery the end user often initiates the request.
- Document delivery is generally perceived to be quicker than ILL.
- ILL often supplies the original item, whereas document delivery invariably provides a copy.
- Within specific limitations (see the explanation for the "Rule of Five" in chapter 8's "Copyright" section), articles can be supplied through ILL without payment of a copyright fee, but with document delivery a copyright fee is almost always added. Parenthetically, some librarians have argued that use of document delivery results in the loss of the five free request per journal that the library would be entitled to receive without paying a copyright fee under ILL.

Numerous entities offer document delivery services to libraries. Some leading services are mentioned in this section, but it is not the author's intention to offer evaluative commentary or endorse one commercial service over another. In the mid-1990s noteworthy document delivery player include national libraries, for example, the Canada Institute for Scientific and Technical Information (CISTI) or the British Library Document Supply Centre; commercial vendors, for example, DIALOG Information Services or EBSCO publishing; and not-for-profit entities such as the Educational Resources Information Center (ERIC) Document service or the Research Libraries Group (RLG). These services typically charge as set fee for each delivered article plus a copyright fee that various according to the publisher's charge. A 1993 Library Journal article by Mounir Khalil summarized 26 document delivery services that were operating or in the planning stage, including ADONIS, the OCLC Dispatch Service, and the UMI Article Clearing house. Addresses, phone and fax numbers, coverage, and cost were generally provided for each.[34] Tuttle provides detailed descriptions of seven such services; UnCover, OCLC's ArticleFirst, UMI Infostore, the Genuine Article, Faxon Finder, EBSCODoc, and Sweets and Zeitlinger's SwetScan.[35]

Some publishers offer document delivery services for articles from their own publications. For example, Haworth Press advertises in its journals the "Haworth Document Delivery Service" for all Hawroth-published articles. The cost is comprised of a "set-up charge per article," photocopying charges per article based on the item's length, an optional "flexicover" charge per article, postage, and handling, and an optional same-day fax service charge based on the number of pages. Likewise, the New York Times advertises an "Articles by Fax or mail" service whereby previously published articles on high-interest topics, such as AIDS, can be ordered for$3.95 each.[36]

An April 1994 survey of 90 Association of Research Libraries (ARL) libraries found that 78 (86.7) percent0 used commercial document delivery services to obtain items for their patrons. In terms of the number of supplied items, the most frequently used services were CISTI, 11,630; the Genuine Article, 3,092; UnCover, 3,012; DIALOG, 1,853; the British Library Document Supply Centre, 1,843; and UMI ARTICLE Clearing House, 1,776. According to the number of libraries using their servies, the top-ranked suppliers were the British Library Document Supply Centre and UMI Article Clearing house, both used ą 64 libraries; Chemical Abstracts Service, 532 libraries; UnCover, 38 libraries; and the Genuine Article, 30 libraries. Not unexpectedly, given the increased emphasis on access rather than ownership, 73.7 percent (56 of 78 respondents) reported an increased use of document delivery suppliers over the previous fiscal year; 77.8 percent (63 of 81) projected an even greater use of document delivery services in the coming fiscal year.[37]

Document Delivery Versus Subscription

Libraries have traditionally used ILL to procure articles from serials they cancelled or never subscribed to in the first place, but commercial document delivery is now a strategies alternative to subscription; and, for a given title, the choice between the two is a fundamental serials collection management decision. The criteria for reaching this decision are examined below.

- *Availability from document delivery services.* Document delivery is not an option for titles that are not offered by document delivery services.
- *Level of use.* Document delivery is most appropriate for infrequently used titles.
- Need for immediate access. Subscription is the logical option for titles to which immediate access is required, as most document delivery services take one or two days at a minimum.
- *Purpose of use.* Apart from usage level, the purpose of use is a crucial factor. Titles needed to support the teaching process, which requires rapid access to materials, are better suited for subscription. Moreover, document delivery is not a good option if brows ability is an important consideration. In contrast, serials supporting research are strong candidates for document delivery because immediate access is usually not necessary.
- *Political considerations.* This is another self-evident factor. As Bill Coons and Peter McDonald ask, is the decision to use document delivery in place of subscription "likely to adversely affect a powerful department chair?"[38]
- *Cost-effectiveness.* A major question concerns the break-even point at which a library should subscribe to a journal rather than rely on commercial document delivery. If financial considerations are the sole criterion, three major variables would affect the decision: (1) cost of each document delivery; (2) cost of an annual subscription; and (3) number

of demands for document delivery within the year. The mathematics are simple, even though the decision making is complicated. If each document delivery costs $9 and an annual subscription 450, it appears cost-effective to subscribe if there will be six or more uses of the journal within a year. (Five uses would cost $45, and six would cost $54.) However, such a crude analysis does not consider the relative staff cost of maintaining a subscription versus reliance on document delivery. In any case, the decision can not be made on cost-effectiveness alone. Unfortunately, one of the most important considerations, use convenience, can not easily be quantified.

Various decision-making policies have been suggested, but there is no consensus. Official standards offer some limited guidance. The 1995 Association of College and Research Libraries (ACRL) standards for college libraries state:

> In general it is good practice to consider owning any title that is needed more than five times per year... It may not be necessary to subscribe to certain less frequently used titles if they are available at another library nearby, or if needed articles may be quickly procured through a reliable delivery system or by electronic means.[39]

Coons and McDonald recommend that a subscription be considered in every case where the annual document delivery cost is greater than half the subscription price.[40] A study at the Columbia University Libraries of biology journal requests during 1993 found access through either commercial document delivery or interlibrary loan to be far more cost-effective than subscription for all titles requested 10 or fewer tiems.[41] Carol Tenopir and Donald W. King likewise assert that ILL or document delivery is less expensive than subscription for journals "read" fewer than 10 times a year.[42] Eleanor A. Gossen and Suzanne Iriving conclude that document delivery is preferable for every title used fewer than five times per year regardless of subscription cost.[43]

Bruce R. Kingma and Suzamnner Iring's decision model

concerns the "economic efficiency" of ILL versus subscription, based on analysis of mathematics and science journals at the State University of New York SUNY) at Albany, Binghamton, Buffalo, and Stony Brook Libraries during fall 1994. They outline three sets of decisions rules:

1. based on the financial cost to the library
2. based on the cost to the library and its patrons
3. based on the cost to the borrowing library, its patrons, and the lending lirbary[44]

Because this relatively sophisticated model does not lend itself well to succinct summary, the interested reader should consult Kingma and Iriving's original publication for full details.

Several studies have demonstrated that substantial savings can be derived from substituting document delivery for subscription. The Columbia study found that for the titles from which one article was requested in 1993, the estimated total cost of subscription was $244,917 compared to $11,421 for docuemtndelivery.[45] Donna Goehner, dean of libraries at Western Illinois University, revealed at an ALA conference that during an 18-month period, the library had paid $703.70 o access articles through commercial document delivery for faculty requests for items from recently canceled serial subscriptions; the subscriptions for those serials would have cost approximately $50,000.[46] In late 1995 Forbes magazine reported that the Louisiana State University Library had paid $25,000 during the preceding two years for commercial document delivery, yet two years earlier $446,000 worth of scholarly journals had been canceled.[47]

The perceing analysis presupposes that the library bears the whole cost f document delivery. Actually, this issue raises a host of questions. Should document delivery costs be recovered, either wholly or partially, from the patron? If the library picks up the cot, which budget should be charged; materials, interlibrary loan, serials, or some other department? Or should a separate line item be created? Should certain categories of patrons receive a higher priority than others? Should a limit be placed on the number of patron requests? Should document delivery be paid for or subsidized for all titles or only certain ones; if the latter, which ones? What criteria are used in determining subsidized ad paid-for titles?

Commercial document delivery services available on the Internet, such as UNCover, allow the patron to order articles directly without the intervention of a library staff member. This concept, often termed dis-intermediation, presents an interesting set of issues. One could argue that a library is not necessary if the end user can directly order needed articles. Yet a library can still play a vital role in dis-intermediated document delivery by paying the fee (ether fully or partially). Most of the questions outlined in the preceding paragraph would clearly apply to disintermediated document delivery.

The previously mentioned April 1994 Survey of ARL institutions indicated that 54.2 percent of the responding libraries (45 of 83) paid the complete cost of commercial document delivery, whereas 12 percent (10 of 83) passed the full cost on the patron. Further, 24.1 percent (20 of 83) split the expense between the library and patron, and 9.6 percent (8 of 83) responded "other," which was not explained. Perhaps the latter category included cases where different patron types were treated differently, that is, subsidizing faculty, but no student, requests,[48]

Table of Contents Services

Table of contents services are a relatively new development on the library scene, although they might be viewed as a modified form of Selective Dissemination of Information (SDI) introduced several decades ago. In essence, these services send to designated recipients—usually through Electronic mail (e-mail) or fax, sometimes on tape, disk, or in print—the table of contents of recent journal issues or citations to journal articles based on a subject profile. These services, usually with there own distinctive names, are offered by commercial document suppliers and serial subscription agents. The former includes UnCover Rever and the latter, Faxon FlashTOC or Swets and Zeitlinger's SwetScan.

Although the precise details vary from service to service, one can cite UnCover Reveal as an example. For a $25 annual fee (as of March, 1998), an individual can have the table of contents of 50 journals and the results of 25 search strategies sent to his or her e-mail address. Through the Table of Contents Redistribution Service, an organisation can centrally receive tables of contents for its own redistribution at an annual cost of $10 per title. Institutions (including libraries, universities, and academic departments) can get a site license that allows each user to receive the table of contents for 50 journals of their choice, and the licensing fee is calculated according to a sliding scale based on the number of subscribers. For example, the fee is $750 per year for up to 50 subscribers and $4300 annually if there are more than 400 subscribers.[49]

Table of contents services are inextricably connected to the document delivery concept because many commercial document suppliers also provide this service. For document delivery to work well, library customers must know what articles have recently been published in their areas of interest. Research has yet to be published concerning how libraries actually use table of contents services for serials collection management. Nevertheless, one can speculate that these services

1. provide current awareness that assists access to journals to which the library currently subscribes;
2. help identify articles in journals not subscribed to by the library so they can be obtained through document delivery;
3. sometimes help ordering of documents by the end user without mediation of library staff;
4. as a serendipitous spin-off, provide data about faculty or other patrons' interest in journals.

Key decisions for a library include whether to use a table of contents service, which one to select, an how to finance it. No guidelines or explicit methodologies exist for determining whether a library needs a table of contents service. Basically, the decision is a judgment call. If library staff are satisfied the present journal collection adequately meets patron information needs without procuring documents from external sources a table of contents service would probably not be especially useful. In contrast, the greater the use of document delivery, the more benefits would be derived from a table of contents service (e.g., identifying articles to be requested and compensating for the fact users can not browse journals to which the library does not subscribe). The budgetary questions about document delivery, discussed in the above section, also apply to table of contents services. Criteria for selecting a table of contents service include cost, coverage, currency, ease of use and ability to customize service for local needs.

With increasing regularity journals have been making their table of contents available on the WWW or through listservs. Yet it seems doubtful that their separate efforts could be used for systematic serials access with the same effectiveness as a commercial document delivery system.

Access versus Ownership: The Arguments

This section summarizes the arguments concerning the two basis strategies for meting patron information needs; access and ownership.

Pro-Access Position

This position assumes that as long as the library or information center can provide the patron relatively quick access to a document that meets his or her information needs, it is irrelevant whether the item is owned and housed within the institution's four walls or procured from and external source. The ownership concept often wastes scarce financial resources by purchasing materials that are seldom if ever used, as demonstrated by the Pittsburgh study (discussed in chapter 6) and numerous other investigations. Moreover, access through external sources saves shelf space. New technology, including fax machines and the Internet, facilitate access. For example, Ariel, a system developed by the RLG for transmitting documents over the Internet, provides rapid, cost-effective, and high-resolution document delivery. Access proponents often denigrate the ownership concept as "warehousing" and point out that even if a document is owned, it may not be available to patrons.

A distinction between bibliographical access (knowing what has been published) and physical access (having the information source in the patron's hands) should be noted. One of the first consequences of the introduction of electronic media into libraries was that bibliographical access far exceeded immediate physical access, as CD-ROM indexes and abstracts provided citations for serial articles that were not contained in the local collection. This may make patrons more aware of the collection's inadequacies and lead to increased demands for external access through ILL and document delivery.

Pro-Ownership Position

Ownership represents the traditional paradigm of librarianship. Critics of the pro-access position argue that some of its underlying assumptions—that patrons already know which items will meet their information needs and can wait a reasonable amount of time for access—are not always valid. In reality, patrons sometimes need nearly instantaneous access to information As an extreme example, one sometimes hears the anecdote about the doctor who requested a journal article be delivered to him during surgery and when it was returned to the library, it was covered with blood! Furthermore, clients frequently do not know which documents will meet their information needs. The access concept does not allow for browsing, serendipitously finding relevant items, or directly viewing the range of materials on a particular topic. Although perhaps suitable for supporting research needs, access is less appropriate for such other purposes as teaching, entertainment, or ready reference. Moreover, Rudolf Jacob Penner's research has demonstrated a significant correlation between ownership and accessibility of matrial.[50]

Analysis.

The "Access versus ownership" issue represents a continuum rather than a dichotomy. In other words, it is not a question of wholly one or the other, but rather of the proper balance between the two. It has been observed that the slogan should read "access and ownership," not "access versus ownership." In receipt years the balance has clearly been shifting from ownership toward access—a trend that will surely continue. Nevertheless, it seems highly unlikely (at least to this author) that access will totally displace ownership within the foreseeable future.

In the short term, the increasing emphasis on access makes serials collection management more challenging because librarians have more options (e.g., ownership, ILL, or commercial document delivery) in deciding how to best meet patron information needs.

Budgeting for Serials

Budgeting is inextricably connected with collection management. The budget process is traditionally viewed as a mechanism for setting priorities and helping shape the collection, although, as explained below, these concepts may be less applicable to serials budgeting. Nevertheless, many serials collection management decisions (e.g., cancellation projects) are driven by financial decisions. Fundamental budget issues relating to serials are the budgets composition (what budget lines are included) and division (allocation of funds among budget lies); provision for such special categories as new subscriptions, electronic journals, and document delivery; projection of the funds required for the next fiscal years serials costs; and ex-post facto analysis and evolution of serials expenditure patterns.

This section covers the major budgeting issues pertinent to serials collection management. The effect of the so-called serials crisis on library materials budges has been analysed in the preceding chapter. Serials financial accounting is addressed in chapter 8, and budgeting for electronic journals is in chapter 9. In depth discussion of basic library budgetignprinciples and procedures is beyond this section's scope. The reader is referred to recent texts on the topic such as Murray S. Martin's Academic Library Budgets,[51] Ann E. Prentice's Financial Planning for Libraries,[52] or Basic Budgeting Practices for Librarians, by Richard S. Rounds.[53]

The ALA's Guide to Budget Allocation for Information Resources lists several intended benefits of a budget document, including translating "collecting priorities into a concrete form," serving as a device for requesting funds, communicating budget information, and casting "as an historical record showing actual expenditures, including variances form the initial budget."[54] Budgeting is commonly viewed as an opportunity for planning and setting priorities, predicated on the assumption that various budget categories will receive support in approximate proportion to their perceived importance. Yet it is questionable whether this assumption applies to serials because of the unique budgeting problems they present.

For most formats, such as monographs or audiovisuals, the library begins with an allocated amount and orders the number of items necessary to expend the allocation. In contrast, a library begins the fiscal year with a set number of serial subscriptions and must expend whatever amount of money is required to meet these ongoing commitments. This, serials budgeting is more likely to involve estimating the funds required to pay for the library's serials list than determining the collecting priority of the serials format. This explanation is, of course, an oversimplification, but it helps clarify the inherent dilemma of serials budgeting and the common perception that for academic libraries serials expenditures may be out of control.[55] The fact that a Brown university library budgeting document, reproduced in an ARL SPEC kit, uses the phrase "serials commitment" illustrates the concept.[56]

The Composition of the Serials Budget

The organisaiton of th serials budget is mor eof an administrative than a collection management issue,so it willonly be briefly touched upon her.e A fundational issue concerns what line items are included in the serials budget. Traditional expenditure categories include current periodical subscriptions, memberships, backruns, replacements, newspapers, microformt, refrence serials, standing orders, and binding. In th ecurrent environemtn, docuemtn delivery, table of contents services, and electronic journals could conceivably have separate budgetary liens. A related issue is the possible breakdown of th serials budget among branches or departments. Inconsistency in the makeup of th serials budget among libraries complicates the comparison of srials expenditures. For example, some libraries count standing orders as monographs, but others consider them serials. (The ARL attempts to address this problem by providing precise instructions to reporting libraries.)

It is not uncommon for a libraryto have a single periodicals or serials budgt or expenditures line, undifferentiated by subject. A 1987 CLIP Note found that only 42.8 percent (%) of 116) of college libraries allocated periodical funds by discipline or department.[57] However, responsible collection management calls for an analysis of serials expenditures by subject. nearly two decades ago, Edward S. Warner and Anita L. Anker wrote, "It is becoming increasingly desirable—every required, as a result of economic and political imperatives—that the cots of [scholarly journal]collection support be attributed to academic programmes."[58] In fact, for may libraries assigning current subscriptions to departmental or subject categories.

Many journals can readily be assigned to subject areas (e.g., the American Historical Review to history). For less obvious titles, Library of Congress (LC classification or Dewey decimal classification (DDC) numbers or subject headings in Ulrich's can lend assistance. Warner and Anker describe a method used at the University of North Dakota library in which a journal's cost is apportioned among departments according to their perception of the journal's importance, based on a faculty survey.[59]

Breaking down the serials budget by subject involves some practical problems. Many interdisciplinary journals cannot be pigeonholed into specific subject categories. Scholars in one discipline use journals that belong to other disciplines. Some departments play political games by contriving to have a serial they want charged to another department's budget.

Two theoretical approaches analyze serial support for a subject area—content analysis and component analysis. In a content analysis, every title would be assigned to some subject, but each can be assigned only once. Thus, a journal on economic history would have to be assigned to either economics or history, but not both. In a component analysis, all journals supporting a subject are assigned to it even if it means assigning a single title to multiple subject areas. Accordingly, the title mentioned above would be assigned to both economics and history. Paradoxically, a content analysis may be more practical for serials review projects because each title is sent to a single department; but for collection analysis reasons, component analysis more accurately depicts serials support for various subject areas.[60]

Project of Funds Required for the Next Year's Serials Expenditures

Estimating the cost for the library's serials subscription lists in the forth-coming fiscal year is one of the most difficult serials budgeting functions. Some strategies and tactics are summarized below:

- Take into account changes in the library's subscription list by adding the cost of new subscriptions and subtracting the price of canceled and ceased titles. Do not forget to calculate the cost of serial subscription agent fees.
- Consider the general makeup of your library's subscription list in terms of U.S. versus non-U.S. subscriptions and Science, Technical, and Medical (STM) versus other subjects.
- Be conscious of the mot-current pricing trends (appendix 1 annotates several sources of data on serials pricing trends, including the Bowker annual and the ALA and ALCTS Library Materials Price Index committee's annual report).
- Pay attention to serial subscription agent projections of the year's serials inflation rate, which appear in timely fashion on listervs.
- Ask you serials subscription agent to provide an estimate of the inflation rate for your library's subscription list.

Budgetary Provision for New Serial Subscriptions

Given that new serial titles are constantly coming into existence and that client information needs evolve over time, responsible serials collection management requires that new serials subscriptions be ordered fairly fairly regularly. Hawthorn found that in 1990, 36 percent of larger libraries and 31 percent of smaller libraries had a budget allocation for new serial subscriptions.[61] A number of strategies can ensure funds for new subscriptions.

Many libraries use what might be termed a "Cancel to reorder" policy whereby fund managers can generate funds for new subscriptions by canceling present subscriptions. Hawthorn's research indicated that 48 percent of large libraries and 51 percent of small ones spent money form cancellations on new subscriptions, although some permitted only a fraction of the freed-up funds to be so used.[62] As a variation on this theme, the cost of ceased periodical titles might be earmarked for new subscriptions. (For many libraries, however, serials price inflation consumes any savings from cancellation and cessation.)

Some libraries solicit gift or endowment funds dedicated to serials. For example, an "adopt a serial" programme allows a donor to donor to sponsor a specif serials subscription.

Academic libraries can allow individual selectors or each academic department to allocate its own materials budget between monographs and serials, thus possibly freeing funds for new serial subscriptions. A 1987 CLIP Note revealed that the Missouri Western State University library in Saint Joseph, Missouri, allowed departments to apportion their annual materials allocation however they wised among formats, provided no more than 60 percent was used for journals.[63] Delegating the responsibility to academic departments would help educate faculty concerning serials budgetary problems and remove some of the political pressure from library staff. However, there would be some associated disadvantages. A considerable amount of professional responsibility for serials management would be transferred to faculty, and interdisciplinary journals might fall through the cracks.

Frederick C. Lynden cited examples at the Cornell, Iowa, and Minnesota university libraries whereby selectors were allowed to apportion budget cuts however they wished among serials and monographs.[64] Beverly P. Lynch reported that bibliographers at the University of Illinois at Chicago are also responsible for dividing their funds between serials and monographs with the stipulation that the library's total serials expenditure does not exceed 50 percent of the materials budget.[65]

Delegation of serials budgeting authority to the selector or bibliographer level offers several advantages, for example, more flexibility in responding to the unique needs of different subject areas than with an "across the board" approach, and the danger of shifting materials funds from the humanities to the sciences would be alleviated.

Budgeting for Document Delivery

Budgeting for document delivery represents a particularly significant issue in the current environment's emphasis on access. It is intimately connected with serials budgeting because one presumes that in most libraries the majority of document delivery requests are for serial items. Because it is a relatively new issue, little has been published on document delivery budgeting. Key questions would concern whether to create a separate document delivery budget in and, if so, how much money to allocate and where to get it.

A serials cancellation project effects these questions two ways: a greater need for document delivery is created because there are fewer current periodical subscriptions, and the project may have freed funds to use for document delivery. The aftermath of a major cancellation project may therefore be an appropriate occasion for creating a document delivery budget line or increasing an already existing one.

A January 1995 SERIALIST contribution reported that after a serials cancellation project, and unnamed library used the following formula to calculate the document delivery budget:

Whereby:

X equals the uses of canceled titles

Y equals the amount allocated for serials document delivery

Thus:

$X/2 \times 15 = Y$

In other words, the number of times canceled titles were used is divided by two and then multiplied by 15, equaling the presumed dollar cost of document delivery.[66] No time period for recording use is stated, although one assumes it would be a year: It was stated that any dollar amount for document delivery cost could be plugged into the formula. There may be some flaws in this model (e.g., the presumed 2:1 ratio of canceled journal use to future document delivery request is problematic). Moreover, the model assumes the library will bear the full cost of document delivery for cancelled titles. If part of the costs are charged back to patrons, the library's budgetary requirements would be reduced. Nevertheless, the formula represents one of the first primitive attempts to quantify document delivery budgeting—an issue requiring more research before definitive answer are available.

The April 1994 survey of ARL libraries found that 53.6 percent (45 of 84) did not have a separate document delivery budget line. Of the 39 that did, exactly two-thirds (26) allocated the funds from the acquisitions or materials budget or both, one allocated them from general administration funds, and 9 responded "other," which was to explained.[67]

Analysis of Serials Expenditures

Several related questions will be answered in this section: how much to spend on serials, what portion of the total materials budget to devote to serials, and how to analyze the serials-monograph ratio by subject area. The answers to thee questions varies depending on such key variables as library type, library size, and subject area. Note that in almost all budget categories the final expenditure figure at the end of the fiscal year will not precisely match the original allocation—a phenomenon that can be particularly pronounced for serials. Obviously, collection management analysis should be based on actual expenditure rather than the budgeted amount.

Many libraries allocate the materials budget by the "historical precedent" method, a type of generic drift in which each area receives the same proportion of the budgetary pie year after year. Although this approach might work for monographs, it does not lend itself well to serials budgeting. Continuous renewal of all serial subscriptions will eventually shift funding support from the humanities to the sciences because science journals inflate in price at a significantly higher rate than humanities periodicals. Almost inevitably, most libraries (or at least most academic libraries) will sooner or later be forced to examine their serials expenditure patterns. Such analysis often results in serials cancellation projects or reallocation of funds.

Many authors have quite correctly reflected on the difficulty of ascertaining proper serials expenditure patterns. As succinctly observed by Peggy Johnson, "The search for the perfect allocation formula or the ideal ratio between serials and monographs is a frustrating process."[68] Siegfried Feller likewise states, "There can be no definitive answer, even for a given type and size of library."[69] Robin B. Devin asks, "How much is too much?" referring to the proportion of the materials budget devoted to serials.[70] Considerable professional judgement is required. Although there are no right or wrong answers, such methods as standards, comparative data, citation studies, and formulas can provide assistance.

Standards

For a few libraries, standards provide some insight for evaluating total serials expenditure levels. For illustration, the budget section of the 1994 ACRL, ALA, and association for Educational Communications and Technology (AECT) standard for junior and community college libraries stipulates that a "minimum" collection (at the 50th percentile) should spend $8.70 per Full time Equivalent (FTE) student on "current serials," and an "excellent" collection (at the 90th percentile) should spend $22.20 for each FTE student.[71]

Information Power: Guidelines for School Library Media Programmes, the 1988 American Association of School Librarians (AAL) and AECT standard for school library media centers, presents as quantitative national guidelines per-pupil current periodical expenditure figures, based on 1985-1986 U.S. department of Education statistics, for "high service" programmes in seven levels and sizes of schools. The Expenditure figures summarized in table 6.1 were compiled by the author from the seven tables in Information Power's appendix A, which presents data in four categories covering staff, collections, facilities and equipment, and the budget.[72]

Table 6.1: Per-Pupil Periodical Expenditures from Information Power's Appendix A

	Percentile Level		
School Level and Size	75th	90th	95th
Elementary Under 500	$1.31	$1.85	$2.67
Elementary over 500	$0.88	$1.32	$1.70
Middle/Junior Under 500	$3.10	$4.74	$5.89
Middle/junior over 500	$1.71	$2.51	$2.97
High Schools Under 500	$4.72	$8.23	$11.36
High Schools Between 500 and 1,000	$3.40	$5.36	$7.47
High Schools over 1,000	$2.11	$2.94	$ 4.95

Expenditures per pupil on serials range from $.88 at elementary schools with more than 500 pupils (at the 75th percentile) to $11.36 at high schools with fewer than 500 students (at the 95th percentile. It is not worthy but not unexpected that smaller schools consistently display larger per-pupil expenditures. For example, for high schools at the 75th percentile, the expenditure decreases from $4.72 to $3.49 to $2.11 as one proceeds from smaller to larger schools.

As an alternative to analysis of expenditures per pupil, Information power includes the cost of current periodical subscriptions as part of a four-factor model (along with replacement books, additional books, and reference materials) for calculating the recommended budget for print materials. Unfortunately, the instructions for calculating the periodicals component are not especially helpful. They merely state one should begin with the number of subscriptions that "need to be renewed or started" and multiply it by the average cost of a periodical subscription (for the appropriate school level) or use the actual subscription cost. The document also asserts that the collection's strengths and weaknesses, changes in the student body makeup, and inflation should be considered in calculating the periodicals budget.[73] Information Power was the current standard when this book was written. A revised edition, issued in the summer of 1998, was unavailable to the author.

Comparative Data

It might be of some value to compare a library's monographic and serials expenditures with the ratios in other libraries of a similar type, size, and purpose. Comparison could be made with data from specific libraries or collective data from a group of peer institutions. Such data can be found in a variety of sources listed in appendix 1, including ACRL University Library Statistics and the early Statistics. State agencies, as well as regional or local consortiums, might also be a source of data. Alternatively, a library could conduct its own survey. For example. During the 1980s the Indiana University library surveyed expenditure patterns in 80 peer institutions.[74] For libraries not wishing to undertake such an extensive effort, one might obtain expenditure and budgeting data through informal contacts with a small number of similar libraries. It should be noted that a 1990 survey of 34 ARL libraries found that the monographic-serials expenditures ratio ranged from 50:50 to 15:85, with 40:60 the most frequently reported ratio (by eight libraries).[75] Comparative data provide a context for evaluating a particular library's expenditure pattern but not a definitive answer. Each library has its own unique mission. Furthermore, the patterns in other libraries are not necessarily "correct," as they also confront similar pressures from serials price inflation.

Citation Studies

For university and research libraries, the large number of published citation studies for countless subject areas can provide guidance concerning the materials budgets' division between monographs and serials. Several authors, including Robin B. Devin and Martha Kellogg,[76] Michael Bowman,[77] and Devin,[78] have published tables summarizing the proportion of citations to serials from numerous studies. Chapter 5 presents a more-detailed discussion concerning the pros and cons of using citation data to assist the serials budgeting process. As a slight variation on this theme, Tony Stankus and William Littlefield advocate allocating the science journal budget according to the number of researchers in each specialty and their publication productivity.[79]

Formulas

A large number of so-called allocation formulas for divising the monographic budget among subject areas have been published and debated by the profession. These formulas typically incorporate data on student enrollment, faculty, courses, degrees, publications pout put, cost, circulation, etc. (For more specific details, see the literature reviews by Mary Sellen80 and JohnM. Budd.[81]) Similar formulas for serials do not abound in the literature—probably because the unique budgeting problems associated with serials are not conducive to setting priorities among subject areas. As stated by Stankus and Little field in 1987, "apart from the voluminous price 'complaint' literature, there is little devoted to actual allocation schemes for serials."[82]

In fact, research indicates that only a minute fraction of academic libraries use allocation formulas in periodicals or serials budgeting. The precise figures were 7.6 per cnet (9 of 118) in an October 1986 CLIP Note survey;[83] 10.4 percent (37 of 357) in John M. Budd and Kay Adams's 1987 survey of academic libraries with materials budgets exceeding $100,000; and 12 percent (23 survey of academic libraries with materials budgets exceeding $100,000;[84] and 12 per cent (23 of 192) for periodical subscriptions and 13.5 percent (26 of 192) for serials in a December 1994 survey of college and small university libraries.[85] The previously mentioned 1990 survey of ARL libraries found that only 13.9 percent (11 of used a formula in allocating or reallocating materials funds, although specific data for serials were not reported.[86]

A 1987 ACRL CLIP Note contained periodical allocation formulas or budget policies used at some academic libraries (e.g., Franklin and Marshall College, Oberlin College, Missouri Western State College, and Shepherd College).[87] Recent reports include the development of allocation formulas covering both monographs and serials at George mason Univrsity,[88] the University of Southern Mississippi,[89] Central Missouri State University,[90] and Monash University in Australia.[91]

Perhaps the best-known formula pertaining to serials is Charles B. Lowry's so called matrix formula, used at the University of Texas at Arlington and other institutions. Book and serial funds are distributed to each department according to a formula incorporating 12 variables: FTE faculty, freshman-sophomore credit hours, junior-senior credit hours, master's credit hours, doctoral credit hours, library use, graduate degrees, under-graduate degrees, book cost, serials cost, faculty publications, and faculty external grants. A "Book/Serial Dependency Index" is then used to divide each department's allocation between monographs and serials in proportion to the total cost of current books and serials subscription sin the area, using Blackwell North America approval plan book statistics and serials data from Faxon.[92] Thus, for a subject where the cost of books was \$40,000 and serial subscriptions \$60,000, the monograph-serials budgetary ratio would be 40:60 perçent.

Benefits of the formula approach are a complex array of variables is considered; a seemingly objective and equitable method is used; favoritism and politics are presumably eliminated from the process, or at least reduced; and, if applied on a regular basis, changing trends in the parent institution and the external environment (i.e., production and cost of materials) can be incorporated. On the negative side, formulas may work better for allocating book funds than serial funds; be time-consuming to implement; fail to adequately address document delivery and electronic journals;

and not be appropriate for interdisciplinary subject areas.

REFERENCES

1. Margaret Hawthorn, "Serials Selection and Deselection: A Survey of North American Academic Libraries," *Serials Librarian* 21, no. 1 (1991): 31. Also, 10 percent of the large and 13 percent of the small libraries reported written policies were under development or revision; 6 percent of the large libraries indicated all serials decisions were under the faculty's control with no policy input from the library. Her figures do not add to 100 percent.

2. G. Edward Evans, *Developing Library ad Information Centre Collections*, 3d ed. (Englewood, Colo.: Libraries Unlimited, 1995), 188.

3. Selma K. Richardson, *Magazines for Children: A Guide for Parent, Teachers, and Librarians*, 2d ed. (Chicago: American Library Association, 1991), xxiv.

4. Hawthron, "Serials Selection and Deselection," 37

5. Steve Black, "Summary: Collection Development and Indexing," SERIALST (February 14, 1997). The percentage is my own calculation from the raw data (16 of 21). Black speculates that indexing may increase in significance as budgets tighten.

6. American Library Association, *Guide to the Evaluation of Library Collections*, ed. Barbra Lockett (Chicago: American Library Association, 1989), 12

7. Hawthorn, "Serials Selection and Deselection," 36

8. Bill Katz and Linda Sternberg Katz, *Magazines for Libraries*, 9th ed. (New Providence, N.J.: R.R. Bowker, 1997).

9. Bill Katz, Magazine Selection: How to *Build a Community-Oriented Collection* (New York: R.R. Bowker, 1971), 27

10. Phyllis J. Van Order, the Collection Programme in Schools: Concepts, Practices, and Information Sources, 2d ed. (Englewood, Colo.: Libraries Unlimited, 1995), 161. The other five criteria were the contents' interest, appropriateness of format for the magazine's purpose and audience, whether any users require large print items, and index in.

11. Ross Atkinson, "The Citation As Inter-text: Toward a Theory of the Selection Process," *Library Resources and Technical Services* 28

(April/June 1984): 109-19.

12. Hawthron, "Serials Selection and deselection," 37, 39.

13. Bernard M. Fry and Herbert S. White, Publishers and Libraries: A study of Scholarly and Research Journals (Lexington, Mass.: Lexington Books, 1976).

14. Sandra R. Moline, "the Influence of Subject, Publisher Type and Quantity Published on Journal Prices," *Journal of Academic Librarianship* 15 (March 1989): 12-18.

15. Kate McCain, "refereed Journals, "SERIALIST (March 26, 1996).

16. Luke Swindler, "Serials Collection Development," In Managing Serials, by Marcia Tuttle (Greenwich, Conn.: JAI Press, 1996), 65-100.

17. Loriene Roy, "Weeding," *Encyclopedia of Library and Information Science* 54, supplement 17 (1994): 380-82.

18. Association for Library Collections and Technical Services, guide to Review of Library Collections: Preservation, Storage, and Withdrawal, ed. Lenore Clark (Chicago: American Library Association, 1991).

19. Thomas E. Nisonger, Collection Evaluation in Academic Libraries: a Literature Guide and Annotated Bibliography (Eglewood, Cle.: Libraries Unlimited, 1992) 167-76.

20. Judith A. Segal, "Journal Deselection: A Literature Review and an Application," Science and Technology Libraries 6 (spring 1986): 31.

21. Robert N. Broadus, "A Proposed Method for Eliminating Titles from Periodical Subscription Lists," *College and research Libraries* 46 (January 1985): 30-35.

22. Maurice B. Line, "Use of Citation Data for Periodicals Control in Libraries: A Response to Broadus, *College and Research Libraries* 46 (January 1985): 36-37.

23. Tony Stankus, "Journal Weeding in Relation to Declining Faculty member Publishing," *Science and Technology Libraries* 6 (spring 1986): 43-53.

24. Sherrie Schmid, Jane Tredwell, and Gloriana St. Clair, "Using dBaseIII+ to Create a Serials Review List," *Microcomputers for Information Management* 5 (September 1988): 169-82.

25. Stanley J. Slote, *Weeding Library Collections; Library Weeaing Methods*, 4th ed. (Englewood, Colo.: Libraries Unlimited, 1997).

26. Joseph P. Segal, *Evaluating and Weeding collections in Small and medium-Sized Public Libraries: The CREW Method* (Chicago: American Library Association, 1980).

27. Slote, *Weeding Library Collections*, 4th ed., 26.

28. Stanley J. Slote, *Weeding Library Collections: Library Weeding Methods*, ed e. (Englewood, Colo.: *Libraries Unlimited*, 1989), 15.

29. Segal, *Evaluating and Weeding Collections*, 15.

30. John Urguhart, "Relegation," in *Periodical Administration in Libraries: A Collection of Essays*, ed. Paul Mayes (London: Clive Bingley; Mahden, Conn.: Linnet Books, 1978), 117-18.

31. Association for Library Collections and Technical Services, *Guide to Review of Library Collections*, 26

32. Jamie Webstr Hastreiter, Larry Hardesty, and David Henderson, comps., Periodicals in college Libraries, CKIP Note 8 (Chicago: Association of college and Research Libraries, (1987), 9-10. Some of the percentages are my own recalculations from their raw data.

33. Dennis P. Carrigan, "From Just-in-Case to Just-in-time: Limits to the alternative Library Service Model," *Journal of Scholarly Publishing* 26 (April 1995): 178.

34. Mounir Khalil, "Document Delivery: A Better Option?" *Library Journal* 118 (February 1, 1993): 43-47.

35. Marcia Tuttle, *Managing Serials* (Greenwich, Conn.: JAAI Press, 1996), 314-20.

36. New York Times 143 (January 10, 1994): A5.

37. Mary E. Jackson and Karen Croneis, comps., Uses of Documen: Delivery Services, SPEC Kit 204 (Washington, D.C.: Association of Research Libraries, *Office of Management Studies*, 1994), 3-4. The percentages are my own calculations form the raw data.

38. Bill Coons and Peter McDonald, "Implications of Commercial Document delivery," *College and Research Libraries News* 56 (October 1995): 627.

39. Association of College and Research Libraries, *College Libraries Section* , standards Committee, "Standards for College Libraries,

1995 Edition," *College and Research Libraries News* 56 (April 1995): 247.

40. Coons and McDonald, "Implications of Commercial Document Delivery," 626.

41. Paul McCarthy, "Serial Killers; Academic Libraries Respond to Soaring Costs," *Library Journal* 119 (June 15, 1994): 44, citing Anthony w. Forguson, Kathleen Kehoe, and Barbara A Lit, Columbia university Scientific Information Study (New York: Columbia University Libraries, 1993).

42. Carol Tenopir and Donald W. King, "Setting the Record Straight on Journal Publishing: Myth vs. Reality," *Library Journal* 121 (March 15, 1996): 32.

43. Eleanor A. Gossen and Suzanne Irving, Ownership Versus Access and Low-Use Periodical Titles," *Library Resources and Technical Services* 39 (January 1995): 43.

44. Bruce R. Kingma with Suzanne Iriving, The Economics of Access Versus Ownership: The Costs and Benefits of Access to Scholarly Articles via Interlibrary Loan and Journal subscription (New York: Haworth Press, 1996), 39. Also issued as *Journal of Interlibrary Loan, Document Delivery and information* Supply 6, no. 3 (1996).

45. McCarthy "Serial Killers," 41.

46. Thomas E. Nisonger, "Access and Holdings: Integrating Issues of Access and Collection Development," *Library Acquisitions: Practice and Theory* 19 (spring 1995): 118-19. I summarized Goehner's presentation at the ALA 1994 Annual Conference.

47. John R. Hayes, "The Internet's First Victim," *Forbes 156* (December 18, 1995): 200-201.

48. Jackson and Croneis, *Uses of Document Delivery Services*, 5-6. Again, the percentages are my own calculations from the SPEC Kit's raw data.

49. CARL. Reveal Home Page. Available:http://uncweb.carl.org/reveal/index.html (Accessed March 8, 1998).

50. Rudolf Jacob Penner, "Measuring a Library's Capability," *Journal of Education for Librarianship* 13 (summer 1972): 17-30.

51. Murray S. Martin, *Academic Library Budgets* (Greenwich, Conn.: JAI Press, 1993).

52. Ann E Prentice, *Financial Planning for Libraries*, 2d ed. (Metuchen, J.J.: Scarecrow Press, 1996).

53. Richard S. Rounds, *Basic Budgeting Practices for Librarians*, 2d ed. (Chicago: American Library Association, 1994).

54. *American Library Association, Guide to Budget Allocation for Information Resources*, ed. Edward Shreeves (Chicago: American Library Association, 1991), 1-2.

55. Beverly P. Lynch, "A Library Director's Perspective on Collections and the Library User," In *Collection Management for the 1990s Proceedings of the mid-west Collection Management and Development Institute*, University of Illinois at Chicago, August 17-20, 1989, ed. Joseph J. Branin (Chicago: American Library association, 1993), 14. Lynch asserts, "Libraries must get control of their serials budgets."

56. Frederick C. Lynden, "Preliminary Estimate of the 1991/92 Serials Commitment," in Materials Budgets in ARL Libraries, SPEC Kit 166, comp. Peggy Johnson (Washington, D.C.: Association of research Libraries, *Office of Management Studies*, 1990), 97-104.

57. Hastereitr, Hardesty, and Henderson, *Periodicals in College Libraries*, 7. One library (0.8 percent of the respondents) reported it allocated periodical funds per faculty member.

58. Edeward S. Warner and Anita L. Anker, "Utilizing Library Constituents' Perceived Needs in Allocating Journal costs" *Journal of the American Society for Information Science* 30 (November 1979): 325.

59. *Ibid.*, 325-29.

60. The distinction between content and component analysis is briefly discussed by Thomas E. Nisonger, "Editing the RLG Conspectus to Analyses the OCLC Archival Tapes of Seventeen Texas Libraries, *Library Resources and Technical Services* 29 (October/December 1985): 322, based on Glyn T. Evans, Roger Gifford, and Donald R. Franz, Collection Development Analysis Using OCLC Archival tapes: Final Report (Albany, N.Y.: SUNY Office of Library Services, 1977). ERIC Document ED 152 299.

61. Hawthron, "Serials Selection and Deselection," 33.

62. *Ibid.*

63. Hasteier, Hardesty, and Henderson, Periodicals in College Libraries, 69.

64. Frederick C. Lynden, "the Impact of the Rising Costs of Books and Journals on the Overall Library Budget," of *Library Administration* 10, no. 1 (1989): 89.

65. Lynch, "A Library Director's Perspective," 7.

66. Jeanie M. Welch, "Document Deliver," *SERIALST* (January 31, 1995). Unfortunately, the posting is ambiguous is regard to whether X represents the number of items cancelled titles were used, or the number of canceled titles multiplied by the number of their uses.

67. Jackson and Croies, *Uses of Document Delivery Services*, 5-6. Again, the percentages are my own calculations from the SPEC Kit's raw data.

68. Peggy Johnson, "Materials Budgets in ARL Libraries," SPEC Flyer 166 (July 1990): 2, in *Materials Budgets in ARL Librâries*, SPEC Kit 166, comp. Peggy Johnson (Washington, D.C. Association of Research Libraries, Office of Management Studies, 1990).

69. Siegried Feller, "Developing the serials collection," In *Collection Development in Libraries*: A Treatise, pt. B, ed. Robert Do Stueat and George B. Miller Jr. (Greenwich, Conn.: JAI Press, 1980), 508.

70. Robin B. Devn, "Who's Using What?" *Library Acquisitions: Practice and Theory* 13, no. 2 (1989): 169.

71. "Standards for Community, Junior, and Technical College Learning Resources Programmes," *College and Research Libraries News* 55 (October 1994): 577. [Prepared by a Joint Committee at the Association for Educational Communications and Technology (AECT) and ACRL, Co-chairs, Marilyn McDonald and Gretchen H. Neill.]

72. American Association of School Librarians and Association for Educational Communications and Technology, *Information Power: Guidelines for School Library Media Programs* (Chicago: America Library Association: Washington, D.C.: Association for Educational Communications and Technology, 1988), 117-23.

73. *Ibid.*, 127-30.

74. Stella Bentley and David Farrell, "Beyond Retrenchment: The Reallocation of a Library Materials Budget," *Journal of Academic Librarianship* 10 (January 1985): 323.

75. Johnson, "Materials Budgets in ARL Libraries," 2.

76. Robin B Devin and Martha Kellogg, "the Serial/Monograph Ratio

in Research Libraries: Budgeting in Light of Citation studies," *College and Research Libraries* 51 (January 1990): 46-54.

77. Micheael Bowman, "Format Citation Patterns and Their Implications for Collection Development in Research Libraries," *Collection Building* 11, no. 1 (1991): 2-8.

78. Devin, "Who's Using What?" 167-70.

79. Tony Stanks and William Littlefield, "One Researcher, One Journal, One Research Paper: Workable Budgeting schemes at the Science Departmental level," In Scientific Journals: Issues in *Library Selection and Management*, ed. Tony Stankus (New York: Haworth Press, 1987), 199-208.

80. Mary Sellen, "Book Budget Formula Allocations; A Review Essay," *Collection Management* 9 (winter 1987): 13-24.

81. John M. Budd, "allocation formulas in the Literature: A Review," *Library Acquisitions: Practice and Theory* 15, no. 1 (1991): 95-107.

82. Stankus and Littlefield, "One Researcher, One Journal, One Research Paper," 208.

83. Hastreiter, Hardesty, and Henderson, *Periodicals in College Libraries*, 7.

84. John M. Budd and Kay Adams, "Allocation Formulas in Practice," *Library Acquisitions: Practice and Theory* 13, no. 4 (1989) 383-85. However, 145 (40.6 Percent) used a formula for materials fund allocation, primarily for books.

85. Jane H. Tuten and Beverly Jones, comps., *Allocation Formulas in Academic Libraries*, CLIP Note 22 (Chicago: Association of College and Research Libraries, 1995), 16, 21. The percentages are my own calculations form the raw data. In total, 40 Percent (76 of 192) of the responding libraries used an allocation for at least some type of information resource.

86. Peggy Johnson, comp., *Materials Budgets in ARL Libraries*, SPEC Kit 166 (Washington, D.C.: Association of Research Libraries, Office of Management Studies, 1990), 13. Four additional libraries had future plans to use of formula.

87. Hastreiter, Hardesty, and Henderson, *Periodicals in College Libraries*, 66-74.

88. Laura O. Rein and others, "Formula-Based Subject allocation: A Practical Approach," *Collection Management* 17, no. 4 (1993): 25-48.

89. Carol cubberley, "allocating the Materials Funds Using Total Cost of Materials," *Journal of Academic Librarianship* 19 (March 1993): 16-21.

90. Mollie Niemeyer and others, "Balancing Act for Library Materials Budgets: Use of a Formula allocation," *Technical Services Quarterly* 11, no.1 (1993): 43-60.

91. Merran Evans, "Library Acquisitions Formulae: The Monash experience," *Asustralian Academic and research Libraries* 27 (March 1996): 47-57.

92. Charles B. Lowry, "Reconciling Pragmatism, Equity and need in the Formula Allocation of Book and Serial Funds," *College and Research Libraries* 53 (March 1992): 121-28.

CHAPTER 7

Collection Development and Information Management

When it comes to the school library, the collection must reflect a balance between supporting the teaching and learning in the school and providing resources to meet individual needs and interests. *Selection* of materials however, should not be limited just to information needs, but should include resources that will challenge and inspire students and staff alike. Collection development is the process of developing and maintaining a range of resources that will meet the information needs of the library's users.

The collection development policy should be evaluated on an annual basis to meet the needs of the changing curriculum framework and teaching needs. A useful way of doing this is to ensure that it is presented for discussion at a staff meeting towards the end of the year. Provide copies of the document prior to the meeting, so all staff have an opportunity to contribute. Along with *library staff*, members of the *library committee*, teaching staff, the Principal and other school community members should be involved in ratifying the document.

A collection development policy is essential for all school libraries and should be written to outline what the collection will contain and why it exists. It describes the underlying principles and parameters of the school's collection of information resources. It should be developed as part of the school plan.

A collection development policy can:

- Describe the scope and purpose of the collection and how it relates to the school's purpose and goals.
- Encourage the development of a relevant, quality collection, including the selection of new resources and the withdrawing of inappropriate resources.
- Ensure equity of access to information for all users.
- Define the roles and responsibilities of people involved in collection development.
- Guide *budget* planning and facilitate future planning.
- Assist in the *evaluation of the collection.*
- Guide the decisions about the acceptance and recording of *gifts and donations*.
- Assist in the review of *disputed materials* and outline procedures for resolving issues regarding disputed materials.

ALIA's guidelines for the development of a collection development policy can be found at: http://www.nla.gov.au/libraries/resource/acliscdp.html

Sample collection development policies are included at: http://www.sldirectory.com/libsf/resf/coldev2.html.

A comprehensive collection development policy may include criteria for selecting various resource formats, including physical and digital resources, and another separate set of criteria for selecting *suppliers*. Conversely, these criteria may be encompassed in separate policies – the Selection Policy and the *Acquisition* Policy. In a small school library the collection development policy will probably be all inclusive. Whichever policy format is used, subscriptions to online information services, CD-ROM purchase, networking of information resources across the school and the library policy of collecting digital resources should be included.

Collection Evaluation

Collection evaluation is a good way to make sure that the

needs of the students and staff of the school are being met and resources are being kept up-to-date. The purpose of collection evaluation is to ensure that the collection reflects the reasons it was established and maintained.

This process should be ongoing and it should take into account the following:

- Capacity of the collection to meet the school's needs.
- Need to maintain up-to-date resources.
- Age and condition of the resources.
- Resources which are no longer relevant to the school's need.
- Resources are in a variety of formats.
- Technological developments.
- Online subscriptions versus hard copy
- Online subscriptions versus access to hard copy materials.
- Library staffing, space and funding levels.
- Licence and access conditions for online resources.

By continually monitoring the collection it is ensured that:

- An up-to-date collection with an average age of less than 10 years is maintained.
- Relevance of resources is reconsidered after approximately six years. The rate of change of knowledge in some specific areas may determine that a resource is obsolete before 10 years.
- *Worn and inappropriate material* is discarded, with at least 10 % of the items being replaced annually.
- Journal and electronic resource subscriptions are relevant and cost effective.

In *Learning for the future*: Developing information services in schools (ASLA, 2nd ed. 2001, p. 30) recommended standards for the size of the collection compared with student numbers are given. For example, in a school of 450 enrolled students there should be a school library collection of approximately 10,454 resources (including all formats) which are up-to-date and less than 10 years old.

Figures for additional access to electronic resources such as CD ROMs, electronic subscription services and the Internet are also included and must be considered when evaluating the collection.

Criteria for Selection

The selection of resources for the school library is an important task. Selecting the right resources for the library, whether through purchase or other means, is the key to success. Selection should be based on the school's *collection development policy* and should take a systematic approach to ensure currency and relevance.

While the teacher-librarian has overall responsibility for selection of resources, staff, students and other school community members may have the opportunity to suggest titles or items. A suggestion box could be set up in the library or staff room. A web based form can also be set up on the *school library home page* encouraging students and teachers to make requests for purchase (NB the form needs to be carefully worded to ensure that staff and students are aware that making a request does not guarantee purchase).

Sample request form:

REQUEST FOR SCHOOL LIBRARY PURCHASE

Please circle Staff/student

Name ……………………………………………

Please give details of your request. Fill in as much information as you can

Title & Author if you know

It………………………………………………………

Subject……………………… Format (e.g., book/dvd/cdrom)………………

Cost………………………ISBN………………………………………………

How did you find out about it?

....

Date..................... .

NB This is a request that will be considered for purchase if it meets the collection development policy and sufficient funds are available

Selection is a process that is based on:

- school priorities
- the budget
- recognized selection criteria
- school library's collection development policy

A variety of tools are available to help in the selection process:

- Bibliographies like Global Books in Print.
- Review journals like Magpies at http://www.magpies.net.au/
- Internet sites
- Books
- Other advertising pamphlets and leaflets.

Use the State Library of Tasmania website to locate some useful tools to help in the selection process http://explore.statelibrary.tas.gov.au/Nav/Topic.asp? Topic-Books%2C +magazines+and+literature.

The DELIC Electronic Software Acquisitions Programme (ESAP) can also provide guidance. The ESAP evaluated electronic resources have already been selected according to specific criteria relating to school libraries. Substantial discounts have also been negotiated by DELIC for site licenses for Tasmanian schools. So it is always wise to go to the DELIC ESAP site when considering the purchase of electronic resources. See http://www.education.tas. gov.au/esap/default.htm.

When deciding on which resources to acquire a set of criteria should be used to evaluate each item. A general set of criteria can be used for all resources, or a specific one may be used for specific formats or genres, for example for fiction, non-fiction, CD-ROMs, URLs, kits, etc.

An example of some general selection criteria:

- Purpose
  - Is it relevant to students or staff?
  - Does it achieve what it sets out to do?
  - Does it appeal to the target age group?
  - Does it fit in with the *collection development policy*?
  - Does the library have the appropriate equipment to use the resource?
- Suitability
  - Ease of use
  - Clarity of illustration
  - Use of language
  - Target audience
  - Are special storage or shelving requirements needed?
- Production
  - Quality
  - Ease of use and safety
  - Durability
  - Accessibility
  - Attractiveness
- Value for money
  - Standard of production
  - How many years will its context be relevant for?
  - Library need
  - Minority appeal
  - Authority (credentials) of creator
- Equal opportunities
  - How are cultures, religions, ethnic diversity, gender and disabilities presented in text and image?

Criteria for evaluating specific types of resources can be found at; http://www.eddept.wa.edu.au/cmis/eval/library/selection/index.htm*cmissel

The Queensland Education Department has a draft set of guidelines for evaluating resources to suit the Queensland curriculum:

General Criteria
http://education.qld.gov.au/information/service/libraries/reosurce/evalc-core.html.

WWW sites: http://education.qld.gov.au/information/service/libraries/resource/e/valc-site.html

There is also a section on developing a section policy: http://education.qld.gov.au/information/service/libraries/resource/evalg-develop.html

Suppliers

Library suppliers offer a wide range of materials, which can be viewed in catalogues, on CD-ROM or the Internet or by bringing them into the school. A school library visit to a remote school by a library supplier is an excellent service as materials may be purchased straight away. It is essential that the supplier notifies library staff of a planned visit well in advance to ensure the proposed date for the visit is suitable and to enable library staff to alert teachers of the visit.

The new resources can be displayed in the school staff room and teaching staff given an opportunity to make recommendations for selection. This can also be a useful device for promoting the school library. Libraries can also invite students and/or parents to assist in selecting library materials. This has the added benefit of ensuring that the library stock is relevant to the users and fostering relationships between students and library staff. Often the library supplier will stay for the afternoon or day that the display is being held. Adequate security measures should be taken to ensure no displayed items are lost.

Stock may be purchased from suppliers at their location, especially if the school is located nearby to the outlet.

Before purchase, it is important to check the library catalogue to ensure an item is not already held by the library. It is also important to ensure that any new purchases fit in with the library's *collection development policy*. The library manager should guide the purchases.

Any items selected by teaching staff should be purchased if funds allow (professional judgement on the part of the teacher ensures that the resource is relevant to the curriculum), but if funds are running low at the time, the title may be noted and placed in a Desiderata file for future purchase.

There are basically three types of suppliers and these may provide different levels of service:

Retailers (Booksellers/Distributors)

These are useful for commercial (popular) publications and there are some Tasmanian bookshops that specialize in providing services to school libraries.

Most retailers will:

- Supply any items which are currently available in Australia
- Order from overseas and handle any overseas payments

Publishers/Producers

These are useful for publications in a specific subject area – i.e., Scholastic Press publishes material especially for school libraries at http://www.scholastic.com.

Most publishers/producers will:

- Supply only items which they publish/produce or for which they hold the Australian agency
- Immediately supply any items in stock or can give immediate information on future availability of these items.

Wholesalers/Discount Houses

- Can only supply what is available at the time.
- Can be a source of bargains, but this can encourage impulse buying.

Libraries may stick with the one supplier or they may use a variety of supplier according to their particular needs. When choosing a supplier the following should be taken into account:

- Are they accurate in filling orders?
- Are they accurate in accounting?
- Are they willing to offer discounts?
- Is the service fast and accurate?
- Do they provide status reports?
- Will they back order?
- Do they allow for cancellation of orders?
- What is their returns policy?
- What add-on services do they provide –i.e. can they provide items shelf ready?

To be a good buyer the following points should be considered:

- When ordering, provide enough accurate information for the supplier to be able to identify the item.
- Pay promptly.
- Be specific about any instructions such as where to send goods, invoices, correspondence.
- Ensure that there are sufficient funds to cover any purchases by keeping accurate records of encumbered funds.

Useful website for specialist subject suppliers:

For out of print or rare books Try http://www. biblioquest. com.au/

Some format specific suppliers in the educational area include:

Videos http://www.actf.com.au/learning centrenew/catalogue/ htm/about.htm

Educational software http://www.education.tas.gov.au/esap/ default.htm.

Maths and science kits http://www.klikkomath.com/enquiries-

and-ordering-aus.html

Historical kits and CD ROMs http://www.naa.gov.au/education/education.html

Suppliers of equipment for use within the school library should be evaluated before purchase. Some criteria for evaluation includes:

- Price
- Capability of equipment
- Durability of equipment
- Maintenance and service back up
- Ease of use.

If you are a TALIS library, check the equipment list for TALIS on the Systems Support web page:

http://www.statelibrary.tas.gov.au/systems/contacts/schools.htm. >Software and networking > Equipment list for TALIS before purchasing computer hardware, software and accessories. With the increasing opportunity for online shopping, it may be possible for school library staff with access to a school credit card to purchase materials online.

Online ordering may be possible from Tasmanian distributors.

Gifts and Donations

The school library may receive donations or gifts of material from other sources. These gifts may be solicited or unsolicited.

Unsolicited gifts/donations may be accepted by the library. Conditions for the acceptance of gifts or donations into the school library's collection should be clearly stated in the *collection development policy*. In particular, school libraries should decide:

- Whether all gifts will be accepted regardless of conditions imposed by donor
- Whether gifts/donations will be accepted only if there are no conditions attached.

Some donors want their bequests to be publicized. This is

best achieved with a book plate and the library may like to design or purchase some for inclusion in the donated items.

However, it is important to carefully consider the gift in the light of the library's collection development policy. It is essential that the inclusion of the donation into the library's collection meets the criteria set out in the policy. If the gift is not suitable, the collection development policy should clearly and sensitively state *methods for disposal* of unwanted gifts and donations.

Solicited donations can be a useful way of increasing the resources of the school library with a limited *budget.* Annual reports from major Tasmanian companies in the school library's area may be useful for the World Futures essential, for example. Other solicited gifts/donations can be obtained through researching your local area and contacting community groups. Once again, however, it is essential to ensure that the resources are appropriate to the information needs of the school library group and as such must always be evaluated against the collection development policy.

Budgeting

Budgeting is a managerial tool used for planning and facilitating decisions about the allocation of available funds. The purpose of the budget is to express financially how the library will achieve its outcomes. As such, it must be linked to the school's priorities and plans. By keeping a detailed budget the library manager is able to clearly demonstrate the *collection development policy.*

What have a Budget?

- To justify the allocation of funds.
- To provide accountability for items of expenditure.
- To set planning parameters for the school administration.
- To identify priorities of the library and school.
- To develop school awareness of the financial requirements of the library.

Scope of the Budget

A budget includes costs associated with:

- Collection development
- Building/furniture/equipment maintenance
- Growth in priority/areas
- Administration costs of the library
- Projects e.g. automation, security system
- Whole-school site licences or subscriptions to on line materials
- Some school libraries may have to include staff salaries in their budget planning.

Characteristics of a Good Budget

A good budget.

- Is an ongoing process.
- Includes all relevant items.
- Is clear and easy to read.
- Is well documented and publicized.
- Ensures that forthcoming needs are clearly identifies and costed.
- Is fair and appropriate.

In order to assess adequate funding for learning resources consider:

- The cost of replacing outdated or worn out resources and filling stock gaps.
- Learning resources need to be regularly replaced in order to be relevant to the needs of the curriculum and the reading and information needs of pupils and teachers.
- The importance of planning ahead and costing for ICT developments including: Internet access, CD-ROMs, online databases.
- The proportion of funding required for developing new curricula areas.
- The need for funding both books and non-book materials.

Acquisition Budget

- A detailed budget showing encumbered funds should be kept for all orders sent to suppliers
- The budget should show at a glance how much money has been encumbered.
- The budget should also include provision for GST and the astute Library Manager will ensure that any GST paid from the library budget comes back into the library budget by liaising closely with the Bursar
- The budget should be linked to the various collections in the *Essential Learnings Framework* so that a balanced collection is developed
- The budget should be kept as a separate document for use by the library even if the Administrative Officer is responsible for paying the *orders* and keeps her/his own records as it demonstrates the principles behind collection development.

Example

Collection code	Order/Supplier and date	Title	Amount encumbered (includes GST)	Balance ($2,000)
WF (World futures	Sandy Bay News agency 223/9/02	Belgium: a political Perspective	$58.90	$1941.10
T (Thinking)	Dymock's 30/9/02	Six red hats	$22.50	$1918.60
PF (Personal futures)	Amazon.com 2/10/02	Acne and how to treat it (includes CD ROM)	$100.00	$1818.60

Ordering

After the *selection* process when resources have been selected to meet the needs of the collection, or when a request has been received, an order must be placed with a particular *supplier*.

Before an order can be placed, if the purchase is based on a request, bibliographic verification to establish the correct title, author, etc details must be carried out. The library's catalogue must also be checked to ensure the item is not already held in the collection.

A number of sources can be used for bibliographic verification including other union catalogues like the *National Bibliographic Database* or *TALIS*.

The order is then prepared with sufficient details to initiate and track the order, including selecting the supplier, finding the *funds* and issuing claims if necessary.

Methods of ordering are commonly automated, including dispatching the order. Orders may be sent by post, fax, phone or online methods, but details must be filed to enable order tracking. There are also different types of orders, which entail special methods of ordering such as standing orders, blanket orders, standard orders and subscriptions.

It is important that the library establishes the most appropriate supplier for the material it is ordering. Very different suppliers from those supplying normal orders generally handle subscriptions, rare books and government publications.

Problems in Ordering

- *Cancellations* – funds allocated for expenditure but not expended during the financial year usually revert to the general school fund. Therefore it is very important that school libraries carefully monitor outstanding titles when the end of the financial year is approaching. They may choose to cancel the order and re-submit in the new financial year to avoid losing funds, or they may arrange a credit note for the items to be supplied later. Long-standing outstanding orders particularly need to be followed up.
- *Failure to publish* – sometimes and order is placed with a supplier on the basis of pre-publication Information. It can

happen that the item is never published. When this occurs, either a credit note is arranged or the order is cancelled. Regular supplier reports are essential to inform of the progress of outstanding orders.

- *Out of print material* – if a school library has a desiderata file of out of print material that it would like to obtain, it may place this with one or more specialist suppliers. The desiderate file should always be checked as part of the pre-order process as occasionally the items may be requested.
- *Grey literature* – literature which is not normally available through normal bookselling channels and therefore difficult to identify and obtain such as conference proceedings, annual reports or items that are published in developing countries without an established book trade. Like OOP (out of print) resources, these orders may need to be placed with a particular supplier.
- *Claim periods* – the time during which a supplier will replace a damaged item or supply one that has failed to arrive, varies considerably. It is essential that claims are made in a timely manner and that items received are carefully checked before any marking is done on them.
- *Title changes* – in the interim between the order being placed and the arrival of the item itself, especially for items that have not been published, titles may have changed. It is important that school library staff are aware of this possibility and check all details carefully for items received against outstanding orders.

Receiving Orders

Checking new materials is a task that usually falls to the library technician or library assistant. The procedure may be:

- Sort mail before opening and ensure correct destination.
- Open deliveries carefully to avoid damaging contents.
- Locate the packing slip an invoice (sometimes sent separately). Non-urgent materials without accompanying

invoices or a copy of the order can be set aside to be dealt with at a later date or when the invoice arrives.

- Check that the material received matches the packing slip, invoice and order form.
- Check that materials are in good condition.
- Locate any urgent materials or materials require special handling.
- If the material received is satisfactory, the date of receipt and actual cost of the item is added to the order form.
- Update library records to reflect the in-process nature of the item.
- Update the school library budget.
- Send invoice for payment to appropriate authority (usually school bursar).
- Catalogue item.
- Notify requestor of arrival of material or prepare new resources list.

The receipt of library materials also includes other procedures such as:

- *Returns* – even the most reliable library suppliers make mistakes sometimes. Generally an order is considered binding once shipment has been made or the order acknowledged. It may only be cancelled or altered with the agreement of the supplier, unless incorrect items are supplied in which case they can be returned without permission. Mistakes made in placing the order (such as the library supplying the incorrect information) are binding, unless the library and supplier have built up a good relationship.
- *Claims* – a claim is a communication to a supplier regarding the non-arrival of overdue orders. Claiming should be done regularly and amount of time to wait before claiming depends on the kind of order under consideration. For example, foreign orders cannot be filled as quickly as domestic orders.

- *Statistics* – should be kept by type of supplier and speed of service to give an overview and allow for evaluation of supplier performance.

Processing

The processing of library materials should be consistent. It is a good idea to document how each stage of the processing is carried out so that all members of the *library staff* know how if should be done.

The order in which the items should be processed should be established. Shelves in the workroom can be identified and labelled for each stage, e.g. "new Items," "To be covered" or "Needs Spine Labels."

Decisions need to be made about how different materials should be prepared such as kits, AV materials and CDROMs. How they are processed also depends on where and how they will be *shelved.*

All items should:

- Be stamped with the school stamp in a number of places. For a book the most usual places are on the title page or inside cover, halfway through the book, and once more towards the end.
- Be barcoded (if the library is automated), with a barcode that should be attached in the same place on each item (*note*: consider future inventory procedures when making the decision about the placement of barcodes). TALIS school libraries should purchase their barcodes from State Purchasing and Sales.
- Have cards, pockets, date due slips typed and attached if using a manual circulation system.
- Have a tattle-tag placed in them if an electronic security system exists. The types of tattle tag you use will vary depending on the particular format you are tagging. Video recordings and computer discs such as floppy discs or CD ROMs cannot be tagged with security tape that requires

sensitizing and desensitising as information stored on the disc will be erased. (Refer to the manual for your security system or check with your supplier).

- Be covered if they are books or housed in suitable storage boxes or bags if they are other materials that need protection.
- Have a spine label with the Dewey number or location prefix on it attached once it has been catalogued. Spine labels can be printed off from the automated library system.

For book covering and basic book repairs there is a useful instructional video produced by RAECO called *Keeping books alive* – available for loan to Tasmanian schools from the Media Collection at DELIC (Call Number V1731 and V1731A). RAECO products are provided in Tasmania by TOPS – see http://www.tops.com.au – and they are an authorized library supplier.

If you would like some instructions on how to go about covering books and processing other materials contact the *Department of Education Library and Information Centre*.

Useful Websites

Book repair: http://www.dartmouth.edu/~preserve/repair/repairindex.htm.

Cataloguing and Classifying Resources

Cataloguing is the collection of all the information about an item (i.e. its bibliographic information) in a formal way. This includes the author, title, publisher, etc., including the assignment of subject headings and classification numbers.

Cataloguing is a professional activity, with the teacher-librarian having control over the key processes to ensure the quality of the catalogue. The catalogue must be constructed and maintained correctly in order to perform its function of retrieving information. When new items are added to the school library collection, it is essential to ensure that catalogue records for those items can be located in the school's Public Access Catalogue. This usually entails adding holdings to an existing catalogue record, or creating a new one.

Similarly, when items are deleted from the collection, the catalogue record or holding for that item should be deleted. Thus the school library's catalogue accurately reflects the resources held in the school library centre. Systems at the *State Library* may be contacted for more information on 6233 7939. Schools without a teacher-librarian are restricted to adding holdings onto TALIS records and are unable to add original catalogue records to the shared database unless alternative arrangements are made. Contact Systems Support to discuss the range of cataloguing options available to school libraries.

Every item in the collection must be described using a standard format, with the same basic components contained in each description. The descriptions must always be cited in the same order and employ consistent punctuation. AACR2 Rev. ed. (Anglo-American Cataloguing Rules 2nd revised edition), Dewey Decimal Classification and the TALIS cataloguing manual (given to all school libraries at TALIS training) should be used in order to assure consistency. The standardization of procedures helps in the local, national and international exchange of bibliographic data and is essential in computerised systems.

TALIS libraries, including school libraries, use Library of Congress Subject Headings to assign headings to records in the shared database.

School libraries that do not have access to centralized cataloguing have a number of options. They may:

- do their own original cataloguing
- purchase commercially produced cataloguing
- or use a combination of the above

If they create their own records it is advisable to keep a record of decisions that are made with regard to classifying of items and level of catalogue description. AACR2R and DDC should be used, along with appropriate subject heading lists from either SCIS (Schools Cataloguing and Information Service).

http://www.curriculum.edu.au/scis/ or LCSH (Library of congress Subject Headings) http://www.loc.gov/cds/lcsh.html.

Commercially produced catalogue records may be purchased from the National Library through its Kinetica service http://www.nla.gov.au.kinetica/or from SCIS.

Cataloguing Digital Resources

Librarians and teacher librarians are becoming increasingly aware of the growing need to collect URLs, perhaps to include on the school intranet or school library web page. These resources form part of the library collection and should be included in the Collection Development policy.

Metadata provides a system for cataloguing online resources. DELIC's *metadata web page* has information about what metadata is and how it is used.

Cataloguing Library Resources for the Essential Learnings (ELs)

School library resources that are suitable for the Tasmanian Curriculum Essential Learnings Framework can be identified in TALIS by the application of the 690 Essential Learnings Marc Tag and/or Library of Congress subject headings that correspond to the Values of Education, to TALIS title records by school library cataloguing staff.

690 Essential Learnings (ELs) Tag

The Essential Learnings Framework is comprised of five Essential Learnings (Thinking, Communicating, Personal Futures, Social Responsibility, World Futures, each of which is divided into Key Element Outcomes. (Essential Learnings Outcomes Chart: http://www.education. tas.gov.au/ocll/outcomeschart.pdf)

The relationship between the Essential Learnings and the Key Learning Areas (KLAs) is best represented diagrammatically as provided on the Learning, Teaching and Assessment Guide website: http://ltag.education.tas.gov.au/effectteach/units7 10/thinking.htm.

Guidelines for use of the 690 Essential Learnings Tag

The use of the 690 Essential Learnings Tag is optional. School libraries are not required, and are strongly discouraged, from going back through their entire collection and applying this tag.

School library resources can be tagged as either suitable for specific Essential Learnings, Key Element Outcomes or both.

The 690 Essential Learnings Tag can be applied to fiction and non-fiction school library resources, as well as the various formats – videos, DVDs CD ROMs CDs, serials, kits and print items.

Given the nature of the Essential Learnings Framework most library resources can, in some way, be used to support the teaching of one or more Essential Learnings. The aim, however, is that only those resources that have been specifically identified as being useful in the teaching of a particular Essential Learning or Key Element Outcome be tagged to ensure that relevant, useful search results will be obtained by school library patrons.

It is strongly recommended that school library staff seek out and accept recommendations from teaching staff in terms of resources that are suitable to be tagged. Assigning the Essential Learnings tag to a library resource should be viewed as a collaborative effort between school library and teaching staff.

The following may assist in identifying library resources that best address the Essential Learnings.

When to apply the 690 Essential Learnings Tag

For all types of library resources:

- The topic/subject matter of the resource focuses on a issue that is significant within the Essential Learnings Framework and positively builds deep understanding.

Example: Marine Education kit

(World Futures: Investigating the natural and constructed world; World futures: Creating sustainable futures).

- The resource can be used to *directly* teach an Essential Learning Key Element Outcome or Professional Development material that specifically addresses or develops knowledge about the teaching of the Essential Learnings.

Example: Teacher reference book on teaching thinking skills (Thinking)
Picture book that explores bullying (Personal Futures: Being ethical)

For electronic resources, the following criteria may also be of use to support the inclusion of an Essential Learnings tag. The resource:

- caters for diverse learning styles and multiple intelligences
- promotes higher order thinking
- presents authentic learning tasks
- builds on students' prior knowledge

When not to apply the 690 Essential Learning Tag

- Topical resources that would be used to assist in research or to answer a big question.

Examples: Non-fiction book on dinosaurs
CDROM on Astronomy

- Resources that do not *directly* relate to the Essential Learnings but may be used to support the teaching of an Essential Learning.

Examples: Video on cartooning techniques – may be used to support the teaching of "Being arts literate"

Posters of Australian animals – may be used to support the teaching of "Investigating the natural and constructed world"

- A useful educational resource, but no Essential Learnings specific.

Examples: Map of the World
Calculators

Library of Congress Subject Headings for the Values of Education

The Essential Learnings Framework is based on a core set of

values: Connectedness, Resilience, Achievement, Creativity, Integrity, Responsibility and Equity. The following list of Library of Congress Subject Headings, developed by Jennie Bales (Summerdale Primary School) and Michael Baker (State Library – Cataloguing), correspond to the values and may be used to identify suitable library resources. For more information on the Values of Education as defined by the Essential Learnings Framework refer to the Values and Purposes Statement: http://www.education. tas.gov.au/ocll/publications/ valuespurposes. pdf.

Value	*LC Subject heading*
Resilience	Resilience (personality trait) – Fiction
Achievement	Success – Fiction Also See references to this heading from Personal growth and Self-improvement subject headings
Creativity	Creative ability – Fiction
Integrity	Integrity – Fiction
Responsibility	Responsibility - Fiction Also see references to this heading from Accountability and Obligation subject headings
Equity	Social justice – Fiction Toleration – Fiction
Connectedness	Connectedness - Fiction

Unwanted/Inappropriate Resources

Disputed materials are those that may be considered controversial or offensive to students, staff or other school community members.

The way to handle these objections should be documented clearly in the school library's *collection development policy*. A procedure should be arrived at through discussions with the principal, who has responsibility to the school community for all activities conducted in the school.

Whether the objections are on political, racial or moral grounds, by having in place a policy, and procedures to follow, the complaints can be handled in a logical, non-emotive and established way.

The procedures should state clearly:

- How will the objector be asked to document their concerns? (It may be useful to devise a form for objectors to complete)
- What will the process of review be?
- Who will reassess the material?
- Will it be temporarily withdrawn from the collection while awaiting a decision?
- What will happen to the material once a decision has been made? For example, will it be available for all students or only certain students?
- How will the objector be informed of the school's procedures and decision?

A review *committee* should carefully consider the implications of withdrawing useful materials form all students in response to an objection from a minority group. As much as possible the library's collection should reflect a balance of views from different perspectives on major issues.

Weeding

Regular reviews of library stock (both physical and digital) should be carried out to ensure that resources remain relevant and attractive. Culling the resource collection, sometimes referred to as weeding, involves the removal and disposal of materials and cancelling of subscriptions that are no longer considered suitable for the collection. This process is Just as important as the initial selection of materials and should be carried out on a regular basis. *Systems* Support at the State Library of Tasmania have clearly developed criteria for weeding the physical collection.

Guidelines and procedures for culling should be included in the library collection development policy.

Criteria for culling should be established, similar to those used for selection. Schools may find the following suggested criteria useful for physical collections.

Physical Condition

- Torn, scratched or worn out
- Damaged beyond repair
- Unattractive

Content and Form

- Inaccurate, biased or misleading information
- Dated or obsolete formats
- Stereotyping of race, culture or sex role
- Irrelevance to the curriculum and current teaching and learning methods
- Inappropriate or irrelevant to the needs and interests of users

Use Patterns

- Declining because interest has waned
- Declining because materials were acquired to meet specific needs which no longer exist

An interesting and somewhat useful website is the Sunlink Weed of the Month Club based in Florida: http://ww.sunlink. ucf.edu/ weed/

Disposal of Culled Materials

Culled and damaged library materials, should be removed from the collection and disposed of according to approved procedures. Remove the item from the shelves and remember to remove the catalogue record for the item from the library catalogue This may involve simply removing the holdings from a union catalogue, such as *TALIS*, or removing the whole record if your school library is the only school to hold the item. It is also essential to ensure that the item is clearly labelled as having been withdrawn from the collection. A special purpose stamp is often purchased for this purposes.

It the material is found to be offensive, outdated or in poor condition then it should be permanently disposed of. However, if the material has declining use patterns for different reasons, other libraries or collections may find it useful.

Suggested methods of disposal include:

- Pulping
- Waste removal
- Exchange with other schools
- Gift to other school or a more suitable agency such as a charity
- Wiping an reusing video and audio tapes
- School library book/resource sale

If you decide to have a sale, it is essential to ensure that all appropriate procedures for withdrawing the item as previously detailed, have been carried out. It is important to check with other teaching staff and the principal to ensure all are in agreement before the sale goes ahead. This is where a collection development policy that includes criteria for withdrawing items is very important as staff may have a vested interest in some of the material you have decided to withdraw and may challenge your choices. Being able to point to the criteria included in the policy is extremely compelling, especially if the policy has already been approved. Ensure that items are for sale for a nominal fee, thereby ensuring the advantages of the book sale are achieved.

Advantages of holding a book/resource sale include:

- Provides an opportunity for students who may have no books, videos, CDs, etc. at home to acquire some.
- Cost effective as no couriers are required to pick up the resources for exchange/pulping/donation.

- Cost effective as a nominal sum may be charged fo. the item and that money can go back into the school library *budget*.
- *Promotes* the library and may encourage students and staff who rarely use the school library to come into the centre

Weeding of Digital Resources

Donna M. Shannon in her chapter included in *Providing more with less: collection management for school libraries* (2nd ed.), says that 'keeping Web links current is an essential part of maintaining digital resources.' (p. 228).

Link checking software is available to weed out dead links and save library staff time when checking for changed links. It must be remembered that the software is unable to evaluate content.

The library's collection development policy should contain clear guidelines for the selection of digital resources so that the reverse policy might apply to the de-selection of such resources.

Contracts and licensing agreements must be adhered to when weeding digital resources. Some resources will need to be carefully removed once subscriptions have expired.

When cancelling subscriptions to electronic journals, consideration should be given to the lack of access to back copies of the journal once the subscription ends.

Bibliography

Dillon, Henri, J. & Mcgregor, J. (2001), *Providing more with less: collection management for school libraries*. 2nd ed. Centre for Information studies Charles Sturt University, Wagga Wagga.

Stocktaking/Inventory

The purpose of carrying out a stocktake is to identify missing items. It can also turn up errors in *cataloguing or processing* such as a mismatch between the catalogue record and the barcode or call number.

The following points should be considered:

- A policy should be in place to outline the cycle of stocktaking. Should it be carried out every year, or alternate years? In the school library it is strongly recommended that stocktaking be an annual activity performed at the end of the school year.
- Advise library users, particularly teachers, that a stocktake will take place on particular dates and outline the reasons why it is necessary. This will ensure staff cooperation throughout the stocktake period.
- A decision should be made whether to close the library during stocktake, or just to close the section that is being worked on at the time. The process will be quicker without interruptions an there will be less chance of patrons moving items around if the library is closed.
- It may be a good idea to weed the collection before the stocktake, or use the stocktake to look at the resources and weed as you go.
- Before the stocktake commences you may like to retrieve items out on loan to ensure they are not missing. This will involve follow up of *overdues* for both staff and students.
- While it is not essential that the collection be in strict Dewey order, all resources should be *shelved* within the correct collection to reduce problems. A shelf check can be beneficial for following up missing items.
- Make a list of every collection in your library, such as special collections, non-circulating collections and those collections which may be based outside the library. Plan the order by which you will stocktake the collections.
- If items are missing the catalogue records should be amended so that students and staff are able to see that the items are no longer available for loan.
- What will you do with the results of the stocktake? Will the losses be reported to teaching staff, administration or

the wider school community? Is an estimate of losses needed to help in planning budgets for the next year?

See the *Systems support* website for further procedures on conducting a stocktake/inventory using TALIS.

Metadata and Learning Objects

Metadata is data about data. The *catalogue record* you create for the TALIS system is a type of metadata. Metadata helps people searching for electronic information to find what they are seeking more efficiently by providing a structured way of describing electronic resources.

Learning objects are the building blocks of multimedia online learning resources, which are being developed as part of the Learning Federation project to enable schools to deliver modules through a flexible mode. Sets of metadata elements that enable the management, evaluation and retrieval of learning objects have been developed.

When you are creating the *school library website* with links to your electronic resources, you usually create embedded metadata automatically when you use a web authoring tool such as Microsoft FrontPage. For specific guidelines on creating websites from the Department of Education in Tasmania see the Wise Web Weaving information at: http://www.education.tas.gov.au/wiseweb/default.htm. For more information about embedded metadata contact Web Strategy and Support Unit. http://www.educaiton.tas.gov.au/websupport/

If you are unfamiliar with metadata, you may find the ENDA metadata tutorial at http://metabrowser.spirit.net.au/tutorial/EdNA.html. Useful, as it provides an excellent overview of the use of metatada in the school library environment. Information about ENS metadata is also available from the EDNA website directly at http://www.edna.edu.au/metadata The following information about metadata comes form the DELIC home page at: http://www.education.tas.gov.au/delic/metadata/aboutmetadata.htm.

"Without metadata a document is left floating in a cyberspace filled with 550 billion other documents. The chances of it being found by the right person at the right time are greatly diminished.

How does metadata aid resource discovery?

Currently, web "surfers" who type in a search request are often overwhelmed by thousands of responses. The search results frequently contain references to irrelevant web sites while leaving out others that hold important material. Describing information resources in a standard way with metadata saves time and expense in locating those resources and results include select resources only." (DELIC).

Metadata needs to be updated whenever the URL< in this case your school library's website, changes.

Metadata can be held separately from the resource in a repository. This repository store can only be searched from a specific entry point. For example, to search the metadata held in the repository for the Department of Education web site, the user must search using the http://www.education.tas.gov.au web page search engine and/or browse facilities.

Organisation of Resources and Collections

The collections and resources of the library should be arranged in an organized and logical way. The library should be well sign-posted so that users are able to easily locate the collection or section they are after.

Before you can label the shelves and decide on signage, consideration needs to be given as to the number of collections the library will have. For example, decide whether the library's non-fiction collection in its variety of formats would be better shelved as a single, integrated sequence or as separate sequences according to the type of material.

Many school libraries have decided on separate collections for their non-book items as non-book materials have particular shelving and storage requirements. It is quite common in the school library, to find separate collections for kits and video recordings. CD ROMS are also often stored separately in a closed access area that library staff may browse but students may not.

The advantage of an integrated collection is that, in terms of retrieval for clients, a single integrated sequence can ensure that students and staff alike are finding all the materials available in the library on a single subject.

The disadvantage of integrated shelving is that not all items are designed to be shelved. In fact, items like posters and kits are much better if stored on hanging frames, as they are more easily browsed.

It is up to the library manager, in consultation with other teaching staff, to design the shelving requirements to optimize use.

All shelves should be clearly labelled and sign posted. All items must also be clearly labelled. The first part of the items' spine label should clearly indicate to which collection the item belongs, for example, VID for video collection, REF for reference, S for the serials, etc. The spine lable should be identical to the holding on the *catalogue record.*

The main collection of non-fiction resources should be shelved in a single sequence, from left to right within bays and in numerical order. At least 10% of each shelf should be left free for additions to the collection. Bookends should be used to ensure books are packed loosely enough to allow easy removal whilst still ensuring they keep upright. Space behind the books should be left so that air can freely circulate. Big folio or elephant books should be stored horizontally in stacks of no more than three. You may wish to have a parallel sequence running on the bottom shelf of each bay of non-fiction books for the large books that fit into that sequence.

Consideration also needs to be given to the height of the shelves to allow for clients from all ages to retrieve the books without undue physical exertion.

Fiction books should be shelved alphabetically by the author's last name, left to right within the bays.

Any books that can be used as quick reference such as encyclopaedias, dictionaries, atlases and almanacs should be used as the core of the reference section and shelved separately with a spine lable that clearly indicates they are for reference and not for loan.

Audiovisual resources, such as tapes and videos may be shelved together, separately from the other collections. Likewise with other media formats, software, posters/charts, vertical file.

Signage needs to be clear and easy to read and see. All the different collections should be immediately apparent upon entering the library. If not, it is useful to have a plan of the library near the entrance.

Coloured labels to indicate broad categories can be used on the shelving An alphabetical subject index in a range of formats can be developed and made into wall charts or booklets.

Clear guiding and signs will ensure that the library is easily accessible and effectively used. Subjects may be listed on the end of a bay panel and wall subject indexes can also be used.

Many school libraries have separate sequences for different fiction types, for example easy-reads, quick reads, best sellers, picture books, young adults, etc. The decision on the number and types of collections should be based on client needs and should be made to best suit student usage patterns.

Troubleshooting Hardware and Software

The difficulties school library clients experience using networked services fall in two main categories:

- They need help because of inexperience or lack of confidence or over confidence with computers
- There is something wrong with the network, an individual machine, an application or a network connection.

General Assistance

All school library staff should be able to provide general advice, such as which area of the library has computers connected to the network, or how to access CD ROMs. Students may occasionally need help using the computers and there should be clear signage near them, with instructions on how to log onto the network and how to use the digital resources. Students may not be familiar with using the library catalogue and all new students should be given an introduction to using TALIS with a set of notes to help. Although the TALIS system is user friendly, it is important that clear instructions on the various search options are also included near the Public Access Catalogues (and since the library catalogue can be accessed from any PC in the school, instructions should be provided in all classrooms, staffrooms, etc).

Networks

The school's Internet service may become disconnected. Try the following steps before rebooting the computer:

- Click on the stop button on the browser's toolbar then click on reload or refresh. Reloading will actually create a new connection to the site.
- Restart the browser. Click on.exist, then double click on the browser's icon.
- Check to determine whether another network application is working. This will enable you to decide whether the problem is a network problem.
- Check to see if other computers are still using the network and Internet. If this is the case you can try rebooting the problem computer.
- If there is still a problem, ask the student to move to another machine while you contact network support within the school. If the problem is with the PAC you need to contact *Systems support* at the state library on 6233 7939 or state.library@education.ts.gov.au. Systems can explain how to check network traffic at any given time (sometimes the amount of traffic can affect the speed of the catalogues).

CD ROMs

Problems with CD ROMs may be isolated and solved. Try the following:

- Ask the student to try a different CD and if that works you know you have a problem with the CD so supply them with a second copy if you have one. But, if the second CD doesn't work it is a computer problem and you should contact your school's network support officer.
- If you don't have a second copy of the CD the student wants to use, you may try clearing it and then ask the student to try again.
- Ask the student to use a different PC as some PCs have a greater tolerance for error than others.

Printers

Printer problems are usually either because of problems with the printer itself, or with the print server network. With an individual printer the problems are usually:

- Paper jams – check and correct
- Lack of toner – check and replace
- Out of paper – check and fill
- Check power is on and try resetting the printer
- Check student has sent their document to the correct printer. Look in settings at the start menus and check
- Check that other students are able to print. If this is the case, the document the student is working on may be unprintable. You may wish to test the printer by printing a simple text document.

If there are problems with all printers on the network you will need to contact your school's network support officer.

The Information Management Branch (IMB) of the Department of Education is also available for help. http://www. education. tas.gov.au/corporate/imb/ The following excerpt has been taken directly from the IMB home page.

"IMB is the provider of IT services, products and support for the Department of Education. As current and emerging technologies become more vital to the day-to-day operations within the Department, the need for a robust network, dynamic applications and innovative IT solutions becomes paramount. IMB has a range of roles throughout the Department, including:

- Managing IT infrastructure
- Developing and managing IT projects
- Providing technical support through the Help Centre and Support Services
- Providing guidelines for the use of IT
- Developing solutions for storing, accessing and processing data"

Bibliography

General

Anderson, B. "Conser on the Internet: Facilitating Access to Serials Information." Serials Librarian 31, no. ½ (1997): 77-94.

Clasquin, F.F. "Financial Management of serials and journals Through Core Lists." Serials Librarian 2 (Spring 1978): 287-97.

Diodato, L.W. "Serials Claims: Three Perspectives, Library/Publisher/ Vendor," Serials Librarian 21, nos. 2/3 (1991): 201-3.

Harington, S.A. "serials Specialists Are Hard to Fin," Serials Librarian 21, no. 1 (1991): 1-11.

International Subscription Agents. 5th ed. Chicago: American Library Association, 1986.

Katz, William W., and Linda Sternberg Katz. Magazine for Libraries. 5th ed. New York: R.R. Boker, 1986.

Katz, William W., and Linda Sternberg Katz. Mogazines for Libraries, 5th ed. New York: R.R. Bowker, 1986.

Keating, L.R. "Replacement Issues: Where Do You Find them and at What Cost?" Serials Librarian 21, nos. 2/2 (1991): 165-68.

Marcinco, R.W. "Issues in Commercial Document Delivery." Library Trends 45, no. 3 (Winter 1997): 531-50.

Nisonger, T. Management of Serials in Libraries, Englewood, Colo.: Libraries Unlimited, 1998.

Prabha, C., and E.C. Marsh. "Commercial Document Suppliers:

How Many of the ILL/DD Periodical Article Requests Can They Fill?" Library Trends 45, no. 3 (Winter 1997): 551-58.

Quint, B. D "Document Delivery Field Continues to Shrink with Demise of EBSCO Document Services." (September 21, 1998). Information Today NewsBreaks. March 1, 1999, <http// www.infotoday.com/newsbreaks/nb0921-2.htm>.

Stein, L.L "What to Keep and What to Cut?" Technical Services Quarterly 10, no. 1 (1992): 3-14.

Wilkas, L. International Subscription Agents. Chicago: American Library Association, 1994.

Woodward, H.M. "Impact of Electronic Information on Serials Collection Management." IFLA Journal 20 no. 1 (1994): 35-45.

Academic

Alexander, A.W., and J.L. Smith. "Annual Survey of Serials Collection Assessment Programmes, Practices, and Policies in Academic Libraries," Journal of Library Administratin 17, no. 2 (1992): 133-48.

Chrzastowski, T.E., and K.A. Schmidt. "Surveying the Damage: Academic Serial Cancellations—1987/88 through 1989/90." COLLEGE & research Libraries 54 (March 1993): 93-102.

Davis. D. "FIRST Search: Collection Management and Academic Libraries." OCLC Systems and Services 9 (Fall 1993): 43—45.

Dow, R.F., et al., "Commentaries on Serials Publishing," College & Research Libraries 52 (November 1991): 521-27.

Houbeck, R.L. "Locked in Conversation: College Library Collectiosn and th ePluralist Society," Journal of Library Administration 17, no. 2 (1992): 99-131.

Kingma, B.R., and P.B. Eppard. "Journal Price Escalation and the Market for Information." College & Research Libraries 53 (November 1992): 523-35.

McCain, K.W. "Some Determinants of Journal holding Pattern as in Academic Libraries." Library & Information Science Research 14 (July 1992): 223—43.

Welsch, E.K. "Measures of Social Science Collection Development Costs." Behaviour and Social Science Librarian 10, no. 2 (1991): 9-26.

Public

Boyer, R.E. "Serials in the Small Public Library," Library Resources & Technical Services 29 (April/June 1985): 132-38.

Falk, G. "Increase Your budge by Convincing Users to Adopt-a-Magazine." Library Journal 110 (June 15, 1985): 34.

Fyfe, J. "History Journals for a Public Library." Serials Librarian 13 (December 1987): 69-75).

Lenahan, N.M. "Use of Periodicals and Newspapers in a Mid-Sized Public Library." Serials Librarian 16, nos. ¾ (1989): 41-47.

Ostling, E. "Periodicals in Libraries—a Democratic Right." Scandinavian Public Library Quarterly 25, no. 2 (1992): 16-17.

Stout, M.A., and B. Stunz. "Creating Core Serial Lists in a Public Library." Reference Librarian, nos. 27/28 (1989): 267-78.

School

Buboltz, D., and R. Ling-Louie, "A Treeful of good Reading (Magzines as a Way to Promote Reading)." Book Report 10 (January/February 1992: 16-18.

Bury, J.M. "Management of Periodicals in a Small School LMC." In Collection Management for School Library Media Centers. Edited by Brend White, 313-49. New York: Haworth Press 1986.

Clark, M.P. "Young Adult and Children's Periodicals: Selections for the School Media Centr," Serials Review 7 (Obctober 1981): 7-24.

Drott, M.c., and J. Mancall. "Magazines as Information sources," School Media quarterly 8 (Summer 1980): 240-44.

Estes-Ricer, B., and J. Johnson. "Relevant Resources: Periodicals in Elementary Schools." School Library Media Quarterly 19 (Fall 1990): 53-56.

Richardson, S.K. "Magazine Collections in Elementary School Library Media Centers." In Library Education and Leadership. Edited by S. Intner and K. Vandergrift, 373-85. Metuchen, J.J.: Scarcrow Press, 1990.

Swisher, R., et. al. "Magazine Collections in Elementary School Media Centers." School Library Journal 37 (November 1991): 40-43.

SPECIAL

Anderson, D.C. "Journal for Academic Veterinary Medical Libraries." Serials Librarian 18, nos. ¾ (1990): 73-86.

Battistella, M.S. "OCLC-Serhold Connections; An Evolution in Health Sciences Union Listing." Bulletin of the medical Library Association 79 (October 1991): 370-76.

Cawkell, A.E. "Evaluating Scientific Journals with Journal Citation Reports." American Society for Information Science Journal 29 (January 1978): 41-46.

Cooper, E.R. "Simplified Approaches for Serials Management." Serials Review 18, no. 4 (1992): 17-20.

Freehling, D.J. "Cancelling Serials in Academic Law Libraries." Law Library Journal 84 (Fall 1992): 707-24.

Humphreys, B.L., and D. E. McCutcheon, "growth Patterns in the National Library of medicine's Serials Collection." Bulletin of the Medical Library Association 82 (January 1994): 18-22.

Morton, D. "Making the Most of your Serials Budget." College & Research Libraries News 53 (November 1992): 630.

Shalini, R. "Journal Acquisition and Cost Effectiveness in Special

Libraries." International Library Review 13 (April 1981): 189-94.

Triolo, V.A., and D. Bao, "A decision Model for Technical Journal Deselection." Journal of the American Society for Information Science 44 (April 1993): 148-60.

White, B., and J. Tomlinson, "Library Subscription scheme at the Institute of Advanced Legal Studies." Law Librarian 23 (march 1992): 29-34.